Fred H

AN AUTOBIOGRAPHY

Fred Hollows

AN AUTOBIOGRAPHY

WITH PETER CORRIS

KERR

Professor Hollow's royalties from the sale of this book have been assigned to the Fred Hollows Foundation Inc., PO Box 782, Willoughby, NSW 2068. Half of Mr Corris's royalties will go to same. A royalty on copies sold will go to same from the publisher. Cash contributions from Rosemary Creswell Literary Agency and Tower Books Pty Ltd. Many Australian booksellers make contributions on sales.

First published 1991
This edition updated, 1992, 1993
Reprinted 1994 (twice)
Kerr Publishing Pty Ltd
3/37 Duke St
Balmain NSW 2041

Typeset in 11½/16 Goudy Old Style by Bookset Pty Ltd, Melbourne
Cover design by Suzy O'Connor, Sydney
Printed by McPherson's Printing Group, Maryborough, Victoria

Distribution by Tower Books

National Library of Australia
cataloguing-in-publication data:
Hollows, F. C. (Frederick C.), 1929–93
Fred Hollows: an autobiography.

New ed.
Includes index
ISBN 0 9588004 7 2

1. Hollows, F. C. (Frederick C.), 1929–93. 2. Ophthalmologists—New South Wales—Sydney—Biography. 3. Opthalmology—Australia. 4. Trachoma—Australia. I. Corris, Peter, 1942– . II. Title.

617.7092

For Desbele Ghebregiorghis,
front-line Eritrean eye surgeon
and for those who have worked with him

May the peace
for which they have struggled long
endure.

And for Sanduk Ruit,
Sherpa eye surgeon
and one of the greatest

Contents

PROLOGUE

Change of heart: Porirua, 1948

I was dropped off there by a friend of my father who'd run me down from Palmerston North. Porirua, which is a major centre now with a mixed Polynesian, Maori and pakeha working-class population, was then a little seaside town, at the head of an estuary. I was standing outside the front gate of the mental hospital, where I'd got a vacation job as an attendant. It was late on a Sunday night, pretty bloody cold and very dark. I'm standing there with my suitcase — nineteen years of age, green as grass, a small town boy with one year of Bible college behind me. I'm a teetotal, non-smoking virgin and I remember thinking, *This is something different. This is spooky*.

It was, too. Someone came and got me and we walked through the dark gardens, crunching along a gravel path. A bit of wind in the trees and a very strange smell. We went through the main building, down passages and through doors which the bloke opened with a big brass key. It was a bit like a prison where you have to close off one part behind you before you get to the next. And pervading everything was this unidentifiable smell. I don't know whether he was giving me a sort of initiation tour or not, but it put the wind up me. We went out to another building, which they called a villa, and he told me where my room was. He also gave me a big brass key.

And that was it! I was the attendant in charge of a section which was full of madmen. It was the spookiest experience of my life. I got to my room and stowed my things and went to bed. There was a fanlight above the door, letting in some light from the passage. Very eerie. I was tired and went to sleep, but I woke up in the middle of the night when I heard footsteps in the corridor. For a second I didn't know where I was and when I remembered, it didn't help much. Somehow that particular sound fed into my auditory cortex, and when I hear anything like it, even now, I get a quick little surge of terror.

Working in that place for a couple of months completely changed my life. Looking back, I suppose it directed me towards doctoring, but it wouldn't be an easy course to plot. The biggest impact came from the people I was working with, the other attendants. Most of them were British provincials — Geordies, some Scotsmen; rough, knockabout blokes — ex-seaman, some who'd been in the war. But they were terrific men, kind and gentle. I never saw one of them display any spleen or antagonism towards the inmates, no matter what the provocation. It was amazing. I remember one time when I was in charge of a room full of men, all very disturbed and one of them was striding around angrily. He was obviously wild and going off his head. I think he'd just had a visitor from outside who'd upset him. Big bloke. Over six feet and fourteen stone and I'm five foot seven and a lightweight — nine stone nine, wringing wet.

'Mr Hollows,' the attendant in the next room says. 'Come and have your afternoon tea.'

All the attendants addressed each other as 'Mr' while on duty. Not off duty, not when we were out drinking. I said,

'What about these fellows? Some of them look a bit toey.'

He told me just to lock them in for a bit and I did. I'd just turned the key and stepped back from the door when I heard an almighty bloody bang, like an explosion. This big bugger had run at the door and he'd knocked it clean out of the jamb. Heavy door, too. And he was stepping over it towards me. I started to shape up to him. I was too scared to do anything else although he'd have cleaned me up with one hand. And the little red-headed attendant, the guy who'd called me in for my tea, just comes up quietly and gets between us.

'Come and have a cuppa tea, George,' he says. Gives no sign that anything unusual has happened, no anger.

I was very impressed by those men, by their goodness, I suppose. Before that, I had assumed that life outside of the church, away from the comforts and discipline of religion, was the slippery path to perdition. Also, I thought it was miserable, uncomfortable, wretched and unhappy. I'd had a proper job done on me, and I'd gone along with it. I thought the only real joy in life was in the church but I found out differently at the hospital. Those men were good and religion had nothing to do with it. I found out what secular goodness was. And it was an unlikely environment to discover that. That smell, of course, was the smell of institutionalised people. I've experienced it a hell of a lot since — in hospitals, in prisons.

Things were very rough in mental health then — ECT, ElectroConvulsive Therapy, was just coming in, straight-jackets were used and there were virtually no tricyclic anti-depressants. But in the male part of the hospital I never saw any gratuitous violence or sadism. It was a bit different in the female wards where we were sometimes called in to give a hand. There was a lot more anger in there, more repression. Although the staff were mostly psychiatric nurses, it seems they were not as well able to cope with the rather less violent situations they encountered than these unqualified men who rarely raised their voices. I'm not sure why that was.

I don't want to give the impression that the changes that were taking place in my outlook were purely philosophical. I started to drink. I got drunk a few times with the men I was working with. Chundered all over the place, of course.

And I met a nurse, a very lascivious lady whose name, to my great shame, I've forgotten. She was a bit older than me and one night we went out to a cabaret, my first experience of nightlife. We danced and drank a bit and then went up to a hayloft close to the hospital grounds and, after an hour of groping and rolling around, I got it in. Pure ecstasy and not a shred of guilt.

It's funny to think back to those days. There was a kind of English propriety about everything, a properness. But something else underneath. A few days after this frolic in the hayloft, I was waiting at the bus stop to go into Wellington and I was wearing a Donegal tweed jacket, very fashionable at that time, very smart. There I was, at the bus stop with a few people about. Sitting behind me in the bus shelter, a senior attendant from the hospital leaned over to me and flicked something off my shoulder.

'Excuse me, Mr Hollows,' he says, 'but you've got some hay on your jacket.'

Now, everyone around there knew what the hayloft was used for. Everyone!

So, it was at that place that I encountered the facts of life, in the broadest sense, for the first time. One day a bloke jumped up from where he'd been sitting, away with the fairies, and grabbed my tie and slipped the knot hard up against my windpipe. There were two other men sitting beside him, staring into space, and they weren't going to say boo. I got my thumbs on his carotids — didn't know the term then, of course — and squeezed and, thank Christ, he went limp before I did. The point is, there were men in that place dealing with that sort of thing every day. Good men. And no odour of sanctity about them. Ordinary citizens.

I think this realisation must have fused with other, earlier ideas I'd had but not formulated clearly. When I left Porirua to go back to my studies everything was different. I was a different person, behaving and thinking differently, interested in different things. But not altogether. There were all those other influences coming through, the family and our way of life that were still exerting an influence on me. I suppose they still do.

PART ONE

CHAPTER 1

Young Fred

When a Hollows meets a Hollows,
Be it here or far abroad,
You can rest assured there's one thing
That you have that's in accord,
It's your name, because it's special,
Your ancestors' choice for you,
It's unique because it landed
With your forebears firm and true

From 'The Pioneering Hollows' Shirley Hollows,
to the tune of 'Coming through the Rye'

Hollows is an unusual handle because it isn't properly a name at all. When my great grandfather, James Hallows, arrived in New Zealand in the early 1870s, coming via the United States and Australia, someone buggered up the entry forms and spelled his name as 'Hollows'. It was easier to stick with that spelling than get the mistake corrected. Eventually there was a big Hollows clan in New Zealand, and you could be pretty sure if you met anyone else by the same name that you were related. The family, past and present, was the most important factor in your development when I was growing up. Who you were equalled who your family was, where they lived, what they did and how they were regarded.

James Hallows was from Lancashire, the cradle of the modern industrialised working class. He was a coal miner in the Old World and a coal miner in the New, but he found the better life he'd been looking for in New Zealand. His sons didn't necessarily have to go down the pit, although some of them, including James, my grandfather, who'd been born in Lancashire and came to New Zealand as a young boy, did.

He spent most of his working life at the Shag Point coal mine, Otago.

His son and my father, Joseph Alfred Hollows, was a railwayman, continuing the tradition of working at the heart of the industrial revolution. I was born in 1929 in Dunedin. I was my parents' second son and they had two more after me. Dunedin was a major railhead and my father was an engine driver. He owned a house, a small semi-detached, and that's where I spent my first seven years. Dunedin bears some similarities to Melbourne. It too was founded during the gold rush, has a tough Scottish tradition, and acquired some stately Victorian buildings. But it's located 200 kilometres further south than the southernmost tip of Tasmania and the climate is severe. Cold, hard place, Dunedin, at the best of times and they weren't the best of times. The Depression was on and I can remember that there was a lot of poverty. My father was in work throughout the Depression so it didn't touch us directly, but I retain a memory, like a shadow over things, that there were people around who were a lot worse off than us.

I had one year at North East Valley Primary School in Dunedin but I don't remember anything about it. The holidays are much clearer. It's a family thing again. My father met my mother at a place called Ohakune in the North Island where there was a railway junction. It was timber country; one of the biggest stands of native timber in New Zealand was around there and my mother's family were in the timber business. My maternal grandfather, Frederick Cossom Marshall, after whom I'm named, had been a seaman's cook and became what they called a saw doctor, the bloke who kept the saws sharp. Other members of the family were woodworkers — joiners, carpenters and cabinet makers. Woodworking's one of my great interests, maybe that's where it comes from.

My mother's father also leased a tract of land from the Maoris and had a small farm. That's where we went for our holidays. First, we'd travel two thirds of the way up the South

Island of New Zealand, from Dunedin to Christchurch. Then on to the ferry, operated by the railways, at night, arrive at Wellington in the morning and take the train again — an all-day trip to Ohakune junction. It was cheap travel because my father had a railway pass. We did that almost every summer. We camped out, walked in the bush. They were great holidays.

When I was seven my father shifted the lot of us to Palmerston North, a large town in the North Island where there was a railway junction. He'd got a promotion but he became disenchanted with his work. Up to that time, the engine driver, the fireman and a cleaner worked as a team. The locomotives in the system were made in Dunedin. The team would meet at the engine shed; the cleaner would light the fire and they'd bring the engine out and oversee the linking up of the train. They knew the locomotive intimately, knew all about its maintenance and quirks. There was a sort of solidarity to it all. This changed during the Depression. What was called a Put-and-Take system came in. The driver and fireman didn't service their engine any more or assemble the train. They just took off in whatever engine was allotted to them from the pool. The result was that they were alienated from their central work machine and individual pride, and a competitive spirit between the teams went out the window. The Put-and-Take system was the death blow to the bit of Arcadian spirit that remained in railway work.

I didn't know this at the time. It was still a great thrill to me to see Dad driving the express which was a double-header, that is, two JA series locomotives linked together. Two hundred and sixty tons of steam-driven power. And to go up there with him on the footplate was pure joy. But Dad didn't talk about his work at home anymore, I remember that. He had a bad accident too, came off the back of a motor bike, suffered a brain haemorrhage and nearly died. The upshot was he retired from the railways after twenty-three years, went into hock and bought six acres a little way out of town.

This was against all sober and serious advice. He was a keen chrysanthemum grower and he'd decided to go into business at it. The place he bought was very run-down, an old poultry farm, full of what they called tussock — a knotty sort of grass that could only be ploughed by mechanical means. You needed a blade that went down eighteen inches. So he was starting from behind scratch but he made a great success of it. He acquired an international reputation as a grower of chrysanthemums, made overseas trips to flower shows and he wrote a couple of little books about his methods.

That was a wonderful place to grow up in. It had a creek running through it and that's where we learned to swim. We had a lot of friends and did the things country kids do, which is to say, work pretty bloody hard on the farm, milking cows and keeping things clean, and also have a lot of freedom and pick up useful knowledge. You learn to shoot and fix machinery, for example, if that's the way you're inclined, and I was.

The strongest influence on me at that time was my father. He and my mother were members of the Church of Christ — 'very strong in the church', as the expression was. The Church of Christ was rather like the Baptists, believing in total immersion, back to the Bible, fly specks and all. But it wasn't a rigidly fundamentalist sect; there were considerable progressive elements in it and my parents were on the progressive wing. My father in fact was a kind of radical, a sort of Christian Marxist. I remember a time when I was very young hiding behind a couch in the sitting room and hearing my father talking to another man who was joining the International Brigade, going off to fight in the Spanish Civil War. I remember feeling envy for someone facing such a big adventure. Later, Dad staged a protest in Palmerston North when he was rostered to work on a Sunday. As an elder of the church that was against his principles, like the runner in the film, *Chariots of Fire*.

His Christianity shaded into politics. He was a lifelong Labour voter, a pacifist during World War 2, which wasn't a popular stance, and later an anti-nuclear campaigner. He had firm views on some things, such as the basic wage, but he gave them a personal slant. He said the basic wage should enable a man, working forty hours a week, to buy a house, feed, clothe and educate his children without his wife having to work. There are some very conservative aspects to that, but also a sense of the social contract and the responsibility of the employer, and he was ready to march or jump up and down or do whatever he had to, to make sure the terms of the contract were met.

I never knew my father to do anything mean or small-minded. He was generous to a fault with me and others. Later on, he gave me money which I sometimes spent frivolously and he went guarantor for people who didn't do the right thing by him. But he wasn't a wimp. He'd give me a clip over the ear if he thought I needed it. The interesting thing was his capacity to surprise me. For example, you'd think, as a Christian pacifist that he'd have a set against firearms, especially in the hands of youngsters. I suppose I must have thought so because when I got hold of a rifle, a .22, I kept it hidden and tried not to let him know that I had it. One day we were sitting around and he said, 'Go and get that rifle of yours, Fred, and let's see if it's any good.'

No fuss, but he'd known all along that I had it. I got the thing and he tacked up a card in a tree about twenty paces from the back step. It wasn't an ordinary playing card — they were the Devil's pasteboards, you see — it had a mark in the centre of it, the letter 'I', about a centimetre square. They were used in some particular kind of card game. My old man shouldered the rifle and he put three shots, bang, bang, bang, into the centre of the card. I was very impressed.

The atmosphere I grew up in was respectable, teetotal, non-smoking, avoiding bad language but not judgemental. My parents weren't pious; they didn't feel that they had a direct line to God, just a possible approach. And I found that very acceptable, with the result that I attended church enthusiastically and joined the Boys' Brigade and taught Bible classes when I was old enough and was totally absorbed in that kind of life.

Totally absorbed? Well, I was going to school, of course, primary school and then the intermediate school that fed into either the technical school or the high school. I don't remember much about it. I was a good student, I guess. I usually won a prize at something or other. No great shakes at maths, but not a duffer. I took a liking to French one year because we had a good teacher and I thought it would be terrific to be able to speak French. The next year I didn't like the French teacher and I dropped it. I was a bit like that — following my whims without any great plan. Accident and happenchance play a great part in life, I think. For example, my older brother Monty was at the technical school and I was very impressed with a piece of practical work that he'd brought home — a metal bench clasp that you could put a padlock on. He'd drilled the holes in the steel and everything. In Australia they'd call that activity 'metalwork' and in America they'd call it 'machine shop', but at the Tech in Palmerston North it was called 'engineering'. At the end of the second year at the intermediate school we had to decide whether we were going to the high school or to Tech. I was in one of the two academically stronger classes and it was assumed that we'd all go to high school. There was an interview with a teacher which was a bit of a formality, but I threw him by saying I wanted to do engineering, by which I meant that I wanted to shape and control metal — it seemed to me like an incredible thing to be able to do.

'So you want to be an engineer, do you, Hollows?' he said.

Heads were turning and I was blushing and nodding.

'Well, what sort of an engineer do you want to be? You don't want to be a greasemonkey all covered in dirt, do you?'

That didn't sound so good. I shook my head.

'Right,' he says, 'you want to be a civil engineer. You go to High School.'

It was a couple of years later at high school, that I discovered what a civil engineer did and I knew I didn't want to have a bar of it. Very theoretical. Not my sort of thing at all in those days. But I was in the academic education stream by then and that led to other things. If I'd had a few more clues about 'metalwork', and been able to convince that teacher of my interest, I might have finished up as a mechanic. In fact, I've sometimes thought, looking back over the various jobs I *have* done, that if I hadn't become an eye doctor I would have liked to be a bore sinker, a water-driller. But that's jumping ahead quite a long way.

A big part of my life as a teenager was taken up by the Boys' Brigade. One William Alexander, a Scot, had established this arm of the Protestant church, and it was built on the twin pillars of religion and discipline. We wore a uniform, assembled a couple of times a week, did gymnastics, semi-military things like marching and paper-chases — 'orienteering' they'd call it now. And we had speakers from all over the place, some of them interesting. There was a band. I played trumpet in the Boys' Brigade band and I became an NCO. So did Monty, my oldest brother. We went on camps around New Zealand which were something like Scouts' jamborees. Muscular Christianity is easy to parody, but I enjoyed it.

At school I was going along all right. Stayed out of trouble, was on the way to being a prefect in my final year. I played B-flat bugle in the Palmerston North Boys' High School drum and bugle band. Very hard instrument to play, only five notes. I could sometimes manage the top one but it couldn't be guaranteed. We made a lot of noise around the town.

I also played rugby at school and that's where I did get into trouble, physically. I didn't have much natural ability as a footballer, not a lot of clues about what to do with the ball when I got it, but I did get it. I had stamina, didn't tire easily, and I had a hell of a lot of enthusiasm. The result was that I was in the First Fifteen in my senior years which was a big honour, what every kid wanted, but I was there just on heart. I was smaller than most of the other players and I got knocked about a lot. It seems that I spent a good few Saturday nights up at the hospital, in Casualty, getting stitched. My nose tells the story better than I can. It was always getting broken.

There was very little extra-imperial influence on New Zealand in those days, a WASPish environment. Very little contact with Maoris. Jim Larkins was a Maori and I was a sort of friend of his. At school there were the Ponanga brothers who were great sportsmen and became army officers. My mother's family, in fact, were critical of the Maoris, saw them as undeserving landlords, wastrels and so on. Against that, at school, we were told about the Treaty of Waitangi and the Maori resistance to white settlement. The Maoris were given a place of respect in the history of New Zealand. I remember that the national news, over the wirelesss, was always broadcast in Maori as well as English. Maoridom wasn't an isssue at that time.

Still, we were 'British to the bootstraps', as Bob Menzies said and the leading New Zealand politicians would have said exactly the same, probably did. In fact I can remember feeling very proud when I heard that 'we', that is, the English air force, had dropped a load of bombs on Germany immediately after war was declared. I suppose that also means I hadn't embraced my father's pacifism, and there were other things I hadn't taken completely on board.

I'd started to read a bit of theology and to question the bald fundamentalist propositions advanced by some of the people in the church. I had a few rows with the elders and was starting to sort out the people who had closed minds and those I could talk to. A minister named Gordon Stirling made a big impression on me, probably kept me in the church at that time of doubt and wavering.

At some function or other Gordon Stirling sang:

> At the Cross, at the Cross
> Where McGinty shot his hoss
> And the bridle and the saddle rolled away . . .

Not that my people were dour about it, but that was the first time I experienced irony and satire in a religious context and saw that religion didn't have to be humourless and catechistic. I began to see that there were people whose mind-sets were dogmatic and impenetrable, and others who had a questioning sort of faith. And I got interested in that other approach.

At much the same time, accident again, I was having trouble with English at school. There was a lot of grammar in it, parsing, conjugating and such, and I found it dead dull. Maybe I mucked up a bit, showed my impatience and lack of interest, because I fell foul of a teacher named MacDonald, 'Soapy' MacDonald, who was very big on this sort of thing. He barred me from the English class and said, 'Hollows, you're out. And if you ever go to university, not that you'd do any good there, don't ever attempt to study English.'

Well, that was a bit of a facer, because you *had* to do English to get any kind of a qualification. But there was another teacher, Guthrie Wilson, a new teacher who'd returned from the war, who you had to see if you were presenting discipline problems. (I suspect he was having his own problems with Palmerston North Boys' High School; he later became headmaster of Scots College in Sydney and I learned he'd written novels about the war.) What he cared about, obviously, was writing. He heard me out and he said, 'Have you read this, Hollows?' and he took *Tom Jones* by Fielding off his shelves.

I said, 'No.'

'Go away and read it, and come back next week.'

I read it and thought it was a great yarn. We had a bit of a talk about it and next he gave me *To the Lighthouse* by Virginia Woolf which I didn't enjoy nearly as much. But for the rest of the year I just did that — read novels and poetry and developed a taste for writing, particularly verse. The funny thing was, I found out much, much later, just before my father died, that he'd had a lifelong love of verse and could recite reams of it. And his father before him was the same. I thought I was the first of the Hollows to take an interest in poetry. Wrong.

So I was getting on top of things at school and about the same time I sat some Bible study exams and finished top of the list in New Zealand. I was very surprised because I hadn't studied particularly for those exams. Well, it looked like I could get into university and you go with your strengths, don't you? So I went off to university in Dunedin, back down south, to study Arts and Divinity. I was going to become a minister of religion.

CHAPTER 2

Out of the Nest

At the Cross, at the Cross
Where I first saw the light,
And the burden of my sins rolled away.
It was there by my faith
That I received my sight,
And now I am happy all the day.

Hymn 'At the Cross'

My parents' education had ended with the Proficiency Certificate, eighth grade. My father had gone into the railways and my mother, who was the oldest of ten, had become a second mother to her younger siblings. Monty had gone to Tech. I was the first Hollows to go to high school and on to university, but it wasn't treated as a big thing. There was no pressure put on me one way or the other. I was going into the church and would enter Glenleith College in Dunedin, a Church of Christ theological college attached to Otago University, so that might have alleviated any misgivings that might have been felt about my going to university.

Nineteen shillings a week it cost to live at college. My father paid that. Pretty cheap for food and board. The food was frugal but adequate, and it was a good place to study. Quiet. I did six Divinity and four Arts subjects in my first year and I passed them all. In terms of academic qualifications, that was the solidest year I ever put in. I enjoyed it up to a point. I was interested in some of the subjects and I was seeing some new things. My class consciousness got sharpened.

I think I'd always been relatively class conscious, but in an unformed way. When I was young I had the thought that people who were rich were somehow very clever. At university I saw some people who were very, very rich but I found out they certainly weren't very, very clever.

But I began to feel oppressed by the cloistered atmosphere in the college. The piety of some of the students really pissed me off. I still think piety is one of the cardinal human crimes and the symptoms of it are fairly disgusting. There were blokes in that place who washed their underpants twice a day. Church attendance began to irk me a bit. Some of the senior students and staff were bigots. I think I must have been reading some of the more sceptical theologians. Fortunately, the principal of the college, the Reverend A.L. Haddon, was of a liberal temperament and he didn't offer any objection when I came up with something a bit out of the ordinary.

The usual thing for students of Divinity was to spend their annual holidays doing a sort of locum for a minister somewhere, to give him a break. I told the principal that I didn't want to do that.

I said, 'I'm going into the ministry and that's what I'll be doing for the rest of my life. Just now, I want to do something else, see something of the world other than school and university.'

Haddon gave me the nod and I wrote away applying for a job at a mental hospital. I don't remember why I lit on that. I fancy I might have become a bit interested in psychology through my reading and that might have been the link. Casual jobs were easy to get in those days and I landed the position of temporary assistant attendant at the Porirua Mental Hospital . . .

I came back from Porirua a very changed character indeed, and I kept on changing. Sex, alcohol and secular goodness are pretty keen instruments, and they surgically removed my Christianity, leaving no scars. I was an agnostic by the time I returned to Dunedin. I went back to the same college, because it was cheap to live there, but I gave up Divinity and went for a straight Arts degree. Again, Haddon OKed that although some of the less enlightened had problems with it. My parents didn't object; they hadn't pushed me into the ministry and they weren't going to hold me to it now that I'd changed my mind.

I could always talk to and with my Mum and Dad, explain things. I was sure I wanted to do psychology by this stage. The stint at Porirua had reinforced that interest. However, at that time in New Zealand there were no psychology departments in universities. The subject was seen as an addendum to philosophy, a branch of speculative study. But John Passmore, an Englishman who later went on to hold chairs in Australia, changed that. He said that to study psychology you had to understand how the human brain works and that meant knowing something about chemistry, physiology, zoology etc. So I started doing those subjects along with the other Arts things, like English and history and education and in fact, in a piecemeal sort of way, I was doing what was called a Medical Intermediate — the course of study that led to medical school — but didn't know it at the time.

That second year was very different from the first. I was drinking a bit, and one time I vomited drunkenly in the main hall of the college. The wowsers got up a delegation to have me thrown out of the place but Haddon didn't back them. Interesting man, A.L. Haddon. I'd also started rock climbing. I met someone who invited me to go on a climb and when I found out what it was like, that was the end of playing rugby. I loved it. I bought an Indian Scout motor bike with some of the money I'd earned during the vacation, and I used to take off during the weekends and go rock climbing around the Otago Peninsula, much to the annoyance of the God-botherers.

That second year, I was sharing a room with Len Wilson. Len wasn't a Divinity student, he was just doing an Arts degree. He kind of tutored me in Anglo-Saxon and we talked about books and he helped to shape my literary interests. He's been a lifelong friend. He also introduced me to pipe-smoking. Those college rooms in Dunedin were unheated — cold as a witch's tit in winter — and I'd be sitting there at my desk, Len's at his, smoking his pipe, and the window is closed. Well, you either beat 'em or join 'em. Tobacco's been a great friend to me. I even cultivated the stuff in Wales, but that's jumping a long way ahead again.

I did all right that second year and when I went home I found that my father had picked up some intelligence about me.

'I hear you like a drink these days, Fred?' he said.

I hummed and hah'ed and the upshot was we went to the pub in Palmerston North and he outdrank me at a canter. I think that was a useful experience. In his later years, my father drank occasionally, got drunk, threw up and was OK the next day. He wasn't addicted to the stuff and that makes a big difference. Most doctors drink. The addicts are useless, dangerous even. The non-addicts, who pick their times and places, can do their jobs unimpaired.

I worked in the bush at the end of the second year, at some kind of forest survey in the North Island, and then I went up to Wellington, to Victoria University, to finish my Arts degree. I can't remember why I went to Wellington, probably something to do with university regulations. Len Wilson made the transfer, too. We had a good year, worked and played, sat the exams. I was a part-time student then, working at this and that and I was still close to my family although I wasn't going to church. My father and I still agreed about a lot of things and I admired him. For example, he used to call the rich 'Tories' and, as a chrysanthemum grower, he came into contact with some wealthy people. They had the big gardens and the money for the special cultivation the flowers needed. When he gave a talk or a demonstration to these people, he'd throw in references to capitalists and Tories, talk about how working people in fertiliser plants and seed-packaging factories contributed to the beauty of gardens. I thought that was a pretty good line to take.

I wasn't involved in radical politics at Victoria, although there was a fair bit of it going on. There were ex-servicemen doing degrees, older, more mature blokes, and some of them were radical and I respected them. The Cold War was on and there were some fierce debates. I remember one to do with the visit of the Dean of Canterbury, 'the Red Dean', who'd been refused permission by the Americans to land at Honolulu on his way to Australia and New Zealand. The proposition was that the student body should demonstrate outside the American embassy. That debate went on all night.

Then I went off to work in the South Island again, mapping and surveying the stands of indigenous timber. We lived in a very isolated place, there was no motor vehicle road to it — you could get in and out by foot, along a cattle track, but that was it. We had 'Maori Jack' as a packhorse and anywhere it was possible for a four-legged creature to travel, 'Maori Jack' would go. He was a big strong horse and we'd load him with gear and supplies, take him to wherever we were setting up camp, unload him and he'd wander back to base. For 'rapid' transport there was a boat that came once a month, or irregular flights in and out on a little De Havilland Rapide. That was a two-winged plane that had to locate and put down on a little airstrip in the forest. Pretty hairy, what with the tricky light, trees and ferns and mist.

It was a good time though. We did a lot of shooting when we weren't working. In those days, the South Island was overrun by deer and goats — chamois and tahr and the like. After the extermination of the moa, a three-metre-high grazing bird, there were no large animals in New Zealand, no herbivores, to make an impact on the vegetation. The soil and the hills and everything else was held together by the herbiage which the deer and goats threatened seriously. So there was a bounty on them and you could make a bit of money shooting them and cutting the ears off to claim the bounty.

So I'm down there, working my arse off, making good money, all primed to finish my Arts degree and do God knows what, probably psychology or teaching, and the plane comes in with the mail. It turned out I'd failed Education 3, which wasn't a great shock because I'd never got a handle on what the bloody subject was all about anyway. Educational psychology had interested me, but theory of education? I don't think anyone knows what it is to this day.

But I got something else in the mail — an invitation from the University of Otago to take up a place in the medical school. I'd done the subjects that constituted a Medical Intermediate and I'd been placed in the top one hundred students in the country. That brought with it the offer of a place because New Zealand was very short of doctors at that time and the medical schools were looking to train people fast. I hadn't ever thought of being a doctor but there was a fourth-year medical student in the work camp, Trevor Gebbie, and I asked him what it was like.

'It's bloody good,' he said. 'You'll always get a fuckin' job. Not only that, but you'll get a well-paid job.'

By this time I was feeling guilty about bludging on my old man for three years, and I was facing the prospect of going back and studying this bloody awful subject. Not appealing. But I had to decide on the spot, because the plane was going out straightaway and the letter from the university made it clear that they wanted a quick reply, yea or nay. If I knocked it back, they'd offer the place to someone else further down the list. So I scribbled out a reply and that's how I got to go to medical school.

The next job I had was building a spillway for the Lake Pukaki diversion in the South Island. At that time New Zealand was

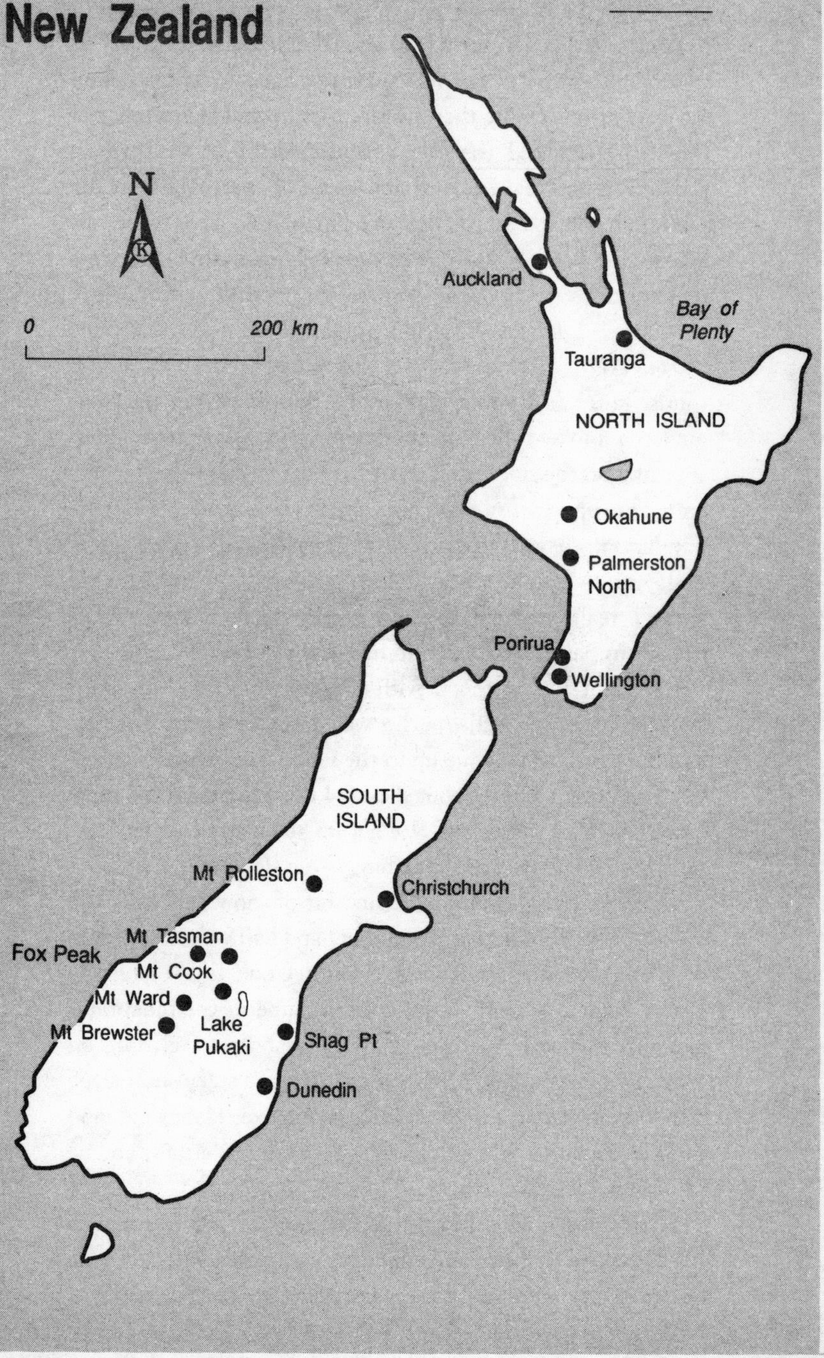

New Zealand

N

0 200 km

Auckland

Bay of Plenty

Tauranga

NORTH ISLAND

Okahune

Palmerston North

Porirua

Wellington

SOUTH ISLAND

Mt Rolleston

Christchurch

Mt Tasman

Fox Peak

Mt Cook

Mt Ward

Lake Pukaki

Mt Brewster

Shag Pt

Dunedin

damming rivers and trying to tame the wilderness, divert its natural energy for industrial use. It was hard work; sometimes we were at it for more than twenty-four hours at a stretch, but one day I realised that I was within sight of the highest mountains in New Zealand and some of the highest in the world outside the Andes and the Himalayas. They were just across the water, these very symbolic mountains that were represented on the New Zealand five pound note. And I thought, *If I don't do something about it, I'm going to leave here without ever getting close to those bloody things*. So I went to the tourist hotel at the foot of Mount Cook and I met the head guide, a bloke called Mick Bowie, and asked him about shooting on the slopes and getting up the mountains a bit. He paired me up with another shooter and we shot a lot of tahr — a mountain goat imported from Nepal and a great land destroyer — over the next couple of days, but I realised that what I really wanted to do was get up over one of the mountain passes, really get up into the clouds.

Mick put me in touch with 'Happy' Ashhurst, so-called because he never smiled, who was an experienced climber, and he agreed to take me up to the Copeland Pass for a price. We went up to a hut, about sixteen kilometres from the hotel and slept there overnight. We got up about three o'clock the next morning and started climbing — up slopes and then onto a rocky ridge and then to the first bit of snow and ice. And there's Mount Cook rearing up there and La Perouse and signs of glacial avalanches around. Mount Cook is 'Aorangi' in Maori, 'cloud-piercer'. It was my first time in the mountains and it was bloody frightening — thousands of feet drop on either side of you. Well, we had to traverse a steep snow slope to get up to the pass. I didn't have an ice axe, Happy did; and I didn't have the right sort of grips on my boots either, and he said, 'Use your rifle.'

So I slogged up, digging the butt of my cut-down Lee Enfield into the snow, and hauling myself along. We got up to the pass and we could look out right over the West Coast which is a seldom-visited part of New Zealand, steeped in folk lore. And there was cloud below us.

Happy says, 'Well, this is where I leave you, son.'

And I thought, *Shit, I'm up in the clouds. Don't leave me here!* But I asked him what to do and he said, 'Look, just glissade. You know how to glissade, don't you? Just slide on your boots down that snow slope into the clouds. Slide down there, stick your rifle out behind you, doesn't matter if you go arse over tit. Down the bottom of that snow there's the run out. You get down there, turn left, go over some snow grass mounds and you'll come to a cliff edge. Somewhere along that cliff edge you'll find a path down. Hut's about three hours away.'

Then he said, 'I'm off,' and he scarpered.

I've never forgotten that — sitting alone on the top of the Copeland Pass in the clouds. Great feeling of misgiving. But I did what he said and I got down all right. Mountain climbing got into my blood then and it was important to me for the next thirty years. It puts things into perspective — risks and skills, life and death, gives you the measure of problems and people.

CHAPTER 3

Hippocratic and other Oaths

axilla *n* (*pl* axillae) the armpit — axillary *adj*.

Concise Medical Dictionary, *Oxford University Press,*
3rd ed. 1990, p. 61

I turned up for the first medical school lecture along with a hundred and nineteen others. Mostly men, about twenty women. We walked into a lecture room with an ampitheatre arrangement, staggered rows of seats. I sat fairly well up the back and talked to a couple of people I knew. I'd come through three years of Arts, where you smoked your pipe, sat around, handed in work to your tutors and discussed it. You were thought capable of analysis and argument, and lectures were rather informal. So I was sitting there chatting and there's a lot of noise, excitement at being in medical school.

A man walked in. He stood dead centre at the lectern in front and yelled, 'Silence!'

I thought, *What's this?*

Everyone shut up.

He yells, 'Abernathy.'

Silence for a while.

'Abernathy!'

A bloke pipes up, 'Yes, sir?'

'Answer your name when it's called!'

He ran through from Abrahams to Zimmerman and I was thinking, *He's calling the roll. Kid stuff.*

Then he spun around to the blackboard behind him and he wrote, 'The return of the U-shaped loop.'

Now I'd studied physics, chemistry, zoology, botany, literature, history, education and all that stuff, and I knew absolutely nothing about human anatomy and physiology. Nothing. And this bloke, Professor Bill Adams, head of the Department of Anatomy as we later found, launches straight into a fifty-five minute lecture, complete with diagrams, on a stage in the development of the foetus. The intestines develop outside the developing abdominal cavity of the foetus; they take a loop shape, expand, develop and gradually return and the abdominal wall closes around them. We got all this in graphic detail. It was a shock to the system.

He finished the lecture, cleared his throat, and said, 'You will now go to dissection. Go down to the room at the end of the corridor on this floor. There you will find twelve bodies. Alongside each body on the wall you will find a list of ten names. Locate your cadaver and dissect the axilla according to the dissection manual.'

This is Day One! Within the first two hours!

So we all trooped out, not really knowing what was going on, whether he was kidding us or not, but, sure enough, there's twelve bodies laid out on slabs. I'd never seen a dead human body before and I doubt anyone else there had. So I found my body and the first question of course is, what the hell's the axilla? We figured out it was the armpit and the first part of the dissection was to take the skin off. Remember, I'd been shooting deer in the summer. In fact, I was still living off the money I'd made shooting deer — sometimes I made three pounds a day — and I knew a bit about skinning. So I made a start on the dissection of the axilla. That was the beginning of the medical course — right in at the deep end.

Pretty exciting kick-off, and I responded well to that, like being told to slide down into the clouds off Mount Cook, but I didn't show any great promise at medical school. I was twenty-two, getting a bit long in the tooth to be an undergraduate perhaps, and I always did just enough to pass. The subjects were graded A, B and C, pass, and D and E, fail. I might have got one B, I don't guarantee it; all the rest were Cs. I was doing a lot of other things — drinking, chasing women, rock climbing, playing billiards. If you'd come looking for me in those days, your best bet wouldn't have been the library or the lecture theatre, it'd have been the pub or the billiards room.

A group of us shared a house in Dunedin — a spec builder had put it up and couldn't sell it. Californian bungalow with a verandah across the front, lean-to's out the back, fairly vulgar taste. But it was solid brick and five of us moved in — all medical students. The house is still there and I've got a painting of it that was given to me for my sixtieth birthday. There was Bill Glass, Peter Brandt, Barry Colls, Dennis Fogg and me. Barry Colls is the professor of medicine at Christchurch Public Hospital; Bill's the Professor of Occupational Health at Otago University in Dunedin. Peter Brandt, in some ways he was the brightest of us, became New Zealand's first cine-cardio-radiologist. He perfected the technique of photographing the heart as it beats. Dennis Fogg, who was very bright in a way, pursued a full medical course.

A diary I kept for part of my second year as a medical student has survived the ravages of time and, looking through it, I see that I attended lectures and demonstrations pretty assiduously, but didn't care to comment on them. The entries about the weekends spent rock-climbing are more detailed. I enjoyed everything about that — the preparation of equipment, the gathering of supplies and the trip to the area of the climb.

I was also a keen, and critical, film-goer. I see that I liked Olivier's *Hamlet* and didn't care for Vivien Leigh in *Dark Journey*. Money was tight — I jotted down the prices of things bought the way people short of cash do. I read D.H. Lawrence that year — *Sons and Lovers* and *The Rainbow* — and attended a few concerts. I went on an occasional shooting trip and shot at the University Rifle Club range ('did poorly, but enjoyed myself'). Entries which include the words 'worked' and 'swotted' became more frequent as the end-of-year exams approached.

We lived in a sort of moderate squalor, I suppose. Studied hard in bursts, played up a bit. Otago University was a very conservative place and there wasn't a lot of political or interesting social activity on the campus. I didn't have any problems with authority though, didn't have any confrontations with the academics. Off campus was a bit different. I ran around with a few wild types, blokes with Irish names — Duffy, Kelly, McMahon — and we'd get into a bit of trouble for drinking after hours. By law, pubs closed at six o'clock then. You had to be careful with those blokes as drinking companions; they were always spoiling for a roughhouse and if you ended up as the only other person around you could find yourself in a fight.

My class consciousness was heightened during this time. There were a lot of rich people in the medical school. I observed them but didn't aspire to join them. I would've had Trevor Gebbie's remarks about doctoring as a good job in mind, but I had no idea of using medicine as a stepping stone into the middle-class. I was voting Labour, my father's son. Money was always a problem although I took a scholarship in second year which obliged you to take whatever post the government allotted you after graduation. That paid the fees and brought in a bit, but the key to survival was to work all through the long vacation and eke that money out through the next year.

I always tried to work near the mountains and at the end of my third year I got a job as a guide on the Fox Peak. I had to get up early in the morning, collect the tourists who were staying in a hotel, drive them down to the lake and row them out to a point where they could take ooh-ah photos of the mountains reflected in the lake. Then take them back, get them breakfasted, fitted out with boots, a climbing pole and a parka and take them up the glacier. Right up to the pinnacle was the go, about three miles up, and the trick was not to lose any of them down the crevasses. The walk was along a series of ridges and some of the crevasses were over a hundred feet deep. The guide carried a pack with a bit of rope sticking out of it, but that was just for show. The rope was only about forty foot long and if one of them had gone over, goodbye.

I met Mary, my first wife, when I was running those tours. She became ill one night and I was the nearest thing to a doctor around. She had renal colic and was in a pretty bad way and I did what I could for her and that was the beginning for us. Mary was a great woman, a wonderful woman, but she had a lot of problems. She was addicted, intermittently, to opiates like pethidine, which she could sometimes get doctors to prescribe for her. She suffered from Munchhausen's syndrome — a propensity not to tell the truth, particularly in regard to medical matters. Sufferers tell lies to get medical attention they don't really need and exhibit other irrational behaviours. For example, Mary told me she was a doctor and I believed that for a number of years, before I found out differently. She'd studied medicine, hadn't qualified, but she could hold her own in any medical company, no worries. An extraordinary woman. I loved her and my family loved her and we moved into a flat. We lived together while I went on with my studies.

Mary was at the centre of my life — we were married in 1958 — for almost the next twenty years and we had some wonderful times together, working, climbing, everything. But she was also the cause of many disruptions, two of them pretty early on in our relationship. She was older than me, had two children from her first marriage, and she was involved with a man in New Guinea. She'd come to New Zealand from Kavieng in New Ireland, Bismarck Archipelago. Not long after we started living together, she left me and went back there and I was full of juice and jealousy and I went after her.

I had to borrow a hundred quid from my old man to do it — hop across the Tasman in a Sunderland flying boat, fly up to Brisbane, on to Moresby and Goroka. The most interesting part of the trip was the ride I hitched on a DC3 across to Rabaul. The plane had been chartered by a man named Dick DeLisle who was a labour recruiter. He was taking mainlanders across to the island coconut plantations and being paid thirty pounds per head for every one he delivered. Conditions on the plantations weren't good and mortality rates were high but that wasn't Dick's concern. He was in it for the money, like the old-time blackbirders. He had to make sure the recruits were OK while they were in his charge and he had his work cut out on that flight over the Owen Stanleys.

We ran into a severe electrical storm — lightning all around the plane, thunder, sheets of rain — and the New Guineans were terrified. In a DC3 you sat along the sides, everybody facing everybody else, and the fear was infectious. It was their first plane trip; I was scared myself — it was only the third or fourth time I'd been up. Dick DeLisle was a little chap, shorter and lighter than me, pale and red-headed, and he had to pacify his recruits, some of whom were big, strapping men. The plane was lurching and bucking and Dick was hopping around, talking Pidgin and patting these black blokes twice his size on the head.

We made it to Rabaul and I met up again with Mary. Emotional stuff, violent. I nearly damaged the man I thought was sleeping with her. He probably wasn't. It was the first time I saw what a powerful emotion jealousy is. Mary had malaria which was a big killer at the time, and I got interested in it. I called in at a few hospitals and saw some of the effects of severe malaria, like spleens the size of footballs. This experience stood me in good stead later when I had to sit an oral examination in pathology. I was very under-prepared as a result of having haired off to New Guinea, but the one subject they asked me to discuss was malaria. I was full bottle on it and passed without trouble.

I brought Mary back to New Zealand and when we hit Auckland I had tenpence in my pocket. That wasn't enough for two pies, which cost sixpence each, so we bought one and shared it. I never remember feeling as destitute as that before or since. We had a long walk before we reached my grandmother's place where we could get a meal and some money.

I couldn't understand why Mary didn't get herself registered as a doctor in New Zealand. Here we were broke, in debt. I got onto her about it and after a while she did get registered and we went off to work in my vacation at Porirua Mental Hospital. In those days, medical students could work in hospitals, under supervision, doing pretty much the things qualified doctors did. Mary, passing herself off as a doctor, administered ECT to a patient who died. All hell broke loose when they found out that Mary wasn't properly qualified. I was hauled up by the Medical Council as an accessory to a fraud, and Mary pissed off to Australia.

I got a job on a construction site, working on the building of a paper mill, to make some money and I went after her again.

Mary was travelling north in Queensland and the Burdekin river was in flood at the time, making getting around difficult. You had to cross the river in lifeboats fitted with outboards and you couldn't be sure when you'd be where. Mary and I just missed each other a couple of times, but we met up again in Ayr or Homehill, up in the sugar country. We regrouped, but I didn't have enough money to get back to New Zealand so we got down to Rockhampton on the skin of our arses and I went into the employment office to ask for a job for my wife and myself. A bit cheeky, because we weren't married at that stage.

The bloke at the office looks at me and he says, 'There's seven hundred men out of work in this town, laddie.'

At that time the sugar cane was all cut by hand; it was seasonal labour, and some of the cutters stayed around the sugar districts for a while looking for work, before they moved on. They got first call on any work going. Not such a good start for me, so I said it didn't necessarily have to be here in town.

'That's different,' he says. 'There's work at Yaraka.'

He said it as if the name of the place meant something, but I didn't know where the fuck Yaraka was so I just said, 'Is it a long way off?'

'It is, actually. There's a job for a cook and a tractor driver and we'll give you train tickets to get there.'

I said, 'That'll do me,' and we went. Took us a fortnight to get there because of the floods. Meals on the trains were paid for and I nearly won a good bit of money playing billiards in a place called Jericho, but the train left and I couldn't clinch it. We travelled to the end of the line — Yaraka was on a spur from the main line to Longreach. We were the only people left on the train, and we were met out there by a bloke in a Land Rover. We confirmed that we were the new station hand and cook and we got into the Land Rover. He's barrelling down the road which had been all cut up by 4WDs, huge ruts in it, one of the roughest roads I'd ever seen, and this maniac of a driver, dropping in and out of these bone-cracking ruts, turns to me and he says, 'Station hands are scum.'

CHAPTER 4

'On the outer Barcoo'

On the outer Barcoo where the churches are few,
And men of religion are scanty,
On a road never cross'd 'cept by folk that are lost
One Michael Magee had a shanty.

A. B. *Patterson, 'A Bush Christening'*

That's great country out there, slap-dab in the middle of Queensland. It deserves better verse than the above. We stayed bush for quite a few months. I've always looked back on it as an idyllic time and thought I must have idealised the beauty of the land, but I went back, about twenty years after this episode, and found that it was just as good as I'd thought.

The Korean War had brought on a wool boom and this bloody great property was being converted from a cattle station to a sheep run. That meant putting through roads, fencing, getting in dingo-proof fences, sinking bores, a lot of hard work. We got to the homestead and Mary hopped straight into the cooking. There were only twelve people on the station, but all the proprieties were observed. The station manager and his family fed in one place, the overseer and the head stockman in another and us plebs in a third. No democracy there.

The bloke who had brought us in took me around the back and showed me the tractor. I had worked on my uncle's farm a bit in New Zealand and I'd driven four-wheel tractors a few times. Fuck me, the thing he pointed out was a bulldozer — a bloody great two-tracked monster with a blade. I knew a bit about them, all bad, but I had never driven one.

I tried not to show any concern and asked whether it ran all right.

'Oh, it's never been used,' he said. 'It was dropped off a low-loader a couple of months back and we've been waiting for an operator.'

Well, that helped a little. I figured that if no other bugger had ever driven it, I wasn't starting from behind scratch. So I just took a look at it and asked for the log-book, the operating manual. That came to light and I took it away to study as if I was sitting for an exam the next day. The tricky thing about those machines was that they had a starter motor that was independent of the rest of the 'dozer. Get that going — it had a small petrol engine, like half of a Volkswagen motor — and you were in business. You could turn over the big motor in the bulldozer and get going. If you couldn't get it going, you were buggered. So I swotted up the manual that night and went out very early to have a go at it. It was sort of make or break. Mary could cook all right, but if I couldn't get this fucking thing going, God knows what'd happen next.

There was a strap that ran round the fly wheel and hooked down into a clip. You had to pull that to get it started. I made sure that there was petrol in the thing . . . maybe I prayed . . . I yanked the strap and the starter motor purred into life like a fucking Rolls Royce. After that, you couldn't stop me. I tore into the work, loved it. I was called a ringer tractor driver and my wages were twelve pounds a week of which I got eight in the hand — they took four out for board and the company store docked you for tobacco and other things.

It was a great time. I spent a lot of time under the vehicles, putting in clutches that were always getting burnt out by the rough work. I'd had a couple of old cars in my later years as a medical student and had taken them to bits as a matter of necessity, to keep them going. So I knew how to do that sort of thing. Like all hard work though, bulldozing was dangerous and I lost one of my nine lives when I bogged the tractor and went back to get a Land Rover to pull it out. The bugger wouldn't start and I got into it to prime the carburettor with petrol. The other bloke hit the starter. I jumped back, the petrol can spilled and the thing went up like a rocket.

You need to be quick-thinking and lucky in those situations. I knew that what you didn't do when you were alight was run. So I rolled on the ground and beat at my clothes and hair and got the fire out. I was burnt to buggery, all over my face and hands and chest and I had to get some help. We were miles from the station but we got the Land Rover going and it was easier for me to drive than to get in and out to open the gates. The other bloke was sometimes a bit slow with the gates and I got on his back about it. The driving was all right because the Land Rover didn't have a windscreen and the rush of cool air on the face was good.

We got back and they radioed the Flying Doctor. I was taken into Charleville and spent a few weeks in hospital there. I just lay under a mosquito net while they put ointment over me, tubes into me, serum and stuff. It probably roughened me up a bit further, but with my broken nose and everything, I've never been anyone's idea of the smooth doctor type.

Those bush towns are full of characters. I remember one old bloke who used to come in there who had heard that I was a New Zealander and it seemed to be his mission in life to give me bits of backblocks wisdom. Some of it might have been all right, but I remember he said, 'Never ride behind a blackfella. And don't eat with 'em. Chuck 'em their food like dogs.'

That stayed with me.

A character I met when I got out of hospital was an ex-schoolteacher from Dublin named Paddy O'Kane. Paddy was working as a bore sinker with a man named George Brown. I had put in a road to one of their bore sites and that's how I met up with them. There was good money in boresinking if you worked hard and Paddy's ambition was to get together five hundred pounds so he could marry this schoolteacher in Rockhampton. But she wouldn't marry him until he had five hundred quid saved. Paddy'd make the money OK, then he'd blow it on two-up in Barcaldine or Blackall or somewhere. Finally, he got his stake together and went off, so George Brown needed a partner and he asked me if I would like to come in with him.

The road-cutting work on the station was just about finished and Mary was getting jack of cooking for that mob, so I agreed. We thought of it as a great adventure — camping out, moving around, living off the land to some extent. It was, too, but it was also bloody hard work as well as enjoyable and a good money-earner. It's a good game, drilling. That was percussion drilling: the bit is weighted and a swivel is part of the mechanism so that when the bit drops it also twists, skewering and cutting into the rock. You have to concentrate, keep your hand on the wire cable, check the plant and you get a sense of accomplishment. When I got the hang of it, George and I were doing twelve-hour shifts. I felt really pleased that I could do it. As I said, next to ophthalmology, that's the work I've enjoyed most.

The money was really terrific. We got paid thirty-five shillings a foot. You put a bore down thirteen hundred feet and you're really earning money. One day, I remember, I made thirty pounds. That was two weeks' wages at an ordinary job in those days. For one bore, one hole in the ground, I made four hundred and twenty eight pounds and I went into Blackall and cashed that cheque. I stood there with all these notes in my hands. I know I'd never had a sense of having that much money before, and I don't think I've ever quite had it since.

We had a lot of adventures, Mary, George and me. One night a herd of steaming brumbies came stampeding through the camp and only missed our tents by good luck. That was a terrifying thing to happen at night — we heard them coming like thunder rolling across the plain and then there were showers of sparks from their hooves on the stones. That made me see the point of the bounty the station manager had put on the wild horses. He was offering five bob for a pair of ears and I went out with a rifle and a quiet little kelpie dog one day and shot over thirty brumbies. It sounds brutal, but the horses were threatening the viability of the run as well as carrying disease and so on. The funny thing was that George, who was a competitive sort of bloke, went out horse-shooting too, but with the wrong kind of dog. He had a bull terrier/blue merle cross, only a pup but very uncontrollable, and it chased the bloody horses away so that George hardly got a shot in.

Another time we knocked off for lunch, shut the plant down and enjoyed a bit of tucker and the peace and quiet. I was drinking tea and I looked up and saw some low clouds. I commented on them to George.

'That's smoke,' George yelled.

I climbed up the derrick and I could see this bloody bushfire burning on a wide front with a whole lot of willy-willys pushing it along. It was lightly wooded country all around and the fire was heading straight for us. We moved like lightning, struck the tents, chucked all our gear into the truck along with some food and water. We didn't worry about the rig, that belonged to Godfrey Brothers, it'd have to take its chance. We jumped into the truck, George hit the starter and the bloody thing wouldn't kick. It was like a scene in the movies, but for real. Hit it again, no go. So George, cool as can be, says, 'Right, Fred, we'll have to get a back-burn going. You start there and I'll work here.'

We got our fire going, burning back towards the bushfire, and it was touch and go for a while but eventually the willy-willys pushed the fire around our camp, out on the flanks, and left us safe. Amazingly, when we started burning, the ground was suddenly alive with snakes, dozens of the buggers wriggling everywhere. We'd been sharing that camp site with them for weeks and never saw one. For a fortnight after that the sky to the east was aglow. I don't know, maybe that was the second of my nine lives gone.

I kept getting letters from the university in New Zealand asking me if I had abandoned the course. I'd missed a good part of a year's work by this stage. I kept putting off replying because George and I were on such a good wicket. But eventually the pressure from the university got to me and I decided I had to go back. It was a pity in a way because we'd just got a contract to put down eight holes in the flat country. We'd been working in difficult territory, jump-ups — that is, escarpment country, pretty rough, where you have to work very hard getting the plant into place and making a start on the bore, spudding in. This contract was going to be a piece of piss — quick set-ups, down you go, pack up and spud in again a few days later. We could've made a fortune.

It was a wrench to leave and George said he was going to pack it in, too, when Mary and I left. We'd been a great team. But we went back to New Zealand where I was slated to do Obstetrics and Gynaecology, starting on such and such a date in January. It was the responsible and right choice to go back, but when I got there I found I had a month's dead time in Auckland — we could have put down a few of those holes and made a thousand quid.

CHAPTER 5

The Eyes have It

> Hollows, you're the house surgeon here now . . . you've got an easy job. All you have to do is know everything about these patients every time I show up . . .
>
> *Dr Harry England*

Back in New Zealand I went on in much the same way, working hard enough to pass, rock-climbing in my spare time, getting into debt. I remember that in Auckland in my final year I caught up with a few of my old mates who had passed me while I was going bush. They were working as junior medical officers, or junior house surgeons, and they were slaving their bums off. These were blokes I used to go drinking with, play billiards with, and they weren't drinking or playing billiards now. They were lucky if they got a feed a day. I thought: *One thing's for sure — I'm not going to work like that.*

I passed the final examinations and got a job in the Auckland Public Hospital as a Resident. Before I knew it, I was working as hard as all the others. I remember that the first job I had was in general surgery. Harry England was the senior surgical tutor and he said, 'Hollows, you're the house surgeon here now. I do a ward round at half-past seven three days a week, and you've got an easy job. All you have to do is know all about these patients every time I show up and if I ring in between times. I don't want to hear from any ward sister or registrar or anyone else telling about these patients. Just you!'

There were two wards, thirty males and thirty females — sixty patients to keep tabs on.

Harry England said, 'Apart from that, your time's your own. You can go to the races, go to the beach, go drinking — do anything you like.'

Sixty people, half a dozen surgeons working on them, complications, people coming and going, it was a dog's life, but a lot of it was very good work, good training. The upshot was that I don't think I had a drink for three months, and when I did finally get away with Mary and an old friend to have a few nibbles, I developed a tremendous pain in the gut. We were going at it pretty hard; it was four o'clock and the pub was going to close at six. The pain was so bad that I had to lie down on a sofa in the lobby of the pub while they got an ambulance. A few upper-crust types got something out of that — a doctor, half-pissed, flat on his back in the lobby.

They got me to the hospital and I was in terrific pain. One of the doctors, not a great friend of mine, diagnosed a perforated ulcer and was dead keen to get me into the operating theatre. But Harry England decided they should x-ray me first and I can remember that x-ray, out of the thousands that I've seen, to this day. It showed a hugely dilated stomach; my stomach was blown up almost into my left armpit with an enormous gas bubble on top of it. I had an ulcer all right, and it had gone into spasm, causing the stomach to expand and secrete all kinds of stuff and what with the rum and beer chasers we'd been drinking . . .

'Give him a hundred milligrams of pethidine,' Harry England says, 'and whack a tube down him.'

The pain went when the pethidine hit me; they got off nearly a bucketful of altered blood and I felt tremendous. The patients, the very same people I was supposed to be dealing with on the next shift, were coming up to me and saying things like, 'Gee, must have been pretty crook beer, doc.'

We had a big operating list the next day and I felt well

enough to do what I had to do by then. That really pissed off the guy who'd been looking forward to getting the knife into me. Every medico has those *Doctor in the House* sorts of stories, but we only tell the ones with happy endings. That was a very hard-working year and there were some excellent doctors around and some real characters. The Professor of Psychiatry, one Dr Blake-Palmer, was a character. Inevitably, he was nicknamed Snake-Charmer. Said to be a heavy drinker, he died of pancreatitis (which is often drink-related), and he wore high-heeled shoes because he was very short — we excused him both peccadillos on account of his being a psychiatrist. He was the one who saved the author Janet Frame from being lobotomised, so that was a contribution.

My next job was in Tauranga, a beautiful, sunny seaside resort town, up on the Bay of Plenty in the North Island, which I chose to forestall the government sending me, as one of its bursary-holders, somewhere else. Tauranga Public was a one hundred and twenty-bed hospital and after I had been there a month or so the other house surgeon left. That put the pressure on, but it was at Tauranga that I made my first significant move towards being an eye doctor. A few things came together. I had done what was called 'an eye term' in my medical course, so I knew the language — the anterior chamber, the cornea, the iris, and I knew roughly what was involved in a retinal detachment operation — and as a result of that I had assisted eye surgeons in the Auckland job.

At Tauranga there was an eye surgeon and a chance to do some eye work, but my interest had been intensified by the visit of Garfield Todd to New Zealand. He was a famous New Zealander who had been the Prime Minister of Southern Rhodesia from 1953 to 1958 and my father knew him. I had been interested for some time in practising medicine in Africa. I'd read a bit about it, and there seemed to be a crying need for properly run clinics, free of political or church influence. I got my father to set up a meeting with Todd and a few interested doctors in Palmerston North. I had also been told by someone that if you wanted to be useful in Africa you had to know how to take out a cataract because there was an enormous amount of cataract-caused blindness.

We had a meeting and it was a complete frost because when I said something about working in co-operation with, say, the African National Congress, Todd stood up. 'I will continue this meeting,' he said, 'no longer.' To give him his due, he later loosened up and presented a balanced case for the ANC to the United Nations. So nothing came of that.

Back in Tauranga, I said to Ron Tingey, the eye surgeon there, 'How about I see all your eye cases and help with the notes and assist you in the operations?'

He wasn't strictly speaking entitled to that amount of the house surgeon's time, so he was all for it.

'Providing,' I added, 'that at the end of the year we've got to the point where I can take out a cataract safely.'

So we did that and Ron taught me how to handle ocular tissue. It's tricky. The cornea is very tough tissue and you need a super-sharp instrument to cut it with any precision; the iris is very thin and the capsule of the lens is only fifteen microns thick. Delicate, delicate stuff, and you have to deal with all this in the most basic of eye operations, like cataract surgery. He was a very good eye surgeon and, of course, the way things were then, he was also an ear, nose and throat man. He'd grown a bit tired of that branch of the work, and so we did a sort of trade. In return for getting a training in the eye skills I also put in time on the ear, nose and throat stuff so that I could take some of those cases off his hands. He'd say, 'Well, Fred, I've really got to get down to my rooms. Now, there's only four tonsils and a couple of adenoids and one submucous resection and perhaps one set of nasal polyps. You'll be all right with those, won't you?'

I never regretted that deal because I learned about the upper airway, back of the nose and throat, and the post-nasal space, and one of the few times I'm certain that I saved a life, I owe to that knowledge. One time I was in Casualty and a

Basic structure of the eye

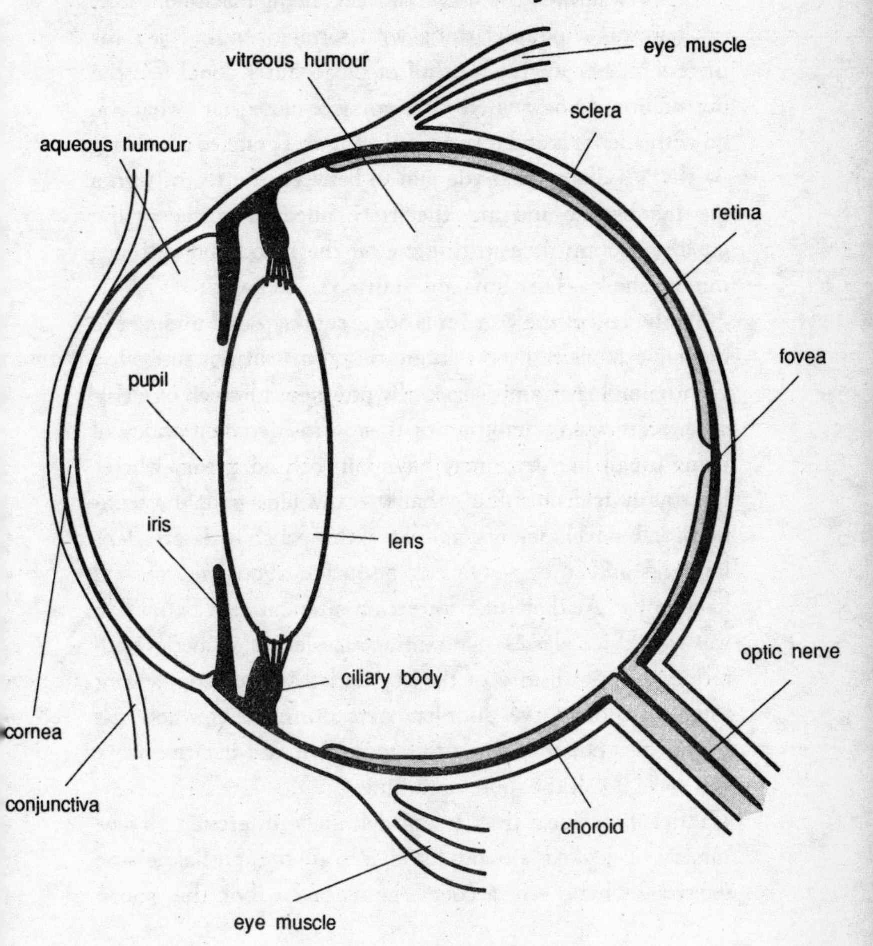

bloke came charging through the doors with his daughter in his arms. She must have been about five years old. She was blue; there was hardly any pulse; her heart was beating but only just. She was bloody near dead.

I said, 'What's happened?'

'She's swallowed the nozzle of a cake-icing machine.'

That was a pointed thing with serrated ends. I put my fingers in; her mouth was full of blood but I could feel the obstruction. I knew where I was going because that's what you do with adenoids and tonsils, feel around. I grabbed a rack gag — that's a device that you jam in between the teeth, turn a big thumbscrew, and open the jaw. I pulled the nozzle out and got the suction tube in to draw off the blood and within a minute she was breathing and starting to pick up.

By the end of the year I was doing cataracts and finding eye medicine more and more interesting. I'm still not sure why. Ophthalmology wasn't a specially prestigious branch of medicine, so it wasn't ambition of that sort. A romantic idea of being useful in Africa may have lain behind it somewhere. I certainly had no inkling that there would be all the technological developments and breakthroughs — lasers, lens implants and so on — that came in the 1960s and are still happening. At that time correction after cataract extraction was with thick glasses — no intraocular lenses; diabetics with retinopathy, a disease of the capillaries of the retina, went blind.[1] A lot of eye disorders were untreatable which was frustrating, but that made the corrective and curative work you *could* do all the more rewarding.

After I decided that I was definitely interested in eye surgery, I looked around for a job as an ophthalmologic registrar. There were a couple going and I took the one in

[1] Modern, microscopic eye surgery has made possible the insertion of a plastic lens, called an intra-ocular lens, to replace the lens made crystalline by cataract. Laser treatment has saved the sight of a generation of diabetics suffering retinopathy.

Wellington. So I was pretty well set on my course by then — doing only ophthalmology. That is, as far as medicine was concerned.

But Mary's daughter Jennifer had come over from Australia to live with us and there was the business of settling her in, getting her back to school after a dropout phase, to cope with. And other domestic matters, like getting out of debt.

Politics, too. It was while I was an eye registrar at Wellington that I joined the Communist Party, along with Bill Glass and six or seven other doctors. The Cold War was on and communists were being persecuted. I joined the Railways Workshop branch of the Party — which suggests there was some connection between my and my father's brand of radicalism. My thinking was simple, pure Bolshie stuff: *If everyone's against them they must have some of the right ideas*. The New Zealand Communist Party was not well organised and they did not find much for me to do until the next year. Not that I would have had much time to do it. Wellington had the biggest hospital in the country and I was kept busy that year, even though I was specialising.

While I was there the first retinal camera to be imported into New Zealand arrived, all crated up. I got a hammer and ripped the crate apart and set the apparatus up. It was a Zeiss Nordenson camera and we used it mainly to photograph the eyes of people with hypertension, then a significant blinding disorder. It is treated with drugs now. So that was the first retinal photography service in the country and I felt I was in the vanguard of eye work and enjoying it. But I wanted to do it properly and I realised there was a hell of a lot I didn't know. There was no post-graduate specialist training available then in New Zealand, and the thing to do was go to the UK and get a Diploma of Ophthalmology.

To do that I needed money and you could make good money as a general practitioner in New Zealand if you played your cards right. I'd done a few short-term locums and heard people talk about them and the general rule was that you were paid thirty quid a week. The practice might be making five hundred, but that was the deal. I thought there should be a bit more equity in it than that. I looked around for a spot and saw an advertisement for a practice in Auckland, available for a year. The advertiser was Dr Robert Bruce. I had read some history; maybe I took a fancy to the name.

I went up there and the first thing he said to me was, 'Young man, general practice is a business.'

I thought: *That'll do me. That's why I'm here.* We haggled for a while in between times while he saw patients. He was an extraordinary man physically — short and burly with an undershot jaw and long, Neanderthal arms — and unusual philosophically — a member of the Plymouth Bretheren sect, people who considered themselves to be in this world but not of it.

'Come on,' he says, 'let's do a few calls.'

We jumped in his car, a big Mercedes 300, the first one I had ever seen, and went roaring off around the suburbs of south Auckland doing calls at a rate of knots. In one big house that had a lot of Maoris in it, he whipped around, remembering the details of the people who he had seen for various things, until he got to the reason for the call — a kid with a huge abcess on her upper arm.

'Hold this arm, Fred.'

Quick as a flash he whipped out a scalpel, lanced the abcess and dressed it and we were on our way.

He was a real operator but a very good, hands-on doctor, very good with kids, skin problems, a whole range of things. We came to an arrangement whereby I would live in his house, he would pay the telephone bill and running costs on my car — I had a flash two-litre Riley then, great machine — and fifty pounds a week. *But*, once I'd seen two hundred patients in any one week, I'd get seven shillings and sixpence for every extra customer. Turned out to be a very good arrangement because it was a busy practice and some weeks I'd be seeing my two-hundredth patient by Tuesday night.

It only worked because Robert had a highly efficient and organised staff, particularly the nurse who lived in the surgery, which was a separate house built on the same block as the one Mary and I lived in. She would have the list of patients to be seen all organised in a logical way to make the circuit of calls efficient. Then she'd deal with the bag — in those days, needles and syringes had to be boiled and there'd be things to replace. I would do a round before breakfast, starting about six o'clock, then a surgery session, then more calls before and after lunch, another surgery and a round of later night calls. It was incredibly hard work — one weekend off in five — but very interesting. Robert took a particular interest in neurotics. He had about thirty of them on his books, people he was keeping out of institutions, and dealing with them certainly broke the monotony.

I picked up some useful doctoring hints from Robert Bruce — two in particular. He said, 'Fred, if you ever get a call when you're about to go to bed, don't get dressed. Just put your dressing gown over your pyjamas and go out like that. It doesn't hurt to remind people that a doctor has to sleep.'

Another time he said, 'Babies can die very quickly. If you're treating a baby for *anything*, don't go to bed before checking on it. And check yourself, not over the phone.'

Some time after that I circumcised an infant. He was the only son in a family of five and the parents, prominent local people, were particularly attached to him. I used a little bit of anaesthetic, what was called rag-and-bottle anaesthesia, and they took him home. I rang up a few times to ask if he was OK and I was told that he was sleeping comfortably. I was about to go to bed after a long day and I remembered what Robert had said. So I went to the house to look at the kid. I had circumcised him at about nine o'clock in the morning and he was still sleeping fourteen hours later. He was white, the colour of a sheet of paper, but still breathing. His mother said she hadn't changed his nappy because he seemed to be dry. I got the nappies off and the bottom one was soaked in blood.

He'd been lying there quietly bleeding to death. I quickly clamped it off and they didn't lose him, but if Robert hadn't given me that advice, they would have.

I actually did some work in the Communist Party at that time, mainly racing around at night painting up slogans on walls and across billboards and putting up posters. I was the only member of the branch who had a car, so when one of these runs was on, no matter if I was knackered after a day's doctoring, I was it. I found out later that NZSIS (the New Zealand Security and Intelligence Service) was keeping an eye on me and the other Communist doctors, but they didn't give us any trouble at the time.

I met Paul Robeson and his wife through that connection. Robeson had gone into virtual exile from the United States and he visited New Zealand, sponsored by some left-wing organisations. He stayed at our house and sang in the Town Hall. I remember he sang 'Joe Hill' and everyone was weeping into their laps. Harry Pollitt stayed with us, too. He was the Secretary General of the British Communist Party and had been a pall-bearer at Lenin's funeral. He was a dynamic little bald-headed man, very impressive. Incongruously, his wife was an extremely proper English lady with an upper-class accent.

So that was a busy, remunerative and stimulating time, but I was dead keen to go to England.

CHAPTER 6

Resisting Pongophalization

Dr Macphail lit his pipe and, leaning over the rail, searched the heavens for the Southern Cross.

M. W. Somerset Maugham, 'Rain'

I had five thousand pounds when I set off for England. That was a lot of money in 1961, but I had got the idea that I might have to do more than just the Diploma in Ophthalmology, which was a six-month course. It looked like it might be necessary to qualify as a fellow in the speciality and that involved a lot more study and time. And I had a wife to support. So I started to economise from the word go by getting a job as a ship's doctor. 'Slow starvation and agony' was the unofficial name given to the shipping line — Shaw, Saville and Albion. Mary and I went to England on the S.S. *Hobart*.

The *Hobart* left Wellington carrying frozen mutton to Britain — twelve passengers, sixty-four crew. We had deck cabins and all I had to do was a surgery in the morning and one at night, an hour or so all up. Plenty of time to study texts on ophthalmology, play deck games, drink and laze around. We set off across the South Pacific. The weather was beautiful and for quite a while there was nothing medical for me to do. The trip took six weeks and it was one of the sweetest times of my life.

The ship was filthy when we left New Zealand, rusted with bloody dunnage all over the place, but within a week it was spotless. The seamen worked like badgers. We hit a storm near the end of the voyage and everything got all fouled up, but, again, the ship was in perfect nick when we got to port. They had pride in their work, those blokes. But they were sailors, just the same. When we arrived at Panama City, at six o'clock in the morning, every man jack of them was lined up ready to hit the gangplank and get into the brothels. Mary and I visited one of the brothels — the Madam performed with a huge dildo on a young girl. It was too much for us so we left the show.

The ship went through the canal to Cristobal Colon at the Atlantic end, which was a rather boring twelve hours, slow going through the locks, a lot of waiting. (Thirteen years later, in 1973, Mary and I went through the canal again after a trip to South America, but by then the cargo ships — we'd sailed on one for nostalgic reasons — were all containerised and you couldn't even get out on the deck. That time I teamed up with a young American student and we ran across the isthmus. Forty-eight kilometres; took us nine hours and the villagers along the way yelled, '*Los gringos son locos*' at us. It wiped me out, but it was better than going through on the boat and it's something to be able to say you've run right across America.)

We docked in the port of London about midnight. This was mid-January and it was freezing cold and sleeting. At that time the port was the busiest in the world but it was incredibly run-down and decrepit — a very depressing place. Someone proposed we have a party until sun-up and that's what we did, drinking all our duty-free booze and generally doing ourselves a lot of damage. In the morning all I wanted to do was sleep, but two relations of Mary's — Englishmen with furled umbrellas — insisted on taking us around and getting us acquainted. It took a few hairs of the dog before London became anything other than an almighty headache.

I enrolled in the diploma course at the Institute of Ophthalmology in Judd Street, North London. I didn't have any particular long-term goals and ambitions. It was a punt: I wanted to find out if I was any good, and Judd Street was the way to do it — to play in the big league. And two things quickly became apparent to me. One was, that through experience and a feel for the subject, I was well ahead of most of the other students. I wasn't going to have any trouble competing with my peers and completing the course. The second thing was that the teachers were streets ahead of me.

The aspects of eye medicine I was interested in — glaucoma, thyroid eye disease, retinal vein occlusions — was stuff they had sorted out long before and could handle without thinking about it. There were higher reaches of the subject, more detailed knowledge of the working of the eye and the nature of eye disorders and treatment, than I'd ever heard of, and that was what I wanted to tap into. It was obvious that I'd have to go the whole hog and get the fellowship qualification.

But first it was a matter of getting the DO and keeping body and soul together. London was an expensive place to live; there were fees to pay, and we were sending money home to Mary's children. So I got work as a radio doctor. It was night call work. You had a radio in your car and did a series of calls relayed to you from a radio base. We were living in Tooting Bec, in the south. About the only doctor I ever met in Britain with a cockney accent, Len Collins, was running this service. Because it was a shock to hear a medico speaking cockney I initially had a slight credibility problem with him. I had run up against the issue of class again, and even more significantly than at home. Accent was part of the iconography of class, and most doctors who began life without a standard southern English accent soon set about acquiring one.

Len Collins drove a big Facel Vega, a French car with a V8 Chrysler engine, very flash. He had a mistress in Italy and was a high roller who did very well out of this strange practice of his. I was good at it, with Mary to help me navigate the streets and do the paperwork. I struck a deal with Len that I would be paid fourteen shillings a case instead of a flat rate. It worked well. We had a front-wheel-drive Mini Minor that was good in the snow. It snowed a lot that first winter. I remember that at one stage, between half-past three and half-past seven in the morning — we did four-hour shifts — I was the only primary care doctor on call for a third of London. It was mostly coughs, colds, sore holes, and pimples on the dick.

I must have made an impression on the teachers in the DO course because one of them, Jimmy Hudson, came up to me after a lecture and said, 'Oh, Hollows, old chap, I suppose you're sitting the Moorfields Prize?'

The Moorfields Junior Prize was an award for the top candidate in the DO examinations. You had to enter for it and I hadn't given it a thought. Prizes weren't something that had come my way since the one I had scored for Bible study, and I was a long way from that. But I thought about this approach and realised that it was an Englishman's way of saying that I *should* enter for it. I did and I shared it with another New Zealander. Good thing to have on the CV. I keep it on my office wall along with a few other gongs and a lot of memoribilia like photographs of Glenleith College, mountains I've climbed and people I've worked with.

After that the fellowship was the obvious next step. It was done in two stages, the first of which was called, somewhat misleadingly, the Primary — honours standard work in anatomy, physiology, pathology and biochemistry at the Royal College of Surgeons. I must have got my second wind as a student because the work very stimulating. It was the most intellectually expanding period of my life, very exciting. I studied in harness with Graham Duffy, a friend from Dunedin, who later became a brain surgeon, and we both worked very hard. The electron microscope had just come into use and there were a lot of developments which were new to me. For example, electron microscopic study had shown how nerve fibres are insulated with spiral rolls of a fatty substance called myelin, and it's this that allows the nerve to conduct electricity. Fascinating stuff.

As it happened, the style of a lot of the teachers appealed to me. For example, the head anatomist was an Australian named John Last. Anatomy lecturers, although they can be droll, are not usually flamboyant. John Last used to pull out a snuff box in the middle of a lecture, put a pinch in the anatomical snuff box — the notch on the back of the hand — sniff it up, all the time talking to three hundred doctors. Then he'd do the other nostril, still talking; then the sneezes would start and he'd pull out this metre-square red handkerchief, have a blow and keep on lecturing without missing a beat.

And he wasn't just a showman. I remember one lecture he gave us on the ventral abdominal wall, the front of the belly. It involved the four muscles and their connections to the sternum, or the bottom of the ribs, the vertebrae and the hip bones. These muscles have sheet-like tendons which have particular origins from above and insertions where they are attached below. This had always been a puzzle to me. After this forty-minute lecture on 'The ventral abdominal wall in relationship to its function' you realised with crystal clarity that the muscles could *only* be that way and the same with the tendons. Anatomy can be dull; you can study a nit on a gnat's knacker *ad infinitum*, but this approach was in terms of the function of the human body and that made all the difference. It was beautiful. I sat spellbound through that lecture, sucked it all in, didn't take a note.

I remember being bowled over by another lecture on the development of the peripheral nerves and how they worked. It was illustrated by magnificent slides and it got right down almost to a molecular level. I was impressed by the fact that the teachers were the men who had set the standards in these subjects — who had actually dissected the nerve supply of the heart muscles, had studied the motor centres, were doing the original research and writing it up. Also, they didn't have a dogmatic, catechistic approach. You could be sure they wouldn't throw something at you like, list the muscles inserting, or taking their origins from, the upper end of the humerus. Instead they'd ask you to discuss the evidence that . . . or examine the argument for so and so . . .

All very well, but the Primary examination was notoriously tough. Only about 1 per cent of candidates passed it the first time up. Now Duffy, who was of Irish extraction of course, had a hankering to go to Ireland and, as it happened, by reciprocal arrangement with the Royal College in Dublin, you could sit the Primary examination there as well as in London. We'd been studying hard for about three months, pretty well cooped up, and Duffy proposed that we go to Dublin and do the examination as a dry run, not expecting to pass. We could have a shot at it, see what it was like, and sit it in earnest later back in London. After the exam in Dublin we could get on the Guinness for a bit.

It was a freezing cold winter in Dublin, and I'll never forget walking into the examination room for the first paper. It was a huge chamber with about four hundred candidates sitting there. There was an enormous fire to heat the place — a couple of square yards of burning coal. I thought, *I'll just take a look at the paper, keep my coat on, and if it's too bad I'll stroll out.* It was an anatomy exam and there were a lot of questions to do with electron microscopy. I hadn't quite cottoned on to electron microscopy then, it seemed too whizz-bang to take on board, and I thought, *Well, shit, I can't answer much of this.* Just then a great groan goes up in the room and I realised that everyone found the paper hard, so I reckoned I was in with a chance and I took off my coat and got on with it.

I don't remember much about the other exams, there were three three-hour papers, but I do remember the last of the vivas, the oral examinations. Every candidate had to face three sets of two examiners for five minutes and a bell rang at the end of your session. High pressure situation. There was an Indian doctor immediately before me, fronting up to the first team, and he got very excitable, waved his arms and was still yelling at the examiners after the bell rang. So I tried to keep calm when my turn came. They gave me a very straight-forward question which I answered quietly. It helped that I could see, among the examiners' notes, the mark I'd got on the paper — 64 per cent and I knew the pass mark was 60 per cent. So unless I completely buggered the oral, I was home and hosed.

On to the next pair and I really got lucky. They showed me a graph of the disassociation curve for haemoglobin. It was a sigma-shaped curve but I wasn't very familiar with it, and they asked me what happens under a certain physiological condition — I can't recall the detail. Now, one of these uptight Englishmen might have just sat there and sweated, but I was a raw colonial and I reached out to grab this chart — just a physical reflex, without another thought in mind.

The examiner said, 'That's it, exactly. You just turn it around, don't you? Quite right.'

I wouldn't have said that in a fit, but luck's a fortune and I went on to the next examiners. One of them was so bored he was sitting there reading a newspaper. The other one asked me what I knew about whole-body radiation. It so happened I had recently read a Pelican paperback called *The Lucky Dragon*, about some Japanese fishermen who didn't get the warning and were in the vicinity of Bikini Atoll, in the Marshall Islands, when the Americans tested a nuclear bomb there. They'd suffered whole-body radiation with a vengeance. I virtually told them the story as it was set out in the book, about the symptoms the Japanese suffered and so on. They listened.

'Have you got any questions for this laddie, Noel?'

Noel had put his paper down. He said, 'No,' and that was it.

We'd been very abstemious through the time of the written papers and the vivas, and so the moment it was over we decided it was time to go and get into a few drinks. The final results would be announced at College Green, the place that housed the Royal College, in a couple of hours. A factotum, all got up in gold braid, would come out and read off the numbers of the successful candidates, no mention of names and dead silence about the people who had dipped out. Three New Zealanders, Graham Duffy, Hilton La Grice (who's now an ophthalmologist) and me, along with Mary, went to the pub. Came the time for the announcement and we sent Mary up to get the news.

We were fairly well away by then, particularly Duffy, who was in his element. He was a wild man, could be belligerent, a great fighter, and here he was in Dublin, drinking Guinness, in touch with his roots. Mary came back and she said, 'Fred and Graham, you've got through. Sorry, Hilton, you missed out.'

At that Duffy, having got his first major postgraduate qualification in one hit and feeling himself to be on his own turf, yells, 'Yippee!' at the top of his voice.

The barman vaulted over the counter, went straight over to Duffy and planted him one. Duffy reeled back but he was too culturally and philosophically confused to fight. I'd never seen such a crestfallen Duffy.

I was riding high — a Moorfields Prize winner who had passed the Fellowship Primary first time up. I started to look around for a good job in ophthalmology and, to my surprise, I missed out on a few appointments I thought I should have got. It was partly a matter of participating in a very competitive, high standard market. My attitude probably had something to do with it. Most of the Australians and New Zealanders qualifying in England at that time were refining their accents. I was known as the doctor 'with the broad Australian accent'. I spoke then the way I speak now. In New Zealand, a disparaging term for an Englishman was a 'pongo'. I called this process of becoming an *ersatz* establishment Englishman, 'pongophalization'. I was still a political animal, a member of the Communist Party. I wasn't going to be pongophalized.

In fact, I did very little in the way of political activity in London. I had presented myself at Party headquarters in King Street, but their attitude to yet another colonial was a bit off-hand. Mary and I were in the Streatham branch and the chairman said, 'And what do you do for a living, comrade?'

'I'm a doctor,' I said.

'Well, that's good, comrade. We've got quite a few doctors in the branch and they don't pay their dues. Your first job's to go around and see if you can't collect some of these unpaid dues.'

I wasn't too impressed. In New Zealand a doctor who was a Party member and didn't pay his dues would get very short shrift. Also it didn't seem like the best job to give a new-chum. Surely, to do it well, you'd need to be acquainted with the characters in, and circumstances of, the area. I did it though, and I remember calling on one doctor and telling him what I was there for. He looked around. 'Shh,' he says, 'I've got some people in for drinks. Would you mind slipping around to the back?'

Not very inspiring. Not much revolutionary fervour there. But bathetic moments like that didn't cause me to have any great crisis of conscience. I just became too busy for politics. I got a job in Cardiff as Ophthalmologic Registrar in the Royal Infirmary. As I see it, it is mainly as a result of the work I did there that I've been able to be of some use in the world.

CHAPTER 7

Epidemiology in Wales

> I had always thought that by becoming a professor I would get good contacts with other academic medical departments and increase the prospects of collaboration in the mounting of surveys and trials. I was, in general, sadly wrong in this assumption, and the origin of the glaucoma survey and trial demonstrates how these things happen in real life.
>
> *Archie Cochrane,* One Man's Medicine

Just after the war, in 1948, a doctor named Sorsby did a study of the blind in England. And he found that more than half of the people who were registered as blind — that is, whose vision had deteriorated to a certain level — were in that condition because they hadn't had their cataracts taken out. Sorsby made a whole lot of recommendations about eye health, one of which was that Britain needed a lot more properly trained eye consultants. It took a while, but resources were eventually channeled that way, and by the early sixties places like the Royal Infirmary in Wales had eye consultants who were looking for junior registrars to train to keep the ball rolling.

That suited me. I planned to sit for the fellowship as soon as possible and continue my run. I had become a rather different sort of fellow by this time — much more serious and convinced that I could really be good at ophthalmology. I sat the exams and I failed. I thought, *Must've been bowled a few wrong 'uns and didn't pick 'em, got a bad bounce.* Six months later I sat again and failed again. Then I realised that I simply did not know enough ophthalmology. These other exams I'd passed didn't tell the story. In terms of the things in ophthalmology that I was interested in, I was a boy in a man's game. So I decided to do as much work as I could, really get the experience. And that's what I did for a couple of years, worked like a dog, and when I sat for the fellowship again I had no trouble. I'd grown up I guess; I wasn't trusting to flair and a bit of luck or blaming the system for anything.

I did a lot of surgery in Cardiff. There was a tremendous backlog of squints in children to be fixed. That was crazy, because the important thing is to correct a squint early so that the child doesn't develop amblyopia, blunt vision. They asked me if I could do three squint lists a week, a total of nine operations. I said I could do five per session. So three days a week I did five squints which meant that I had to have a good look at every patient beforehand to work out the binocular state, and follow up with corrective surgery as required. It was hard work but good work.

Same with retinal detachments. I'd done some in New Zealand and there was no one in the hospital who'd done any. It's not something you can do from a cold start — you need careful guiding through it. Pretty soon I'm doing all the retinal detachments for south Wales and I trained the other registrars to do the operation. There was also a lot of cataract surgery to be done, because the situation still hadn't been rectified even that long after Sorsby's report. There'd been a desperate shortage of eye surgeons in fact, and what we were doing was catching up. For example, Max Graham, one of the senior men, told me that he had a five-year waiting list for corneal grafts. So I did a lot of them too. Terrific experience.

There were some very good people at the Royal Infirmary — Bernie Gluck, the head of the department, two Grahams — a Peter and a Max — and Roger McGuinness, who works with me now, were there. I've got a photograph on my wall of one of our Christmas parties: Mary's there, and me and the other men all in suits and ties, probably Royal College of

Surgeons ties. Nowadays, some of us get around in open-neck shirts and jumpers. Times have changed. Good thing, too. But the most important influence on me at that time came through a man named Archibald L. Cochrane, who was Professor of Respiratory Medicine at the Welsh National School of Medicine and head of the Medical Research Council Epidemiology Unit in Cardiff. Archie Cochrane was an extraordinary man who'd been born into a wealthy Scottish industrial family, had become very left wing, had studied under and been psychoanalysed by Theodore Reik,[2] served in the Spanish Civil War and spent four very rough years in prisoner-of-war camps in World War 2. He'd met George Orwell and Evelyn Waugh and many of the members of the Bloomsbury group and, because he spoke fluent German, he handed over the surrender documents when the Allied forces were captured on Crete.

There are a lot of interesting sidelights to Archie and his autobiography[3] is well worth reading. He didn't take to Orwell very much and had a low opinion of Waugh, who he thought had been pretty inefficient as an intelligence officer. Virginia Woolf seemed to blame Archie for the death of her cousin, Julian Bell, in Spain. Like me, he wasn't able to get much out of her fiction. I was flattered by his references to me in his book, even if he gets the facts a bit scrambled. He refers to me as 'likeable', which is fair enough, but also as 'difficult' — I can't imagine what he meant by that.

Archie was one of the pioneers of epidemiology. Epidemiology simply means study among the people. His unit, into which he'd put a lot of his own money, studied disease and

---

[2] Dr Theodore Reik, an early follower of Freud, was a leading non-medical analyst in the years between the wars. His best-known book, *Listening with the Third Ear* (1948) proved widely popular and and helped to introduce psychoanalysis to the educated public.

[3] Cochrane, A.L. with Blythe, M., *One Man's Medicine* (British Medical Journal Memoir Club), London, 1989.

health care services in the mining valleys of south Wales and employed techniques such as screening and randomised control trials. For his studies of pneumoconiosis, a deadly disease, common among miners, resulting from the build-up of fibrous tissues in the lungs, Archie had isolated the populations of two adjoining valleys — the Rhondda Fach and the Rhondda Faur. The scheme was to survey the populations in both communities, treat the cases of the disease discovered in the Rhondda Fach and use the other community as a control group to study the effects of the treatment.

This was very radical stuff, medically and politically, involving ethical questions and relating to the quality of health service being received by the Welsh people. It involved enormous amounts of work, getting profiles and medical histories for an entire, or 'defined', population. Archie recorded that in a normal day he might interpret about a hundred chest x rays, visit the same number of addresses to persuade people to be x rayed, take forty or so industrial histories and interview thirty or forty miners about what their x rays had revealed.

All sorts of things stemmed from this research in terms of the techniques of epidemiology and the appropriateness of different forms of treatment. Most importantly, it meant that there was this closely studied, well-documented 'defined population' available for other investigations. That was where I came in. I was the senior eye registrar at the Cardiff Hospital at that time, and one day Archie rang me up to express concern about the treatment an outpatient was getting — the mother of Archie's secretary. I said I'd look into it immediately and I told Archie that I'd heard about his epidemiology unit and wondered if we might be able to co-operate on a research project I had in mind: a glaucoma survey.

Glaucoma, a blinding disorder relating to increase in ocular pressure, was very big in the literature at the time for a number of reasons. One was the discussion stimulated by a Swiss, Hans Goldman, who'd published a paper called 'Problems in Chronic Simple Glaucoma'. Goldman argued that by the time a glaucoma sufferer reached an eye clinic it was too late to intervene effectively, and that we should go out into the highways and byways, locate the people who were going to lose vision through glaucoma and save their sight. If you were going to do that, you'd need to know the actual prevalence of the disease in the population, the incidence among the different age groups, sex distribution, the medical histories and so on, the stuff of epidemiological research.

Another influential view at the time was that of Willie Liedecker, a prominent German scientist, who was involved in the mass chest x-raying of the German population after World War 2. The Germans were pretty subdued at that time (all of their dissidents had been killed off, remember) and they got an extraordinary compliance rate for this x ray program which was designed to combat tuberculosis. Liedecker measured the ocular pressures of the people in this very big sample and he came out with the statement that 7 per cent of the population had glaucoma. He was careful not to define glaucoma too closely though. The argument also rested on the interpretation of statistics and graphs which plotted the incidence of glaucoma among different age groups. Liedecker had a view on what a 'normal' eye pressure could be said to be and he attempted to detect 'abnormal' conditions in relation to that.

So it was hot stuff and we set about tackling this 'defined population' to try to sort these things out. I was living in a hospital house in Rhydlava — this was a place built during the war as a rehabilitation centre for wounded troops. It was less than an hour's drive from the Rhondda Fach and we went up there to do the job — working in places like the Tylerstown Chapel — taking pressures with two instruments in three sessions, morning, afternoon and evening. We used the applanation tonometer, which measures the amount of pressure required to flatten a constant area of the cornea, and the Schiotz tonometer which uses a small plunger to indent the cornea, and compared the readings. Every subject had his or her optic discs looked at and one in ten was examined more closely, and we did visual fields for every fourth person. We went through a preliminary process known as a randomised balance block trial to eliminate statistical and human errors in the use of the equipment and compilation of the data, and then we hopped into it.

The important thing was to get as close to 100 per cent of the population as we could because, you never can tell, the significant subjects could be grouped in the last 10 per cent of people. The survey had field research assistants who went around establishing rapport with the people in the valleys and convincing them that there was something in it for them. Every participant who showed up with an eye problem got a referral to the Cardiff Royal Infirmary and a guarantee that if they needed glasses they'd get them. The assistants never referred to the people as 'patients' or anything like that and they were treated decently, given convenient appointments, helped with transport and so on. For the outlying places Archie Cochrane used his Jag to bring some people in. There were occasional hitches; the field assistants threatened to strike when one doctor working on a sub-section of the study, to do with cataract, behaved as if he was 'in his rooms'. I had to take him aside and explain things to him.

In the end we covered 92.8 per cent of the population and we had medical records on most of the other 7.2 per cent — it was an extraordinarily high strike rate. Very tedious and onerous work a lot of the time, but we knew that it had a beginning, a middle and an end, and that made it tolerable. It was useful to do that amount of repetitive work because it made me a very acute observer without actually being conscious of it. I remember going in to do a clinic at the Infirmary where I was the Senior Registrar and one of the doctors asking me to look at a woman whose trouble he couldn't identify. I took a quick look and said, 'She's got corneal oedema.'

'So she has,' he said. 'How did you pick that up?'

It was simply because I'd been looking through a slit lamp — that's a device that throws a narrow beam of light into the eye so that, through a microscope, you can examine the eye structures a layer at a time — seeing hundreds of healthy eyes in a day, and I got so I could recognise a disorder almost intuitively.

Some very important results came from that survey. I remember that when it came for me to write a paper I wanted to do something dramatic about glaucoma, full of missionary zeal, but Archie knew better and the first paper I produced was called 'Source of Variation in Tonometry'. I gave it in Oxford and it went over well. It sounds dull, but it was an important piece of groundwork because it showed that our measurements and graphs were more accurate and reliable than anyone else's had been because we'd isolated factors that tended to skew and distort this sort of data. That meant that when the subsequent papers came out[4] they had an extra credibility.

One of the things we showed was that ocular pressure in a whole population was not distributed in a uniform fashion, that you couldn't plot it on a 'normal' curve. The graph shows a skew to the high side and this increases with age. That had important implications for predicting glaucoma incidence because some of the presumptions about the relationship between pressures and the disease were wrong. Some eyes can tolerate higher pressures better than others, for example. In turn, that was important information if you had to decide how to allot health care resources regionally and nationally.

For my money, it also said things about German science as exemplified by Liedecker. Some phenomena of the human body have very little deviation from the mean and others

---

[4] For example, Hollows, F.C. & Graham, P.A., 'Intra-ocular pressure, glaucoma and glaucoma suspects in a defined population', *British Journal of Ophthalmology*, 1966 and Graham, P.A. & Hollows, F.C., 'A critical review of methods of detecting glaucoma' in Hunt, J., *Glaucoma*, Edinburgh, 1969.

show an enormous range. The total refractive state of the eye is one of the latter. I mean, we found that quite a few of the new cases of glaucoma discovered were in people whose pressures were below the average for the whole population. German science didn't have the flexibility to cope with that. It was still Nietzschean, obsessed with archetypes and models of perfection, but that's by the by.

The work gave me an academic reputation. That's one thing. More importantly, maybe, it confirmed me in some attitudes I already held. If I'd been in Boston in the 1770s and the cry 'No taxation without representation' had gone up, I'd have been at the fucking barricades. The credo of this survey was 'No survey without service' — same sort of thing. Careful recording of results, humane and considerate treatment of the people, and action on the problems disclosed. Without my exposure to that approach in Wales, the trachoma project wouldn't have achieved what it did. I'm jumping ahead again.

I didn't climb in the Alps, which I'd half-thought I might do when I got to Europe and in fact there were very few days off, no substantial holidays for that sort of thing. I went on one trip through Scandinavia, visiting ophthalmological institutions, but there were no junkets. I got drunk a few times but I certainly went weeks without having a drink. The demands of the job were just too heavy.

Of course, it wasn't all hard yakka. I remember going to Cardiff Arms Park to see the New Zealand All Blacks play Wales. The referee had disallowed a couple of New Zealand marks and when the Welsh half-back, a little bloke named Watkins, took a mark, Colin 'Pinetree' Meads, a legendary, big, fast All Black, charged right through him. Meads had calculated that the referee wasn't allowing marks. Meads outweighed the Welshman by about ten stone and the word went round that Watkins had a broken back. He didn't as it turned out, but on the Monday at work a few people grabbed me by the shirtfront, wanted to have a go at me on account of what Meads had done to their precious half-back. Other than that, I never suffered through being a colonial. The Welsh had been colonised themselves, after all.

Mary wasn't working and she and I fostered a couple of children for a time. Raymond and Sarah came from a home that had been destroyed by the father's drinking and the mother's incapacity. I will never forget the first meal Mary set before them. They had their places at the table and their own plates and cutlery. When they got a portion of food they didn't know what to do. One of them said, 'Is that mine?' They had been used to the food being dished up in a lump and fighting for it. Similar culture shock when I took them out to Archie Cochrane's place for a swim in his pool. Archie had a farmhouse with a great garden, expensive sculpture and all mod cons. We passed an apple tree and Raymond said, 'What're those apples doing up there?' He'd never seen apples on a tree before.

I suppose I showed I was still my father's son by growing tobacco when I was in Wales. Pipe tobacco shot up to thirteen shillings and sixpence a two-ounce tin. Impossible price. So I wrote to my old Dad in New Zealand and he got one of his mates to send me over some tobacco seed which is very fine, like dust. I got hold of a book on tobacco-growing in Britain and the hospital gardener and I planted the seeds at the right time of year. You wouldn't think it'd grow in that climate but it did. It shot up in the spring, grew six inches in a day, and one of the theatre orderlies and I harvested and cured it. We got about thirty pounds of smokeable tobacco and saved ourselves a bit of money.

We lived reasonably well. We had a hospital-owned house at a subsidised rent, but the wages were low and there was never money to burn. I remember that I borrowed five hundred quid from Archie Cochrane and never paid it back, but he could afford it.

It came time to move on and I was considering applying for a job at a hospital in East Grinstead where they did a lot of plastic surgery. One Sir Benjamin Rycroft had set up the eye department there and it looked like they were doing interesting work in some new fields. I was mulling this over and Max Graham asked me what I had in mind to do. I told him about the East Grinstead job and he said, 'Fred, you're trained! You should be thinking about a long-term job where you can use your skills, not about running around getting more training.'

I thought about it and I realised that he was right. I'd been on a sort of training conveyor-belt and hadn't known when it was time to get off. There was a job going in New Zealand, a senior lectureship at the University of Otago and the Associate Professorship at the University of New South Wales. I applied for both of them and the balance was tipped by political considerations. It happened that Max Graham was in touch with Barrie Jones who was a New Zealander and the first professor of ophthalmology in Britain. Although he was conservative politically, Barrie was a humanitarian who had worked in eye medicine in the Third World. He was very useful to us later in the trachoma project, but just then he told Max he was worried about my political activities. It had to be something to do with the New Zealand job because I hadn't exactly been politically active in England.

I'd left the hospital and was actually working in the epidemiology unit at the time and Archie Cochrane called me in and handed me a piece of paper.

'Take a look at that,' he said. It was a letter from the New Zealand security service and it ran something like :

> Dear Professor Cochrane,
>
> We understand that you are professionally acquainted with one Dr Frederick Hollows, and we would be grateful if you would be good enough to tell us of his political activities and affiliations while a member of your organisation.

To an old anti-Fascist like Archie, that was intolerable. He showed me his reply. From memory, roughly, it was:

> *Mister* Hollows has been a colleague of mine for four years. His work has been exemplary and he is held in high esteem by his peers. His political activities are no concern of mine nor should they be concerns of anyone involved in assessing his professional abilities.

It really pissed me off though, to think of these numbskulls keeping tabs on me in New Zealand. What bloody subversive role could a senior lecturer in ophthalmology, sitting on the edge of the fucking Antarctic ice cap in Dunedin, possibly play? I got the job in Sydney and I took it. They kept ringing me up from Dunedin, trying to get me to change my mind, and I kept telling them to call the bloody dogs off if they ever wanted to get anyone good down there.

CHAPTER 8

Setting Up and Starting to Stir

Sydney, NSW. First city of Aust., capital of NSW; Aust's busiest and largest port, situated on S shore of Port Jackson. Alt. 42 m, r'fall 1195mm. Mean temp. summer 22C, winter 13C.

The Concise Encyclopedia of Australia, *(Horowitz), 1979, Vol 2.*

I didn't know what to expect when I reached Sydney in 1965. I'd worked in well-established institutions and departments but the University of New South Wales was a different sort of place. It had evolved from the Sydney Technical College and was originally conceived of as a university of technology, without faculties of law or medicine for example, and with a rudimentary arts faculty. That idea was abandoned fairly early on, but elements of it persisted. I was appointed to head the department of ophthalmology which had in its brief the teaching of optometrists, which had been done at the Technical College.

Opticians had begun to call themselves optometrists, following the Americans, and the whole issue of their training and competence was a hot one. I fell right into the middle of it. I thought optometrists should be taught the basics of the visual system and how to detect eye disease. I didn't realise that there were other, more ambitious, ideas about. It was a growth period in universities, money around for this and that, and it was decided that resources for ophthalmology at Prince

Henry Hospital should be transferred to the Prince of Wales. So I was at the centre of a greatly expanded system.

Things started to take shape but the conflict with the optometrists went on. They wanted me to certify that the people who'd done the optometry course were able to decide whether disease was present or absent. It was absurd. I told them, 'I don't certify my registrars as able to do that. Nobody's certified to do that.' It reached a head when they brought out a definition of themselves as an independent clinical science, neither medical nor para-medical, in which the individual optometrist has sole responsibility for the diagnosis and management of his patient.

I couldn't wear that. I thought the optometrist could be a very valuable part of a medical team, but the doctors have to take the overall responsibility. We have nurses here who do things nurses don't do in other departments, we train them in those skills, but the buck stops with us. You can't possibly have someone *on* the team who says he's not *in* it. I copped some heat from the university over that. The Vice Chancellor, Phillip Baxter, was on the side of the optometrists. He was a nuclear warrior, believed everyone should have a nuclear reactor in the backyard, and he swung a fair bit of weight. But I weathered the storm and got my tenure, although I had to pretty well demand it. Tenure's important — without it, you have to watch your *p*s and *q*s; with it, you can say what you think.

It was a time of confidence when you could get things done. I remember that I'd done a retinal detachment on a patient and when I went to see him there was a terrible stench in the air. A patient only a few yards away had had a colostomy and there was shit running out of a loop in his bowel. That was crazy. If you get an infection in other parts of the body, if pus builds up, you can let it out; but get pus inside the eye and that eye hardly ever sees again. So I bailed up Roland K. Webster, who was the medical superintendent, and told him that I couldn't have my patients in with people who'd had bowel surgery and the like.

A terrific character, Roland was a Scotsman who put on a kilt and played the bagpipes once a year. He saw the point and we went for a walk around the grounds. There was a collection of small huts not being used and Roland said, 'Fred, we could fix up these huts, six male beds and six female beds. Toilets here and here, and we could link them up with a little walkway. How'd that be?'

I was for it and a fortnight later that little eye unit opened. But the amazing thing was that I didn't write on or sign one bit of paper to get the work done. Not one! They were the good old days before management interjected itself into everything to the detriment of speed and efficiency.

Looking back, there was a fair bit of improvisation and flying by the seat of the pants. I did the first cataract extraction in the Prince of Wales Hospital and I had an audience — a full theatre of interested onlookers. I had a resident to assist me who'd had personal experience of eye surgery in that he'd suffered damage to an eye himself. I thought he knew a bit about it and would be OK. But when I put the needle in, a long needle, two and a quarter inches, boom, down goes the resident in a faint. They dragged him out. The next problem was that I didn't have precisely the right kind of needle for the next injection and using the one I did have, I cut a blood vessel. A retra-bulbar haemorrhage. The strictly correct procedure is to send the patient back to the ward, put a pad on the eye and do the op in a couple of days. But I had all these people waiting to see the first cataract extraction and I thought, *Shit, I can't very well say I've buggered it up and it's not going to happen today*. So I put pressure on the eye and found after a couple of minutes that it was quite soft and that I could proceed. It was the old type of cataract extraction, quicker than the modern method, more dynamic and requiring a high degree of bi-manual skill. There

I was, twenty pairs of eyes on me, no resident, a nursing sister unfamiliar with all the instruments, and I was one split second ahead of disaster all the time. It took ten years off my life, but it turned out fine. When it was over one of the senior theatre nurses said, 'It's really quite a simple little operation, isn't it?'

The department grew physically and in terms of personnel and research interests. We got a few registrars and some outstanding young people. Paul Beaumont, who's now a leading ophthalmologist, was one. He'd bonded himself to serve in the air force after finishing his training but he couldn't stand the life or the work. Hated the discipline and was a bit of a dissenter — it was the late 1960s and he'd called his dog Ho Chi Minh, partly to suggest to the air force that he was politically unsuitable. The work mainly involved certifying very fit people as just that, very fit — extremely boring. Paul came to me and asked if I could find him a job as a researcher, which I did. I scraped up some money from somewhere and put him on. The air force police pursued him for some time, but he managed to convince the authorities that he wasn't suitable material — keeping a copy of the *The Thoughts of Chairman Mao* on his desk at the air force base probably helped. Paul did some good work in connection with thyroid eye disease and he went on to write important papers with me on diabetic retinopathy and the use of the argon laser to treat retinal disorders. He was involved in the setting up of the Redfern Medical Centre, too. I'll get on to that later.

Shirley Palmer was the first sister in charge of the eye outpatients department that we set up at the Prince of Wales. I'd been very impressed every time I'd had any dealings with her in the hospital. She always knew what I was there for, had the notes and any other information at the ready. Also, she wasn't afraid to tell a doctor who wasn't on top of a case to pull his socks up, diplomatically but firmly. She hadn't done any eye work but when I asked her if she'd like to head up this new division, she agreed and she is still there. We began training the nursing staff to take eye pressure, using the new equipment. We trained our first orthoptists and Shirley Palmer proved to be an exceptional person in every way.

A busy eye clinic is a complex of very different things — some people need very special attention for fluorescein angiograms for example, some have to have their pupils dilated, some just need vision fields or pressures taken, others are on medication and need to be tested for its effectiveness and so on. They're fish and fowl, sheep and goats, and it takes a very skilled organiser to keep track of it all. I might say to Shirley when she sends a patient in, 'Look, there's a bloke who's been sitting out there for hours, so why am I seeing this one?'

She'll say something like, 'Oh, he's having a twenty-four hour urine specimen done, so he has to be here until five o'clock, whereas this man needs to be away . . .' In more than twenty years I've never known her to be wrong over things like that. She has quiet shoes — nothing worse than heel and toe plates clicking when people are trying to get things right — and a quiet voice. She takes the trouble to read the notes and see what sort of a person she's dealing with. No number system and no shouting, 'Phyllis Brown!' to some poor seventy-year-old dear who's deaf and confused. An eye clinic can be a stressful place for everybody concerned and it takes someone like Shirley Palmer to make it run well.

In 1968 Frank Hardy published *The Unlucky Australians*, his book on the strike by the Gurindjis at Wave Hill cattle station in the Northern Territory. I'd read his *Power without Glory* when I was a student in New Zealand, so I was interested to hear that he was talking on the subject of the blacks' strike at the Teachers Federation in Sussex Street. I went along and I found him a very persuasive speaker. When he asked for donations at the end of the meeting I passed in a cheque for $300. They thought it was a bit iffy, never having got a donation of that size before. I told them I was an eye doctor at the Prince of Wales, wrote my name on the back and that was all right. The next week someone from the committee Frank was on rang me and asked me if I'd take a look at two Gurindji men who seemed to have eye trouble.

Donald Nangiari and Vincent Lyngian came along to the clinic. They had three working eyes between them and a lot of problems — some cataract, blocked ducts with regurgitated pus and signs of trachoma. They also had a strange hazing of the cornea, hazing in a place which is exposed when the eyelids are open and is normally clear. I'd never seen it before and I called in Roger McGuinness, the doctor I'd worked with in Wales, to take a look. In Australia, Roger had only practised in Sydney and he'd never seen an Aborigine before as a patient. (Neither had I.) Roger took a look, thought for a second and said, 'That's Labrador keratopathy.'

As soon as he said it I knew he was right. I'd read about Labrador keratopathy but I'd never seen it and never expected to see it. It turned out that Roger had worked in London with an eye man who'd spent some time in Labrador and seen this condition. It had also been described for Africa. It's a function of the reflection of ultra-violet light from snow or sand. I thought this was interesting — the first time the condition had been detected in Australia. My interest was still basically scientific then. I'd read a bit about the plight of the Aborigines but I hadn't taken much of it in. I'd assumed it was a variety of the Maori story where the people had been dispossessed of their land by stealth after a treaty, or something such. I didn't know anything about the doctrine of *terra nullus*, the handy British idea that the land had been unoccupied.

But when the Gurindji committee told me they were taking Donald and Vincent back to the Northern Territory and there were some seats on the planes for a few doctors who were willing to make themselves useful, I jumped at the chance to go. Barry Pascoe, who was an endocrinologist and general physician and Ferry Grundseit, a pediatrician, were interested, so we flew up to the Gurindji camp. It took us three days to get there.

Just before we turned in, Vincent asked me what I wanted to do in the morning and I said I wanted to see all the grown men in the camp. We slept the first night under a tarpaulin, all in together, pilots, a nurse, the lot, and it was mayhem. This was the Watti Creek camp. The bloody dogs fought all night and ran over us and I'd had hardly any sleep when Vincent woke me up with a gentle shake on the shoulder.

'Fred,' he says, 'the men are ready.'

About twenty or thirty men were sitting quietly under a shelter waiting. I got my magnifiers on and went over and had a look at them. Every man who'd been a stockman for any length of time had Labrador keratopathy. It was cattle camp country and the stockmen worked long hours in the daylight. Their hats didn't protect them from this scatter of reflected light from the ground. It wasn't a blinding condition but it impaired sight. As well, there were cataracts that *were* blinding them, and signs of advanced trachoma and other things.

Trachoma is a disease which affects the mucous membrane lining the inside of the eyelids and the front of the eyeball (except the cornea). This is known as the conjunctiva and trachoma is an inflammation of this, associated with the presence of an organism called *Chlamydia trachomatis*.

As a result of infection with this bacteria, usually in childhood, a chronic condition develops which causes scarring of the inside of the lid. Directly or indirectly, this may cause the cornea to be ulcerated, scarred and made opaque, resulting in blindness.

The conjunctiva contains immunologically competent tissue and cells whose function is to protect the eye from bugs. Chronic infection destroys this capacity with the result that, even if a person so affected was given a corneal graft, sight would not be regained because the conjunctiva is the essential support mechanism for the cornea and its destruction means that the grafted cornea cannot remain clear. Corneal blindness from prolonged trachoma is the end of the road.

Trachoma has two stages — follicular, indicated by the presence of small white or creamy objects (collections of white blood cells) found inside the conjunctiva, and cicatricial, referring to the scarring and other damage to the eyelids and eye. When trachoma reaches its vision-threatening stage — characterised by in-turned upper eyelashes and ulceration — it is a very painful condition.

It was a shock to me. I'd been working at the hospital and in my private practice and seeing a parade of eye disorders, but nothing like this. In my training and working in Wales, I thought I'd seen every sick eye condition there was to *be* seen, but I was wrong. It was like something out of the medical history books — eye diseases of a kind and degree that hadn't been seen in western society for generations! The neglect this implied, the suffering and wasted quality of human life were appalling.

The next day I saw all the women. The day after that all the children. They were free of the hazy cornea condition, because they weren't obliged to work in the sun all day, but the women had a lot of cataract and trachoma, and there were signs of the juvenile forms of trachoma in most of the children. I went wild, walked over to Wave Hill station and virtually commandeered the radio. I got on to Darwin and demanded that they send a doctor down to look at this situation. That was when I found out how things worked up there. They sent down an Englishman who was supposed to be a doctor but the only instruments he knew anything about were a desk and a pen — never put a finger up a bum in anger in his life. I showed him the eyes. He wasn't interested, utterly unmoved. All he could talk were rules and regulations.

He got up on the back of a truck and started lecturing the people about their bad health and telling them that, if they wanted medical services, they'd have to attend the clinic at Wave Hill station. One, that was six miles away, no easy trot in that country and, two, Wave Hill was the bloody hole of a cattle station they'd walked off in the first place. No doubt about it, the medical services were being used as a way of forcing the Gurindji back to work. But it was interesting to see their reaction. When someone starts shouting at a Gurindji he just turns away, and that's what they did then — quietly turned their backs on this fucking idiot and left him there talking to himself.

CHAPTER 9

Stirring: the Gurindji, ASIO and Me

> We drove on until we reached the bed of the Victoria River, dry at this time of the year — and I stood recalling that here, almost exactly 20 years ago, the Gurindji tribe camped after they had walked off Vestey's Wave Hill cattle station . . . No white Australian could then have guessed that this was the beginning of the struggle for Aboriginal Land Rights which continues to this day.
>
> *Frank Hardy*, Bulletin, *24 September 1985*

The Gurindji committee was cluey about publicity and when I got back to Sydney they'd arranged for a press conference. I had a good deal to say. For one thing, I knew that the sample of people I'd seen wasn't a misleading one — quite the opposite. Those people had walked a considerable distance from different places and the likelihood was that people with *severe* eye problems had been left behind! I made a statement about the difference between medical services in the city and in the outback, and the discrepancy between eye health for Aborigines and white Australians.

A lot flowed from that in time, but just then there was a personal consequence. Not long after my picture and comments appeared in the press, I got home and Mary told me about two men who'd come to call. She described them — gabardine overcoats, hats. They'd asked if this was the home of 'the Professor Hollows who's interested in native affairs'. Mary thought that was strange for a start, very old-fashioned. By then, the referendum to include Aborigines in the census had been passed and attitudes and language were changing.

Hearing this colonialist term, 'native affairs', with its pejorative overtones put Mary on the alert and she told them where I worked and how to get in touch with me if they wanted me. She virtually told them to bugger off. She followed them up to the road and saw them sitting in an unmarked Holden with a rooftop radio aerial. Mary was sure they were ASIO spooks.

I was ropeable. All I'd done was examine a hundred and fifty blackfellows sitting by Watti Creek and found the amount of disease you'd need to look at a million and a half whites to discover, and talked about the differences. I hadn't incited rebellion or anything, and here they were setting the bloody ASIO dogs on me. I was very sensitive about those things. I knew from my reading about the Gestapo's tactics of social control and I'd met people in Europe who'd been through it personally. I'd lived through the red-baiting McCarthy era which hadn't affected me particularly, although there had been that business about the security vetting for the Dunedin job. I thought, *This is the same bloody thing. What can I do to get back at the bastards?*

We lived in Sans Souci then, in a house on a sandspit overlooking Kogarah Bay, a beautiful place, but earlier we'd rented a house at Como and I'd done some bushwalking in the National Park. I'd been appalled by the huge advertising hoardings that disfigured the entrance to the National Park. As soon as you left Sutherland they started and I think some of them might even have been within the park boundary. A real eyesore and against the spirit of the whole park. More than once I'd said to Barry Pascoe, the doctor friend of mine who'd come up to the Gurindji camp, that someone should pull the bloody things down.

When I was casting around for some illegal act that I could get away with, something that would let me feel I'd struck a blow against these security creeps — more emotion than logic in that — I remembered the signs. I rang up Pascoe and I said,

'Pascoe, be out here at eleven o'clock, we're going to do those fucking hoardings tonight.'

Pascoe had Tic Carroll, who was a farmer and later a top on-location film unit manager, and his architecture student brother Matt, who's a big-time film producer now, staying with him and they came along. We all got into my little Alfa Romeo, about midnight, and drove out to the scene of the crime. I had a chain with a big hook on it, to haul the things down with, and a chainsaw and some axes. I'd had a close look at the signs before so I knew how they were constructed, big solid jobs with stays out the back, and how to get at them. There was a track in behind, below the level of the road, where the billposters took their gear when they were changing the message. So we could work without being seen.

We got the hook over the first one, big bastard of a thing, ten metres high, and you had to be careful because if you were underneath it when it came down you'd be dead. I started the chain-saw — dead of night, very quiet — and you'd swear you could've heard it in Wollongong. We got the first one down in no time and we set to work with the axes, dinging in the galvanised iron so that they couldn't just stick it back up and paste a new poster over it. Tic Carroll was a dab hand at that.

The next one along was made out of two-inch pipe scaffolding and I was dubious about our chances of getting it down. Tic wasn't; he said, 'We can do this with a couple of spanners.'

So I got some spanners from my toolbox and we undid all the bolts and the hoarding came crashing down shooting sparks everywhere as the metal rubbed together. We did another scaffolding one and two more of the wooden jobs, beat the shit out of them, and took off pretty pleased with ourselves. All the hoardings had signs mounted on them informing the citizenry that anyone who interfered with this precious property would be fined two thousand dollars, gaoled for life . . . that sort of thing. We put the signs very neatly in the middle of the shambles.

But they put them up again very quickly and all on pipes this time, with the threads and joints spot-welded so you couldn't just unscrew them.

'Job for pipe-cutters,' says Tic.

I said, 'I haven't got any bloody pipe-cutters.'

'No, but the hospital would have, wouldn't it?'

I borrowed some two-inch pipe-cutters from the hospital engineer and we went out again and cut them off at ground level. I had some climbing mates with me, blokes like Johnny Glasgow, who was a terrific climber and a Swiss named Dave who had made some pretty spectacular climbs. They were good with ropes and generally handy, and we got a whole lot of the scaffolds down. It was easy and very quiet. Just open the cutters, clamp them around the pipe, turn a couple of handles, nothing to it. They put them up again — this time on four-inch pipes. So I asked the engineer if he had any four-inch cutters. He didn't.

I said, 'A great big outfit like this hasn't got any four-inch pipe-cutters? You'd better order some in. You never know when you might need them.'

A couple of weeks later the cutters arrived and off we went again to do the job properly, but they'd anticipated that move. They'd welded a piece of angle iron to the back of every last one of the uprights so you couldn't get the cutters around them. That was the end of it. You'd have needed an oxy set to cut through them and you could hardly work one of them by the side of the road. You might set fire to the bush for one thing. But we gave them a run for their money.

That was a good time in many ways, the late sixties. Lively politics. Good music. The pill and sexual liberation. The house at Sans Souci was really two weekend cottages which had been joined together and I spent a fair bit of time doing it up, work I enjoyed. We made friends around there and the social environment in the hospital was good. I was a keen golfer, playing a few times a week, and I got my handicap down to ten. In those days the doctors had a special mess where you could have a meal when you were here. There was a billiard table alongside it and the eye department had the best billiards team in the hospital. And the era of the collar and tie — as an obligatory part of the doctor's personal presentation — had come to an end.

CHAPTER 10

Stirring: the Aboriginal Medical Service

> Yes, everybody was forever having blues, and Aboriginal people were not yet used to working together in this way, but, my gawd, things were getting done.
>
> *Shirley Smith,* Mumshirl: An Autobiography, *with the assistance of Bobbi Sykes*

Not long after I'd been quoted in the press as saying that the discrepancy between rural and metropolitan health care in Australia was a scandal, Ross McKenna from the French Department of the University of New South Wales began sending me notes inviting me to attend a meeting of the Redfern Aboriginal Legal Service. I knew that the university had helped to set up a sort of shopfront legal centre for blacks in Redfern (along the lines of some of the services set up by the Black Panthers and others in the States), but legal matters bore me to tears so I hadn't taken any particular interest. However, Ross was very persistent; his notes pursued me all over the university and the hospital and one Friday night, after a bit of a drinking session at the pub, I decided to go along and see what it was all about.

After some to'ing and fro'ing, Redfern was unfamiliar territory to me then, I got to the meeting. I took a seat and prepared to be bored for a while. It was a small group — two or three whites, three or four Aborigines — and to my surprise they were talking about medical matters. There were no doctors, maybe a nurse in the group, I was the only medico present and it was impossible not to be interested in what they were saying in general and in particular. In general, the legal service was getting swamped by people with a whole range of social and medical problems. In particular, they were talking about a case in which a sick Aborigine had died in the back of Gordon Briscoe's car. Gordon Briscoe was a field officer with the legal service. He is an Aborigine from the Centre and not many people have had a more profound influence on my life than him. At that time he was one of the very few Aborigines in Sydney who had a car — an old Volkswagen.

Briscoe was at the meeting along with Shirley Smith, 'Mumshirl', who's done a lot for Aborigines over more than thirty years, and Gary Foley, and they asked me if I could help them set up a medical service for blacks. I said that whatever lawyers could do doctors could do, and I agreed to talk to a few people. Next Friday there was another meeting, better attended. The Aborigines started to outline the case for a medical service and they were utterly convincing: blacks weren't welcome in doctors' surgeries, they got pushed to the back of the line in Casualty wards and public hospital clinics and so on. Paul Beaumont stood up and he said, 'You only need six things to start a medical service. Doctors, Fred and I can get the doctors; premises, Len Russell[5] can organise that; Aboriginal receptionists and managers, Shirley Smith can find them; publicity in the pubs and shops, Ross McKenna can do that; and transport, Eddie Newman[6] can handle that.'

Everyone there saw that he was right and they got very excited. Someone said, 'When can we start?'. Someone else said, 'Monday night.' I said, 'Whoa, it might take a bit longer than that.' But in fact we opened just ten days later. One of the first things I did was to check out the one doctor in the

---

[5] Field officer of the South Sydney Council Community Aid Program.

[6] A young lawyer working for the legal service.

area who the Aborigines had any time for. I had to make sure that our service wasn't going to bugger up something that was already in existence. I went to see this doctor who said that he paid calls on Aborigines and collected the tiny fee the government paid GPs for services to 'indigent persons'. It was next to nothing. He admitted that he didn't see blacks in his surgery because if he did the whites wouldn't come and the practice would go broke. He said that a medical service for blacks would be the best thing possible.

So we went ahead. We plundered the Prince of Wales Hospital for equipment — stethoscopes, thermometers, scales, all the accoutrements of a medical practice, we shamelessly stole. And we learnt as we went along. I remember seeing a man, early in the piece, deciding what he needed and writing out a script.

He said, 'What's this, doc?'

'Take it to a chemist and you'll get the medicine you need.'

He shook his head. 'No money, doc.'

We backed a truck up to the pharmacy at the hospital and loaded it half full — tens of thousands of dollars worth of pharmaceuticals. It wasn't always a matter of clandestine raids, there were some sympathetic people around. Pretty soon we had more doctors, GPs, specialists, professors of this and that, volunteering their services than we could handle. The medical service was a great success and there are more than sixty of them now Australia-wide, in the cities and in country towns, all owing something to that original model and the principles on which it was based. One of the most important of those principles was that the Aborigines staffed and managed it to the fullest extent possible.

To me, the experience of working there, doing general practice, making house calls, was a revelation. I just hadn't known that there were people in this big, beautiful city enduring living and social conditions like that. And there was so much talent in the black community — nurses like Dulcie Flowers, Marjorie Baldwin, Sally Gould, organisers like Gary

Foley, Paul Coe and Gordon Briscoe and all-round men like Bob Bellear. Bob came quietly into the centre one day with his box of tools and built us several sets of shelves. He had four trade certificates and he became the first Aboriginal barrister in history. A remarkable man.

We had a lot of problems. The South Sydney Council tried to eject us from the premises Len Russell had secured, claiming that we were practising medicine in an unlicensed manner. But we had too many big guns on our side for that to work. Sometimes we were at the centre until the early hours of the morning and, as the legal service had found, the problems spilled out in all directions. The Aborigines had a chronic lack of money, and you never left a session at the centre with any money in your pocket.

The health of the people was poor and it wasn't helped by the conditions they lived in and their lifestyle. The men brawled a lot, the women and kids got knocked around and the community as a whole was virtually at war with the police. It was accepted that on Friday and Saturday nights the police would put a couple of cars and paddy wagons into Redfern and any black unlucky enough to run into them (let alone one causing any trouble) would get a bashing and a night in the cells. Redfern was used as a sort of training ground for police heavy squads. We were dealing with bruises and contusions and other injuries constantly. I witnessed this sort of thing a number of times — blacks being bashed, plucked off the streets and thrown into the wagons. It used to enrage me but there was nothing you could do. If you remonstrated with the police they told you to piss off and mind your own business if you didn't want some of the same.

Of course there was goodwill, too, but often a big gap between good intention and execution. A classic example of that was the case of the two women from the hospital — a biochemist who was also a dietitian and our head dietitian — who came to see me to offer their help in teaching the Aboriginal women to make nutritious meals. I arranged for them to meet Shirley Smith and it was agreed that the two dietitians would go to Redfern and show the Aboriginal women the ropes. A few days later they came in to see me, both terribly upset. They'd taken the fresh vegetables and other stuff into one of the houses and that was as far as they got. There was a cold water tap, one saucepan and one gas ring! Their middle class assumptions didn't make any sense under those conditions and they understood then why the black women went across the street to buy unhealthy fattening fast food.

Other programs we were associated with fared better. There was a gang of Catholic priests, a bizarre-looking bunch, but some of them were Jesuits and highly qualified men. They wore beards and looked as if the history of the human race was written in their faces. They reminded me of the lines of the Paul Simon song:

> And when the radical priest come to get me released
> We was all on the cover of *Newsweek* . . .

That's what they were, radical priests. They got hold of a truck and went to the Flemington fruit and vegetable markets and bought up the produce very cheaply after the commercial buyers had finished. They took the fruit and vegetables around Redfern, and we helped them to target the mothers with the big families. They charged a dollar a box or just gave it away. That did more for nutrition in the area than a lot of other formalised programs.

Similarly with family planning. The Family Planning Association had been given a grant of a couple of hundred thousand dollars to inform the Aborigines of New South Wales about birth control. The reason wasn't far to seek: some work had been done on Aboriginal fecundity which showed that the Aboriginal birth rate was outstripping the national average. In places like Bourke, mothers with fifteen children were not uncommon. A federal minister had said something like 'we are sitting on a time-bomb' — the old establishment fear and guilt directed at a people they'd failed to wipe out.

The Family Planning Association had the money but they couldn't spend it. The Aborigines weren't going to open their doors to nice middle class white ladies coming around in their brand new cars to tell them what to do. They automatically equated people like that with the landlord or the Social Security Department or the police. The younger, radical blacks saw the whole thing as a racist ploy and, to a degree, they were right. But there was a need — young girls were dying from backyard abortions and the Aboriginal women wanted contraception. We had a meeting at the medical centre and it was unanimously agreed that any Aboriginal woman who wanted contraception should have it in the form acceptable to her and agreed to by her doctor. In other words, no generalised program handing out leaflets and the pill and what have you, but individual consultation and attention.

That was the state of play in the city, some wins and some losses, but things were also happening in the bush. There was a study going on called 'The Human Ecology of the Arid Zone' — in a nutshell, an investigation of mental illness in the outback. Max Kamien, a psychiatrist, did some research in Bourke, and, to his everlasting credit, he recognised that the serious problem there was not white neurosis but the appalling level of Aboriginal health. I met him at a party and he asked me if I could take a medical team to Bourke because of the severity of the eye problems the blacks were suffering.

I said I would and my first thought, after the experience with the Gurindjis, was, *I wonder if they've got trachoma there, less than 800 kilometres from Sydney*? I rang up the ophthalmologist who used to pay periodic visits to Bourke and he said that there wasn't any trachoma there. Max Kamien wanted a wide-ranging medical examination of the Aboriginal community to get a proper understanding of the prevalence of the various diseases, so I went up as part of the biggest medical team ever to go on the road at that time.

This was more than fifteen years after Charlie Perkins and the Freedom Ride, but Bourke was still quite a racist town. We helped to bring down a few barriers, I think. We were issued with honorary membership cards for the town's major clubs — the Bowling Club, the Golf Club and the most exclusive, the Oxley Club. I saw Shirley Smith riffling through the cards and I asked her what club she was going to.

Shirley said, 'I'm going to tell my grandchildren that I've been in the Oxley Club in Bourke.'

Walking into the Oxley with Shirley Smith, getting the barman to back off and serve us, and sitting down with the Shire President and the Town Clerk and the local priest, was an event to remember.

We'd arranged to do the eye examinations at the showgrounds, a place known to everybody and where it was possible to set up equipment and keep records. I remember that it was very hot and that there were dust storms and willy-willys making everything very difficult. The first kid arrived, a five-year-old and I decided I'd examine him for trachoma, which involves everting the eyelid. I did it and there they were — those tiny accumulations of white blood cells, less than a millimetre in diameter, the trachoma follicles. I thought, *Hullo, there's one that hasn't been picked up*. The next five children I examined all had trachoma follicles.

I was very annoyed for humanitarian and professional reasons. There was really no excuse for the complete non-detection of trachoma and I knew it meant that the Aborigines had to be living in sub-standard conditions. Also, we hadn't taken the appropriate holorith cards — the punched cards that were used to process information before the development of microchip computers — to grade and assess the extent of trachoma. We had to stop the examinations until we could set ourselves up to do that. In the end, we discovered that there was a great deal of trachoma among the Aborigines — none among the whites — in Bourke. I photographed it, and whenever anyone expressed scepticism, muttered about conjunctivitis, I just had to show them the photographs.

Max Kamien then suggested that I visit Engonnia, a small Aboriginal settlement about a hundred kilometres from Bourke, a really out-of-the-way place. I took the eye team up there and practically all the kids had trachoma signs. Barrie Jones, who had become the first Professor of Ophthalmology at the University of London, played an important role at that point. He had done important work on trachoma in Africa and the Middle East, and he was one of the few scientists who could grow the bacteria. Word got to him about what I was doing and he wrote to me saying something like, 'I hear you have an enclave of trachoma on the shores of Botany Bay.' I wrote back saying that, while Engonnia wasn't a place Sir Joseph Banks had visited, trachoma was indeed a serious problem in the Commonwealth of Australia.

Barrie Jones came out, went up to Engonnia, took cultures, grew the bug and suggested that we try treating the people systemically — that is, not just with eye drops or ointment, but with something that would operate in the bloodstream to knock the drug out. That seemed like the way to go, and Engonnia became the scene of our first mass treatment of the problem. We performed operations where necessary and gave the people glasses, but the big push was to get everyone in the community to take a mixture of a sulphur drug and a folic acid antagonist twice a day for a month, and in the last weeks some folinic acid and vitamin C. This treatment was designed to lessen the effects of infection and retard it until better household hygiene could be achieved.

A woman who worked in the hospital volunteered to live in the community to supervise the operation, because the doses had to be measured and we didn't want any drop-outs or backsliders. The whole living unit had to get the drugs for a full month. At the end of the time we went back and photographed all the eyes again and there didn't seem to be much change. But the schoolteacher there, who hadn't taken much interest up to that point, came up to me, shook my hand and invited me to visit the school.

'I want to show you something interesting.'

I went into one of the two classrooms in the school, said gidday to the kids, three-quarters of them Aborigines, the way you do, and wondered what next.

The teacher said, 'What do you notice?'

'Nothing. What d'you mean?'

'Listen,' he said. 'You can hear yourself think. No one's coughing. Look at the noses, not running.'

He thought it was the best thing that had ever happened in Engonnia. The drugs did a lot to fight the chronic bronchitis and upper respiratory diseases and nasal discharges. We went back again after six months, twelve months and eighteen months and photographed each time. Three of us graded the photographs for trachoma signs and there was a very substantial effect — a dramatic impact on follicular trachoma. The trial proved that systemic drugs could be given to a community safely and were effective. That harked back to the dictum of Archie Cochrane, my epidemiological mentor in Wales, that only treatments proven to be effective were worth doing on a mass basis, and the good relations we enjoyed with the Enngonia people backed up the other important principle — no survey without service. The Enngonia trial became the model for the Australia-wide trachoma program.

CHAPTER 11

Stirring: the Springbok demonstrations

'We will not stop the tour for anything.'

Charles Blunt, President of the Australian Rugby Union, 21 July 1971

Although processes were in train that were going to change my life radically, in 1971 I was still a Sydney academic and suburbanite. One Saturday I was out cutting the grass around the Sans Souci house, enjoying the air and admiring the view, thinking life was pretty good. For some reason I knocked off and went inside. The television was on but there was no sound coming from it. On the screen I saw mounted policemen beating people, riding their horses into them, bringing their batons down. People were running around, falling and yelling and I thought it was some old footage of workers' demonstrations in the twenties and thirties, when the coppers were brought out to break up picket lines and demonstrations. It was very dramatic, violent stuff. Then I realised that it was a live broadcast. Modern! Contemporary! Now!

It went on for a few minutes. The commentators had been shocked into silence and when they opened up again I found that it was film of a demonstration against the South African rugby team which was playing a game *in Melbourne*! I could hardly believe it. As far as I knew no one in Melbourne cared about rugby union and on a Saturday afternoon everyone who could get out of bed would be off watching the VFL. Also, from my contact with the Gurindjis and Aborigines in Sydney, I accepted that Australia was a racist society through and through. But that's what it was — an anti-apartheid demonstration in Melbourne that had brought a tremendously violent response from the authorities and I thought, *There's an undercurrent of different thoughts and feelings in this country that I haven't detected.*

A few weeks later I was having a drink with Frank Hardy in the South Steyne pub. It was a madhouse because it was full of bookies and gamblers betting on every bloody race meeting going on around the country. Hardy was a mad gambler in those days and he kept one ear cocked to the radio the whole time. You'd start a sentence and he'd say, 'Hang on. It's the third at Eagle Farm.' So conversation would stop while he'd listen to that and you'd just get going again and it'd be, 'Just a minute, Fred, it's the fifth at Caulfield.'

I was getting fed up with it — although they're an interesting mob to watch, a group of drinking gamblers, bizarre — when one of Hardy's mates said he was going to the Springbok game at the SCG to see what happened, that sounded more interesting than conversations interrupted by tote dividends from racetracks, so I went too. I went onto the Hill and the place was packed with everybody shouting abuse at the police. There was a line of uniformed police on either side of the fence which had three strands of barbed wire on top of it. People were throwing things at the cops, blowing whistles, singing protest songs and shouting, 'Who killed Collingwood? Who killed Collingwood?'

Pretty inflammatory stuff. Collingwood was a young demonstrator who'd died after a Springbok protest in Melbourne. He'd been kicked and died of a ruptured duodenum. The duodenum's right up against the backbone and it takes an almighty thump in the belly to damage it. Everyone was chanting and booing and getting very worked up. A bloke just near me shouted something at the police and a plainclothes man came up behind him and belted him with a truncheon right across the top of the head. The cop he'd shouted at took two steps and booted him up the arse where he lay.

An Irishman was standing next to me and he said, 'I'm goin' over that fence.'

By that time I was hot to go over it too and I remembered that I had a pair of bolt-cutters in my car. I'd been laying concrete and using the cutters on the reinforcing rods. I was probably a bit drunk. I went to my car and got the bolt-cutters — big ones, I could only just hide them under my coat — and came back into the ground. I worked my way forward, close to the wire and asked the bloke next to me where the play was. I wanted to cut the wire when the game was on the other side of the field, taking the attention of the police. I was craning to see over the crowd and shouting out, trying to make this bloke hear me above the racket. 'Where are they?'

The bloke says, 'Who? What d'you mean?'

'What part of the field are they playing on?'

'They stopped playing ten minutes ago!'

Next week, down at the medical service, Ross McKenna told me that he was getting up a group to organise a protest against the Springbok tour and asked if I would be interested. After what I'd seen I was anxious to do something and it seemed to me that a little organisation would be a good idea. So I went to the meeting and there were girls in hippy dresses and blokes with beards and pigtails and rimless glasses and top item on the agenda was: how are we going to get on the ground? I remember there was a suggestion that we could float balloons over the field that could drop something to distract the police. Another was that we could cut the wire with nail files — double-stranded, galvanised barbed wire!

I said, 'Look, the only way to cut the wire is with bolt-cutters and we have to know how to do it, when to do it and where to do it.'

The first thing was how, so I got hold of a few pairs of bolt-cutters, bought a roll of barbed wire and we had a training session. There's nothing much to using bolt-cutters on wire, really, but if truncheons were going to be out and boots were going to be flying it was better to have done it at least a few times before. We went to the ground for the next match and the plan was for four of us to hit the wire at different places, starting with Ross McKenna at three o'clock and the others following straight after. I took up my position — with the outsize bolt-cutters under my coat — and three big cops, sergeants, got into position right where I planned to cut the wire. It was too late for me to move and I was shit-scared. At a minute past three I was going to have to pull out these bloody great things and attack the wire and the coppers were already thumping and kicking people who were just shouting at them. What were they going to do to me?

A few minutes before three I saw some smoke fly up from where Ross was and next thing Ross is being dragged past with blood all over him, clothes ripped and stained with orange dye. A couple of things had gone wrong. First, Ross had hit the button early — maybe he got the time wrong or saw an opportunity, I don't know. But, like the rest of us, he had a couple of smoke bombs — Payne Wessex smoke signals, used by distressed yachtsmen and the like — and he decided to throw one of these to distract the police before he cut the wire. He reached into his pocket to pull it out and, being a bit flustered, he pulled the ring that ignited the signal. Smoke and flame and orange gunk went everywhere and instead of distracting the police it focussed their attention on Ross. He pulled out his bolt-cutters to have a go at the wire, but they were on him by then.

The police were very agitated. One of them yelled, 'Look out! He's got a phosphorous bomb!'

The cops came at him from all sides and they walloped him. As he was being dragged past I thought, *Jesus, this isn't on today*, and my bolt-cutters stayed under my coat. They took Ross to the police station in the city and we bailed him out a few hours later. That was the inglorious end of Chapter Two of the story of me and the Springboks tour.

The forces of reaction were in full cry at the time. Bolte, in Victoria, had backed the police and called the demonstrators 'louts and larrikins'; Billy McMahon, the Prime Minister, had said they were rent-a-crowd types, professional agitators. Bjelke-Petersen really let the dogs loose and the Queensland police mounted a military-style operation that prevented the demonstrators from disrupting the games. The last match was to be played in Sydney. A lot of the church leaders were opposed to the tour, but in the end the Christian community decided that it would limit itself to praying outside the ground and not confront the police.

I and a lot of others thought that wasn't good enough and I put forward the idea that there should be a whole phalanx of us, all with bolt-cutters, and if we hit the wire in the one spot some of us would be bound to get over and interrupt the game. I was going to go first. I had a beautiful pair of bolt-cutters — double fulcrum, real strong — and about twenty-four people behind me, similarly equipped. But we played it a bit cunning this time. I wore an expensive suede jacket and the bloke with me, a wharfie, wore a good leather jacket and we were behaving like real rugger-buggers — cheering the play and so on. The people behind us, including Mary, weren't in disguise and were making a lot of noise. The idea was that the cops would watch them and not us.

There were hundreds of uniformed police, paddy wagons, plainclothes men in the crowd and big piles of sand all around the ground to extinguish the smoke bombs. At ten past three I looked at my watch, looked around, pulled out the bolt-cutters and went to the wire. And a big policeman who'd been keeping an eye on the riff-raff behind me saw me and he was rooted to the spot. He just couldn't believe what he was seeing.

He shouted, 'Don't do it!' But he still didn't move.

I cut the first wire. Nothing happened. I cut the second

one. We were going well; we'd thought it might take a dozen or so of us to get each strand. Then the police grabbed me and I started to fight with them. I tossed the bolt-cutters back and Mary cut the third wire. It was on for young and old then, with people trying to get over the fence and the coppers punching and kicking and everyone yelling.

I thought I was going to get away for a minute because the young red-headed sergeant who had hold of me and was trying to pull through the chest-high fence — literally, pull me through it — was so agitated that I seriously thought that he was about to have a heart attack. He was showing a circum oral pallor, a blanching all around the mouth that people display when they're about to suffer cardiac arrest or about to die. I'd only seen it a few times, but I recognised it. I was telling him that this wasn't worth dying for when a plain clothes man came up behind and threw me over the fence. The police got me then and they beat the shit out of me as they did with everyone else who went over.

They dragged me over to one of the paddy wagons that were on the ground. I was struggling and abusing them because they were really worked up and getting murderous. They had hold of a man named James Ricketson who was a gentle-seeming sort — wore wire-rimmed spectacles and a big leather coat, looked like a poet or a stamp-collector — and they were dragging him while a copper walked along punching him in the face, over and over.

They threw us in the paddy wagon and we had to wait there for an hour or so until they drove us out. I could see through the grilled window, and one thing I remember is a man running around with his arms full of bolt-cutters, took him a couple of trips to collect them all up. James Ricketson recovered from his beating and as we were being driven away he shouted out to a kid who was standing near the wagon, 'Hey, son, stay at school, get an education and become a decent person otherwise you might end up like these pig coppers you see around you.' I thought that was a good effort from someone who'd had his glasses broken and who'd taken a real flogging.

They took us to the Jersey Road lockup. I was charged with resisting arrest, offensive conduct, wilful damage to police uniforms, possessing an object capable of inflicting grievous bodily harm (the smoke signals) and possession of a hand grenade. So there we were — fingerprinted, no belts or shoelaces, no tobacco — in this dreary bloody cell with nothing to sit on and a toilet bowl without a seat as the only fitting. An Irishman was chucked in with us (I always seemed to be running into Irishmen) and he was still fighting mad. He stood up on the toilet bowl and was going to throw something at the police in the yard outside.

'What've you got?' I said.

He held up a five cent piece, I told him not to throw it and we used it to etch LAND RIGHTS FOR THE GURINDJIS in big letters all around the cell walls.

People were coming in and out, getting bailed, but they'd put a thousand dollars on me and a few of the other ring-leaders. It was Saturday night. How was anyone going to come up with a thousand bucks? The Springboks were flying out the next day and the idea was to keep us inside overnight to forestall any more demonstrations. But eventaully, quite late at night, they brought me out and Ed Kee, a medical student who I'd taught was there. The cops went through a bit of a rigmarole, 'Do you know this person?' and all that, looking pretty sour about it. The reason was, Ed Kee had a bundle of ten dollar notes with him big enough to choke a bullock. The students had collected fifty thousand dollars for bail and Ed Kee was the bail bondsman.

The coppers took it right down to the wire. The sergeant had Ed Kee count out the money very slowly, a note at a time. I was getting very impatient, sick of the bloody place and wanting to know if Mary was all right.

'One hundred. One thousand dollars,' Ed Kee says, laying down the last note.

The cop says, 'I only make it ninety-nine. Better count it out again.'

There was a report on the demonstration in the *Australian* which carried the headline, 'Professor with hand grenade'. Somehow the story got around that the smoke signal was a hand grenade. It made a good headline but it was obviously nonsense. Still, when the dust settled, I had six charges to face — offensive behaviour, abusive language, resisting arrest, two charges of wilful damage to uniforms and possession of a hand grenade. A solicitor named Brian Vaughan, who was a member of the hospital board, arranged a barrister for me — Bob St John. Vaughan warned me that the business was going to cost me money — St John's fees would be three hundred dollars a day.

I went to court a few times and the case was held over for various reasons. The last charge was the most serious and some friends from the hospital — in the pharmacology and physiology departments — weighed in to help me. We conducted an experiment to see how noxious the smoke really was. We locked ourselves in a small room in my house at Sans Souci, and ignited one of the smoke signals. The smoke billowed out of the windows and the doors but it didn't have any harmful effects. So the senior lecturer in pharmacology prepared a written submission, testifying to the essential harmlessness of the smoke.

I was having trouble getting to see Bob St John, he was always with clients or in court, the old run-around, but I finally got hold of him one hour before the case was finally coming up to be heard. He'd just moved rooms and he was sitting in the middle of chaos, chain-smoking, sifting papers and not paying a blind bit of attention to what I was saying about this highly relevant submission on smoke bombs. I was a bit alarmed. St John was a big, bluff type, looked more like a detective himself than a smoothie lawyer, and I got the impression he wasn't really interested. I could see myself being found guilty and hauled off to Long Bay. I was thoroughly browned off at the legal system by this time as well. The court appearances had messed up my schedules and really interrupted the rhythms of my professional life.

Eventually, St John looked up and said, 'We'd better get into the court, I suppose.'

I can't remember whether he looked at the submission or not, but, if he did, it was just a glance.

We went to Waverley court and it was the usual circus — cops, reporters, the whole shooting match. A glossy magazine had recently been founded for circulation among everyone in the eye medicine game, and its editor was there, ready to tell the profession the latest in the Hollows case. I remember that the young sergeant who'd had the circum oral pallor wasn't present. I'd talked to him before, at my other appearances, encouraged him to diet, exercise, cut down on the booze and tobacco, and he told me about the progress he was making. He looked a lot better. But he wasn't there that day and neither were any other police that I recognised.

The case got underway and it looked as if the cops were serious. The police who claimed to be the ones who'd arrested me weren't in fact the same men, but they told their stories fluently enough. Then the prosecutor called the police ballistics expert and he took the stand, all smart in a suit, and testified that the smoke signals were noxious and highly dangerous to humans. After half an hour of this horrific detail, I was anxious as all hell, but Bob St John scarcely paid the expert any attention. When his time to cross-examine came he leaned casually on the table and said, 'What was the lot number of the object you tested?'

The ballistics man said, 'I didn't record the lot number.'

'What was the lot number of the object that was taken from the accused?'

'I don't have a record of that.'

Bob St John looked at the magistrate. 'Your worship, this evidence is inadmissable. What was tested and what the accused is alleged to have possessed may have been two totally different things.'

The magistrate dismissed the evidence and that charge. I was found not guilty of damaging the tunics and guilty of resisting arrest and offensive conduct.

The magistrate said, 'What is known?' Meaning, what previous offences had I been charged with and what convictions did I have.

The answer to that was nothing. (Just as well they didn't know about the hoardings in the National Park.) And the magistrate indicated that no conviction would be recorded. I wasn't too happy with that because it acted as a sort of good behaviour bond. St John said that if I wanted to appeal the only grounds were 'malicious charging' and this had never been proven in an Australian court. Furthermore, mounting an appeal would take a lot of time and money. I said to forget it.

As we were leaving the court, St John said that he was interested in doing some free legal work for the Aborigines. Also, he refused to take any money for the work he'd done on my case. I put him in touch with some people and he went up to Brewarrina for a month. That was a place where a third of the male blacks were either in gaol or just out, before the court or about to appear. JPs running the courts, shonky evidence, shonky procedures, a sort of racist ritual. St John defended all the Aborigines for a month and most of the cases never even got to court once he'd had a look at them.

CHAPTER 12

Among the Tarahumaras

They lift the hair, put a hardwood block under it and chip it away with a sharp axe. That's what gives them the basin-cut look, but they're beautiful people.

F.C. Hollows on the Tarahumara Indians

In 1973 I took my only sabbatical from the University of New South Wales. I missed out on an early one because I was too late in applying for it and I've never been very interested in these academic perks anyway. But in 1973 I was keen to go. I was casting about for a research project and became interested in a study of the Tarahumara Indians of Chihuahua, a state in northern Mexico. An American researcher had heard anecdotal evidence of an extraordinary fact — that heart attack was unknown among the Tarahumaras, of whom there were about sixty thousand living in virtual isolation in canyon country. He went into the field and did a study of the Indians' blood cholesterol levels. He found that adult male Tarahumaras had significantly lower blood cholesterol than adult male Americans. To get technical, the average among Americans was 250 milligrams per litre as against 135 for the Indians.

There was great concern about heart disease at that time because the rate of lethal cardiac failure among males in the thirty to forty bracket was going up dramatically. Coronary artery grafts, valve replacements and by-passes were things of the future. Women, always less prone to cardio-vascular problems than men, were having more heart attacks at a younger age too, and it was thought that we were on the brink of an enormous epidemic of arterial disease.

The eye is the only place in the body where you can look at small arteries directly, under direct light, and we ophthalmologists were starting to see damage to retinal arteries in patients as young as thirty-five. I wondered whether all human beings were subject to this sort of thing as a matter of physical degeneration, or if there were other factors involved. The Tarahumaras seemed to offer an instructive comparison.

I attended a conference in the United States and went down to Peru to have a look at the Andes. Then I travelled by rail and bus up through Ecuador, Colombia and the Central American countries before entering Mexico through Guatemala. In medical terms the most remarkable aspect of that period was observing a study that some American diabetologists were making of the Pimas, a desert-dwelling Indian tribe who lived around the Gila and Salt Rivers in southern Arizona. The Pima were herded onto reservations fairly early in the piece and not much is known about them beyond the fact that, unlike the other Indians who learned the practice from the Spaniards, they did not take scalps because they considered dead enemy bodies as evil entities. By the 1970s, the Pima had entered the scientific literature as the most diabetic people on earth.

I went to the reservation and located one of the huge caravans, or 'trailers' as the Americans call them, that the US Health Department can put into the field pretty well anywhere. They are virtually mobile hospitals. I stepped up into the caravan and my first impression was that it was full, crowded with bodies. Then I realised that there were only about a dozen people inside. The Pima are the fattest people in the world, topping the most obese of Maoris, Tongans and Nauruans. They have all the problems of reservation Indians in spades — alcoholism, atrocious diet ('frybread' is one of the staples, sliced white bread fried in animal fat and salted), inactivity and despair. As you would expect, their eyes were in terrible shape with a lot of glaucoma and diabetic retinopathy was rampant. This saddened me. The Pima got all the ill-effects of American affluence and none of the benefits.

A mere few weeks later I was with the Tarahumaras, a non-diabetic, super-fit people, less than a thousand kilometres to the south-east. Part of the reason for their good health was their inaccessibility. They lived in a big canyon called Barranca de Cobre, 'the copper canyon' — part of the Sierre Madre Occidental, more than 500 metres deep, with an enormous river running through it. To get into this area you have to take a train on one of the few railways that run across Mexico (as distinct from the north-south line). I went from the state capital of Chihuahua to Estacion Creel, a real Klondike-type town where there were a few trucks and cars — all brought in by flat-bed railway truck — but where most movement of goods and people was by human or animal sweat. While I was waiting for my transport into the canyon to arrive, I hired one of the few vehicles in town — a Volkswagen, cut down and modified to cope with the terrain — and took a drive out into the badlands.

Quite by chance, I came across one of the famous Tarahumara runners. I'd read about them and they were another reason for my interest in the place because I was myself a keen runner then. Moving at a good steady pace, and flicking a wooden ball in front of him with a long stick, this rail-thin man was running along the rough dusty road. He appeared to me to be exhausted and dehydrated, but he kept moving. I drove slowly and kept him in sight. He approached a woman who was frying potatoes by the roadside and for a moment I thought he was going to stop and have a feed. But she scooped up some of the poatoes into a leaf and ran alongside him, feeding him as he went. A bit further on there were a couple of children the runner seemed to know. Again, I thought he might stop, but they trotted beside him, urging him on.

I later found out that this man, who won the race he was involved in, had been running for thirty-six hours at the point where I came upon him. In all, he covered about 200 kilometres, running through the night when the runners use a torch made of a pine branch which burns with a bright yellow flame. They run for these incredible distances, keeping the ball rolling and bouncing along in front of them, through some very rough country indeed. Apparently very heavy bets are laid on these races; sometimes the entire family fortune is riding on the runners, so their motivation and endurance can be understood.

The only way into the Indian settlements in the canyon was by truck. I was put onto a local man called Don Pepe who agreed to act as a guide and interpreter. We boarded a truck, along with about ten other people, which was loaded up with sacks of bean and grain and some boxes. It was a good-sized truck and I was looking forward to the ride, sitting on the boxes and taking in the scenery. But a hundred metres down the road the truck stopped and about twenty people climbed aboard. After about a kilometre, another mob got on with all their bundles and they also loaded on a full-grown cow. It was a twenty-four-hour journey and very uncomfortable with all that cargo aboard.

When we reached the canyon's rim we were tired of being jostled and jolted and cooped up in the truck and one of the Mexicans, named Damien, said, 'Come on, Fred, let's get out of here.'

He climbed down from the truck as it was moving and I followed him. The road into the canyon followed a long series of hairpin bends and the truck had to creep down in low gear with the brakes on. Damien and I just slid down, sort of scuttling from one hairpin bend down to the next. That was a darn sight quicker and more fun. We ended up in a place called La Bufa, where there was an American named Jeff Chandler who was a big help to me. He'd been an airline pilot and had retired to live in this part of Mexico where living was cheap. He loved the Indians and spoke some of their language, Amara.

It was very rugged country. The only vehicle in that part of the canyon was a jeep that had been dismantled and brought in bit by bit. Everybody walked, carried their own goods or used burros. They were subsistence farmers, growing mostly beans and maize. They ate almost no meat. I had some chicken soup in a village once and that was a rarity because they don't kill their animals. On this occasion a fox had done the killing for them. My plan was to walk to as many villages as I could and see as many people as possible. I had an ophthalmoscope, a hand-held instrument that enables you to examine the interior of the eye by using a beam of light, which was all the equipment I needed.

Jeff Chandler knew the country and told me where the settlements were. Don Pepe did the translating. I had an Indian to carry my pack and I did a hell of a lot of walking and climbing over the next month and a half. I was very thin and fit and I thrived on it. The Tarahumaras were in extraordinarily good shape, ophthalmologically. There was plenty of water and their household hygiene was reasonably good so that there was no trachoma. The state of their arteries was remarkable. I was trying to see a wide range of people and one man I examined told me that his grandfather, Martine, was still alive, aged ninety-seven.

Martine lived on his own on the other side of the canyon, quite a few kilometres away and a steep climb to his house and garden. I was very tired when I got there. Martine was a typical Tarahumara — short, thin, wearing the loose loincloth arrangement which gives rise to the name they are sometimes given, the 'diaper Indians'. He was working in his garden when I arrived, and the heavy knife he was using to chip a water channel and a tin billy were the only industrialised products in his set-up. He worked hard, walked everywhere and carried his own loads. His grandson was about thirty so I didn't doubt that Martine was in his nineties. His arteries were beautiful — like those of an Australian twenty-year-old, nice curves, no calibre changes or straightened sections.

The climate in the canyon is very severe and the Tarahumaras move to the higher, cooler parts in the summer and back down to the valley bottom in the winter. They have land in both locations. They were very surprised to find a doctor willing to walk 20 kilometres to see a sick person, cross suspension bridges and ford rivers, all of which I did. Mexican medical services did not reach them and they had some serious problems. There were aenemic children, people with dietary-deficiency illnesses and even with diseases out of the history books, like scrofula. Scrofula is a form of tuberculosis of the lymph nodes, usually in the neck, causing the formation of abcesses. If these are untreated they burst through the skin and cause running sores which leave unsightly scars when they heal. Several people died while I was there for want of very basic antibiotics.

I enjoyed the work and the company of the Indians and I improved my Spanish somewhat. I've never been much of a linguist and in general I've only learned a few words of the languages in places where I've worked — 'Come closer, sit down, look up, look down, look left, look right' — that sort of thing. I caused some amusement a few years later in the Pitjantjatjara country when I said 'enter me' instead of 'come closer.'

As a research project though, the study of the Tarahumaras didn't pan out. Some of the factors contributing to the soundness of their arteries were obvious — diet and a heavy exercise pattern — but they were also a very homogenous people. If you study a batch of portrait photographs or group shots, you'll see that the people are remarkably alike. It may be that their low cholesterol and cardiac health are genetically determined. That's good luck for them but of very limited scientific interest.

PART TWO

CHAPTER 13

The Trachoma Program 1

> The program thought it common courtesy to inform people of its aims and objectives; these concerned old people, children, their parents, their homes, their lands and their lives.
>
> *Aboriginal liaison officer Trevor Buzzacott, 'Report on "Liaison" in the National Trachoma and Eye Health Program'*

It was like an epic movie or a TV mini-series with a big cast of characters, lots of dramatic incidents and sub-plots, personal and political, producing changes in peoples' lives. The difference was that films and mini-series end, whereas the work that was begun in the 1970s goes on as it must until the first of our aims — which I drafted on a flight from Alice Springs to Darwin, is achieved — the elimination of trachomatous blindness from Australia.[7]

The publicity associated with my visits to the Gurindji camps at Wattie Creek and Hooker Creek, the work at Bourke and Enngonia and a trip I made by light plane with several other eye doctors and orthoptists (technicians able to test and record information about a person's sight) through South Australia, New South Wales, Queensland and the Northern Territory in 1974, highlighted the need for a national attack on the trachoma problem. On the 1974 trip

[7] See, *The National Trachoma and Eye Health Program*, (Royal Australian College of Ophthalmologists), Sydney, 1980.

we screened more than a thousand children and found, in some communities, trachoma follicles present in 80 per cent of the kids.

Two important movers and shakers were Gordon Briscoe and Dr S.I. 'Pip' Ivil. Gordon Briscoe, after being a field officer for the Aboriginal Legal Service and president of the Aboriginal Medical Service, had spent some time back in the Northern Territory as a member of the Central Australian Aboriginal Congress. After that he went into the Aboriginal section of the Federal Department of Health in Canberra. He was the only black member of that section. Equally unusual in his way was Pip Ivil, also an officer of the Department of Health. He had been a fighter pilot in World War 2 and later a test pilot for Rolls Royce. Then he'd studied medicine back in New Zealand at the same time as me. We younger students had helped him with some of the academic work that was unfamiliar to him and we'd benefited from his experience and knowledge of the world. After a successful career as a GP he'd moved to Australia and joined the Health Department because he wanted to *do* something, to see changes happen.

That made him very different from most of the medicos in that department who were either superannuated TB doctors (relics from the days when tuberculosis was a major public health problem and a lot of doctors had been recruited to combat it) and career medical diplomats who pushed pens and went to meetings and didn't know anything about doctoring. Briscoe wanted action on Aboriginal eye health in the centre; he talked to Pip Ivil and found out that he knew Hollows from way back and and so these two 'doers' approached me. Their question, briefly, was: if red tape could be cut and bureaucratic objections overcome — there were problems about the limits of federal responsibility for health and the sensitivity of state and territory departments — could Aboriginal eye health be tackled and improved?

That, essentially, was the question Pip Ivil put to me. He could see that the Northern Territory health department didn't actually do anything, apart from move a few incompetent doctors and ill-trained nursing sisters over the landscape, getting to grips with nothing.

I said, 'Of course something could be done. A national campaign to do something sensible about Aboriginal eye health is feasible.'

'Well, Fred,' Pip said. 'Will you run it from your department?'

'No, not in a fit,' I said. 'If a great big team from the University of New South Wales rolled up in the Kimberleys, where they think everyone from the east is strange, or lobbed into backblocks Queensland where they regard all southerners as pinko stirrers, there'd be nothing but trouble.'

'All right,' Pip said. 'How should it be run?'

The College of Ophthalmologists had only recently been organised and it seemed to me that this was the perfect body to organise the program through — totally respectable, national in scope, apolitical, all that. I advised Pip to do what he needed to do administratively at the Federal end — get ministerial support and funding and sort out the state and territory problems — and approach me, through the College, to head up the program. And that's the way it was done.

That sounds very smooth. Actually, it was anything but. These initial discussions and resolutions took place in 1975, not long before the constitutional crisis that resulted in the dismissal of the Whitlam government. That put everything on hold for six months — it took at least that long for the Fraser government to lend its support — and there were other administrative delays and uncertainties. Eventually, Ian Viner, the Minister for Aboriginal Affairs, OKed a setting-up payment of $25,000 and we started to roll. Some funny things happened in the setting-up period. Take the procurement of tents, for example.

Acting on advice, I got in touch with the army and was told

that a representative would come to see me on the matter. I finished an operation list at the Prince of Wales one day and the sister came up and said, 'There's a delegation of gentlemen here to see you, Professor. I don't know who they are but they look very serious.' She behaved as if they were police or ASIO come to arrest the hand-grenade professor. I went out to meet them and you never saw such a stiff bunch of blokes in all your life. Only one of them was in uniform, but the five of them were officers, Captain this and Major that. They told me they were there about the tents and showed me a catalogue of what was available. This catalogue was treated like a top-secret document and all it contained were photographs and descriptions of tents. In my mind's eye the photographs were sepia-tinted. Maybe not, but they were very old pictures of very old equipment.

I said, 'How many men does it take to put up one of these tents?'

The answer was, 'About fourteen.'

'That's no good to us. We need light jobs that can be linked up one to another, put up and pulled down quickly and tossed inside a 4WD.'

'You mean the Vietnam tent. I'm afraid we can't help you with those.'

One of the delegation, presumably the man with the greatest imagination and goodwill, gave me the name of a Colonel at the Ingleburn army base who might be able to help. I rang him and he said, 'I'm retiring in a few weeks. I'd like to help. Send a truck over here.'

We sent one of the vehicles we'd started to get together — a two-and-half-tonne, 4WD International, driven by two good-looking young women, Rosie Denholm and Gabi O'Sullivan — to the base and the Colonel said. 'Here're the stores. Take what you like.' We got a truckfull of tents, tables, chairs and stools and the only requisitioning that happened was in the form of a letter I was advised to write to the Minister of Defence, requesting the loan of certain equipment. Months later, way out in the Pitjantatjara country, I got a very pleasant letter from the Right Honourable James Killen expressing regret that the army was unable to lend this vital, constantly-in-use military gear to civilians.

I took two years' leave to devote myself to the program and that was the source of some difficulties, too. The delays and hesitations brought about by the political turmoil caused my plans to have a first-class man named Peter Watson stand in for me to come unstuck. In the end, my functions were only performed on a part-time basis by various people and I was criticised for that. My personal life was in flux at the time. The volatile relationship with Mary had come to an end. She had left to live in France; she returned briefly to Australia, but she died of a heart attack a few years later in South Africa. I'd had several relationships of varying duration and intensity, and I was in the process of buying the big Victorian sandstone house I now have in Randwick — 'Farnham House'.

Along with other people at the time, I had the idea that the small, nuclear family wasn't the best kind of living unit, not the most socially healthy set-up. Living like that, a lot of people seemed to tear each other apart, and I thought a bigger group was the way to go. For that, you needed a big house. I also wanted a tin roof because I think the noise of rain on a tin roof when you're in bed at night is one of the most soothing sounds the world has to offer. Particularly if it's a bit cold and windy — you can feel the elements, but you have a great sense of protection from them. You lose all that with a tile roof.

A friend who was cluey about real estate located 'Farnham House' which was in a dilapidated state and divided into seven flats — partitions everywhere, built-in balconies, sealed doors. There were seven gas and electricity meters and eleven refrigerators. It had an iron roof all right, but there was more rust in it than the *Titanic*. It cost $90,000, which was very steep at the time, although the land was worth more than $60,000. The site had been scheduled for high rise development but that had been rescinded. I was broke, as always , and I had a hard job raising first and second mortgages. I'd just got the house, on payments of close to a thousand dollars a month, when the program started up and my income took a nose dive. I set the salaries and I allotted myself $30,000 per annum.

This is leading me into consideration of some of the principles that lay behind the operation of the Trachoma Program. There were many, but three of the most important were: (1) that the work should be carried out quickly, within two years, so that the assessment of the situation and the delivery of treatments shouldn't be blurred by time and change; (2) as before, no survey without service; and (3) that we shouldn't be seen to be making money out of the work. Eighty ophthalmologists who worked at different times donated their services which is greatly to their credit; the full-time members of the team worked for what might be called award rates and no more. If we used our own vehicles we had a per kilometre allowance but had to meet our own repair bills.

Vehicles were tremendously important. We were subject to the tyranny of distance. Looking back on the program, with all its highs and lows, it seems to me that one of the dominant themes was the travelling — we belted around over outback roads, month after month, by day and by night — often by night because we needed to be in the next place in the morning when the school opened — working the vehicles as hard as we worked ourselves. I'd sold a well-worn Land Rover and my great old Alfa Romeo to buy a second-hand Range Rover for $10,000. I thought I'd get a bit of comfort and speed out of it. (Land Rovers were too slow and punishing on the body, I thought.) It was a bad buy though; with the modifications I had to make to it and the repair bills, tyres and other costs, just keeping that vehicle running totally consumed my income.

Trucks, Range Rovers, Land Rovers, planes and boats — they were the gristle and sinew of the work, part of the fun and part of the danger. The greatest sadness to befall us was the death in 1977 of Pat O'Shaunessy, our field secretary, who was killed in the Kimberleys when the truck she was driving — the International I've already referred to — rolled over about 20 kilometres from Halls Creek. Sandy road, sharp bend and the truck, with high pressure tyres and a tendency to swing at the back, was a bastard of a thing to drive. Pat was only 31 and she'd been a tireless and cheerful worker under the most difficult of conditions. I had to identify her body in the morgue of the Halls Creek police station. Everyone in the team missed her and when we went back into some of the areas where she'd worked the Aborigines were grieved to hear of her death.

I'm jumping ahead again, the memories are so sharp and vivid. The diagrams give a better idea of the scope of the work in terms of the area covered and the numbers of people seen and treated. I was the director of the program but, of course, we split up into teams and I only know at first-hand about the kilometres I covered, investigations I did, the clinics I conducted and the satisfactions I experienced. However, I participated in the work in every state except Victoria, which was covered by other teams. No work was done in Tasmania. From the start, there was a political dimension to everything and this persisted throughout the period of the program.

For example, at one point there were rumblings of opposition in Western Australia. After completing some work in the South Australian backblocks, I spoke on the phone to Gordon Briscoe who was in Canberra with his finger on the political pulse. In language more forceful and colourful than is appropriate here, he said, 'Fred, get yourself across to the west.'

We were dog tired and surrounded by red dust-impregnated gear and vehicles, but I attempted to rally the troops with something like, 'Pack up, we're crossing the Nullarbor tonight!'. In fact, in those days of striated, unmade road and sand drifts, it took three days to cross the Nullarbor and when we got into Kalgoorlie we booked into a motel to wash the sweat from our faces and the dust from our throats. In the morning I was surprised to be greeted by Ben Mason, an Aborigine who was a Church of Christ minister. I had operated on Ben Mason some time before for a minor eye disorder, and I knew him to be a sophisticated man and an influential community leader. He also happened to be a physically imposing figure, tall and well-built.

The Reverend Mason informed me that our arrival in Kalgoorlie had been anticipated, and that it had been arranged for us to meet with certain people from the state Aboriginal Affairs Department and some health workers. He said he'd like to enter the meeting with the trachoma team as part of a small Aboriginal delegation. That was fine with me so we trooped off to the Department of Aboriginal Affairs building and took our seats in what turned out to be a fair-sized gathering of administrators, doctors and other suspicious and sceptical types.

I was somewhat non-plussed when I discovered that there was a formal agenda for this meeting with minutes to be kept, matters to be discussed listed in order of importance and so on. I was even more surprised when one of the doctors stood up and proposed some adjustment to the agenda — the substitution of item 3 for item 6 or something such.

No sooner had he opened his mouth than big Ben Mason was on his feet. 'You shut up,' he said. 'You have let Aborigines bleed to death in the streets of this town and these people are here to help us with our eye problems. You sit down and shut up.'

I don't remember much more about the meeting. I spoke, outlining what we were on about, and the methods we were using. Not a peep from the chastened white fellers and the proceedings came to an end. Later Ben Mason told me what it had all been about — a concerted attempt by conservative

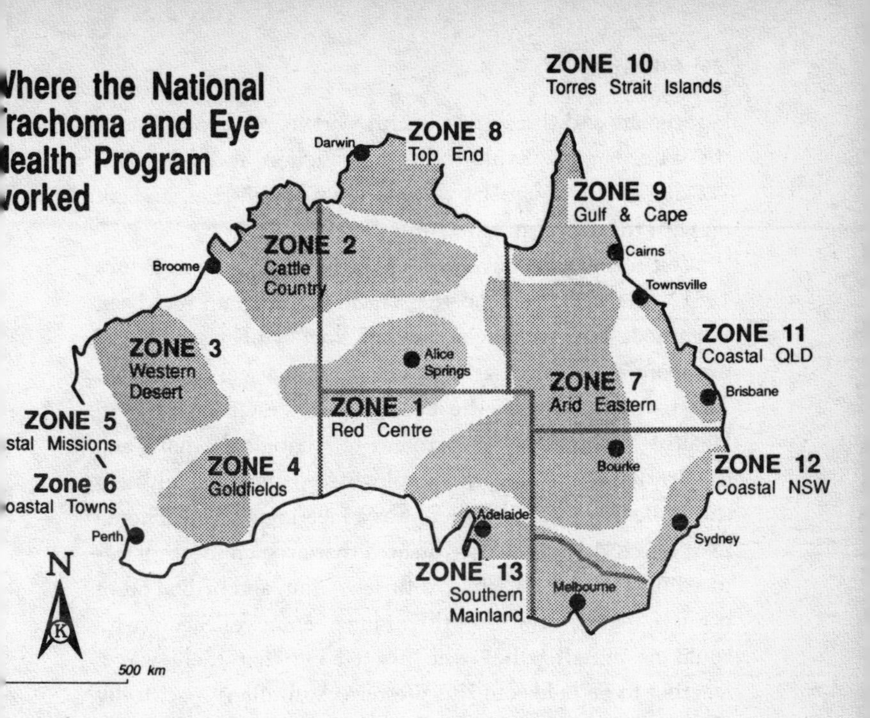
here the National
rachoma and Eye
ealth Program
orked
ZONE 10
Torres Strait Islands
ZONE 8
Top End
Darwin
ZONE 9
Gulf & Cape
Cairns
Townsville
ZONE 2
Cattle
Country
Broome
ZONE 11
Coastal QLD
ZONE 3
Western
Desert
Alice
Springs
ZONE 7
Arid Eastern
Brisbane
ZONE 5
stal Missions
ZONE 1
Red Centre
Zone 6
oastal Towns
ZONE 4
Goldfields
Bourke
ZONE 12
Coastal NSW
Adelaide
Perth
Sydney
ZONE 13
Southern
Mainland
Melbourne
N
K
500 km

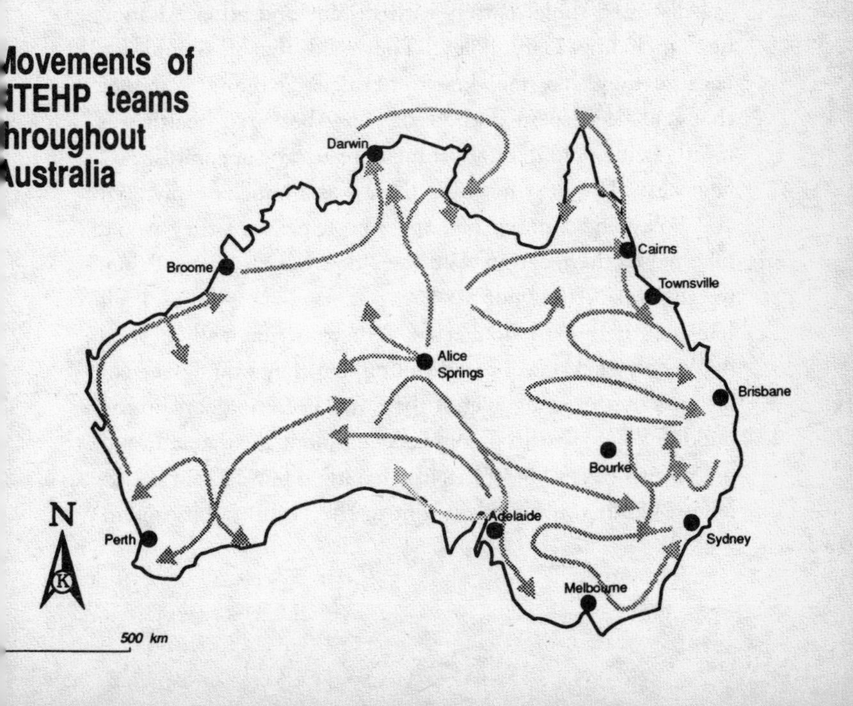
ovements of
TEHP teams
hroughout
ustralia
Darwin
Broome
Cairns
Townsville
Alice
Springs
Brisbane
Bourke
Adelaide
Perth
Sydney
Melbourne
N
K
500 km

bureaucrats and threatened health workers to keep us out of the state. Largely thanks to his direct action, it didn't work. We divided that huge slab of country up into districts and got on with the job in an efficient fashion.

We continued to have trouble in the west, even as late as 1981, after the report on the Trachoma Program had been published. Gordon Briscoe rang me from Canberra, and told me about a meeting that was being held to discuss trachoma. The participants were the Federal and Western Australian Health Departments, Department of Aboriginal Affairs and the Royal College of Ophthalmologists, so I immediately rang the College and asked if there was a meeting about trachoma in Western Australia. I was assured that no such meeting was to occur. However, I spoke to Briscoe again and he had proof it was going to occur. So I then rang a senior colleague (who could never tell a lie) who assured me that there was a meeting to be held, but the Western Australians specifically requested that I do not attend.

I discussed these matters with Briscoe and other Aborigines, including Gary Foley. They said that I should go, because they, like me, knew enormous amounts of money that had been spent purportedly on Aboriginal health was mostly being used in establishing bureaucratic apparatus. So I flew west. The next morning there was a knock on my door and Foley and a group of large Aborigines said they would take me to the meeting. We went down in two cars. When we got outside they put me between two big blokes — I felt like a rather small hooker in a rugby scrum with a good flanker on each side. I recall feeling that they would have got me into that meeting even if there had been no doors on the building. We went in flying-wedge fashion. I was able to put my point of view. Nothing like having a few 185 cm blackfellows beside you when confronting the white establishment.

Top: Me today
Left: Dad and mum: Joseph and Clarice Hollows.
Below: Class of '47, Upper VI, Palmerston North Boy's High School. Young Fred is extreme right, front row.

Top left: My father photographed in 1932 to demonstrate 'the remarkable growth of this *Lilium auratum* grown in a 10-inch "breeze" pot', his own invention.
Top right: Colour Sergeant Fred Hollows, Boy's Brigade, about 1947.
Below: My brothers John and Colin to my right, and Monty (Maurice) to my left in the backyard of our home in Palmerston North in 1953.

Top: With Peter Brandt, in Dunedin in 1953 after a spot of gardening.
Left: Arthur Noorderhaven and me, with our horse Maori Jack — the greatest equine self-starter in the bush.
Below: The epidemiology team in Wales partying at Christmas. I am smoking the pipe; my wife Mary is on my right.

Top: Professor Archibald L. Cochrane, Archie Cochrane, Professor of Respiratory Medicine at the Welsh National School of Medicine and head of the Medical Research Council Epidemiology Unit in Cardiff, war hero, quasi-spy and my mentor — 'no survey without service'.
Middle: A gathering of the Glaucoma Survey Team in Cardiff. A dull formal shot of some usually very lively people. That's the Lord's Prayer in Welsh in front.
Bottom: Lazy weekend at Sans Souci in 1974. See what running does for the waistline!

Top: Shirley ('Mumshirl') Smith and my wife Mary.
Middle: Climbing in the Southern Alps.
Below: This woman at Wattie Creek was the first person blinded by trachoma that I saw.

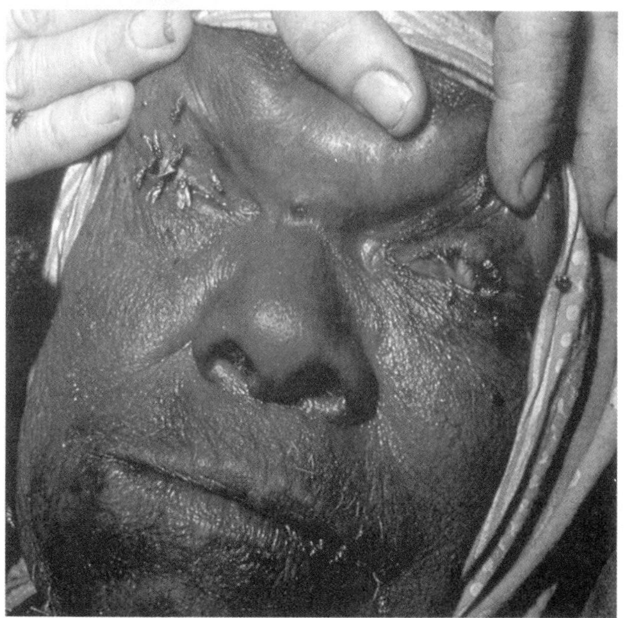

The National Trachoma and Eye Health Program at work.
Top: Outside the dwelling of this *tjilpi* or elder, we discuss the fitting of his spectacles.
Right: The symbol we adapted from the black, red and yellow Aboriginal flag.
Below: Dr David Moran tests the vision of this man in the Pitjantjatjara country of South Australia.

Top: A roadside eye test. The stockman points in the direction of the E letter on the chart.
Above: Transport, 'the muscles and sinews' of the NTEHP teams who travelled over 84,000 kilometres, a lot of it as arid and dusty as this.
Below: The efficient, cheerful and tireless Patricia O'Shaugnessy, field secretary, types up reports in the field. In June 1977 her vehicle overturned and she was killed, 31 years of age.

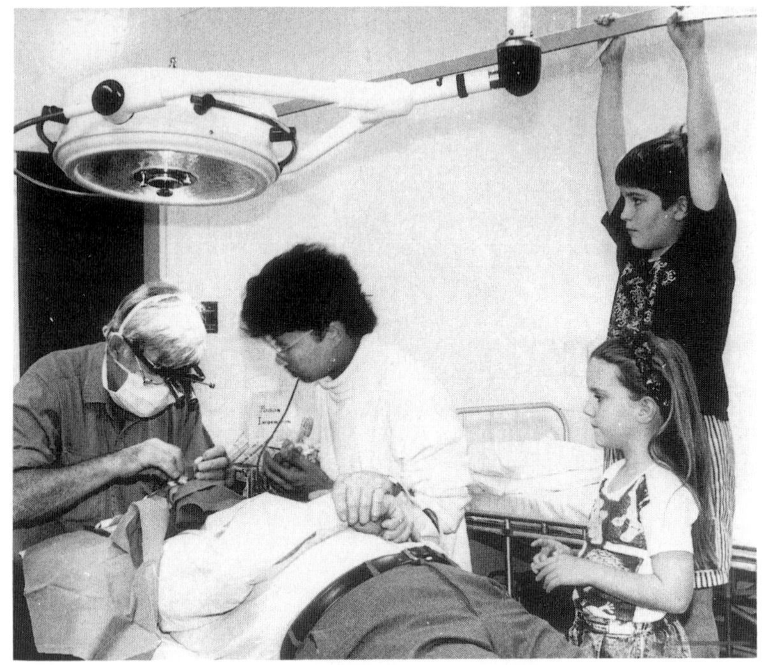

NEWS LTD

Top: Doing an eye operation at Bourke in 1990, assisted by Ranjit Siddhartha, and watched by Emma and Cam.
Above left: Michael Johnson. Runner, scholar, economist and friend.
Above right: Tom Barcham, my sure-footed friend. He got me up and down many big mountains.

Above: Doing my washing in a stream in an Andean village in Peru.
Right: A Tarahumara runner. They run extraordinary distances, hour after hour, using flaming torches at night to see by, pushing the ball before them with the long stick, over rough country, with big bets riding on their endurance and running skills.

Gordon Briscoe. In my opinion Aboriginal Australia's leading intellectual; he instinctively analyses and never confuses semblance with substance.

Reg Murray, an Aboriginal man of many parts, chess player, mechanic and optical dispenser, and he kept the Trachoma Program on the road.

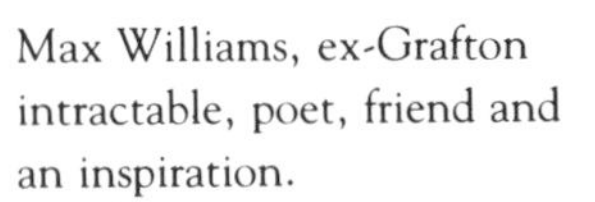

Max Williams, ex-Grafton intractable, poet, friend and an inspiration.

PAT FISKE

Top: Reunion of some National Trachoma and Eye Health Program workers. *From left:* Professor Hugh Taylor, Gabi holding Ruth, me, Sister Marjorie Baldwin, Gordon Briscoe, Sue Bennett and Jack Waterford holding Rosa.

Left: 'I've never been anyone's idea of the smooth doctor type.'

Right: Fessahaie Abraham. An extraordinarily effective lobbyist for the Eritrean cause in Australia. A chemical engineer and the first Eritrean I met.
Below: Fessahaie and his wife Hadas in their Coptic wedding dress at Farnham House. I'm behind the bride and groom. *From the left:* Gabi and Cam, my father Joe Hollows, medical student Sabina Boes, and Michael Johnson with Emma.

Left: Desbele Ghebregiorghis — front-line eye surgeon, a man of enormous commitment.
Below: Desbele standing alongside one of the two tanks that remain a monument for the Eritreans who fought the ferocious battle for Massawa. In the background is the Massawa ice works; although shattered, due to Eritrean ingenuity, the plant was functioning and producing ice at the time this photo was taken.

At the ceremony at the University of New South Wales when I was conferred as a Doctor of Medicine. *From left:* Orthoptist Joe Dalzel, me, Michael Johnson, Rosina Hollows, Colin Hollows, Sister Shirley Palmer, and Ben Hollows.

Left: My daughter Tanya and me at the Christening of the twins, Rosa and Ruth. *Bottom:* Farnham House dinner. *From left:* Dr Nerayo, Eritrea Public Health Program, me Emma; Ascarlu, member of the Central Committee EPLF; Cam; Fessahaie Abraham; Haille Ghebre; and Gabi.

Above: Getting stuck into a bit of woodwork with my assistant, Cam. *Left:* The Randwick house, 'Farnham House'. Lots of rooms, tin roof, terrific home. We flew the Aboriginal flag in honour of Aboriginal guests at the time the photograph was taken. Hopefully, in the future, Aboriginal *householders* in Randwick will seem perfectly normal to all Australians.

Family life.
Left: Gabi and I with our children: *From left*: Emma, Rosa; Anna-Louise and Cam, and Ruth
Middle: Hiking in the Snowy Mountains with Gabi and Cam.
Bottom: With Emma at home.

GREG PIPER

PAT FISKE

Above: Examining eyes in the outdoors, Eritrea 1991. No fear of the MIGs now.

Below: With Desbele, Asmara 1991. He doesn't have an Alfa Romeo and he doesn't care.

JONATHAN CHESTER/EXTREME IMAGES

Above: Post-operative rounds at the Tupche Eye Camp with Sanduk Ruit and Dr Darryl Campbell.
Below: Sanduk Ruit at the Kathmandu Eye Hospital. A great surgeon.

JONATHAN CHESTER/EXTREME IMAGES

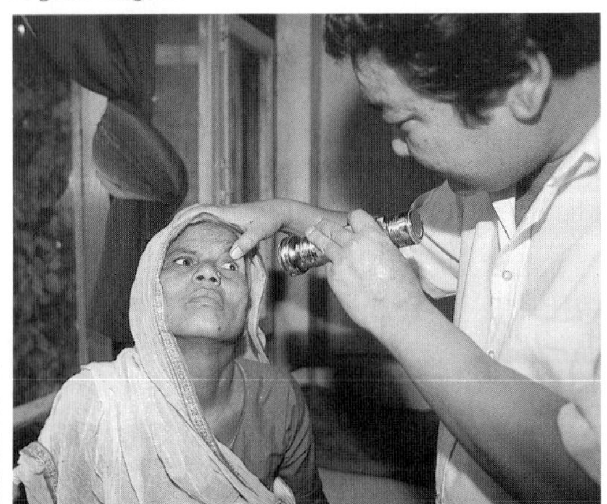

JONATHAN CHESTER/EXTREME IMAGES

Talking with the Hon Koirala, Prime Minister of Nepal. I am convinced Nepal is sufficiently stable, democratic and accountable to be the site of a lens factory for South Asia.

JONATHAN CHESTER/EXTREME IMAGES

Dr Sanduk Ruit, ophthalmologist. His surgical excellence and energy will guide the Nepal Eye Program into a thoroughly modern phase.

JONATHAN CHESTER/EXTREME IMAGES

Hazel Hawke and I prepare to cut a cake that replicated the cover of the first edition of this book — portrait in icing! — at the Prince of Wales Hospital launch. Hazel called me 'a ratbag', which is fair enough. The book raised nearly $100,000 for the Eritrean lens factory.
Postscript: The Eitrean lens factory was installed in 1993. Sales of this book had raised over $165,000 when this edition went to press.

Steven Miller, University of Wollongong, Dr John Cooper and me discussing the building of the lens factory for Eritrea. Steve Miller is an extraordinary machine maker.

JONATHAN CHESTER/EXTREME IMAGES

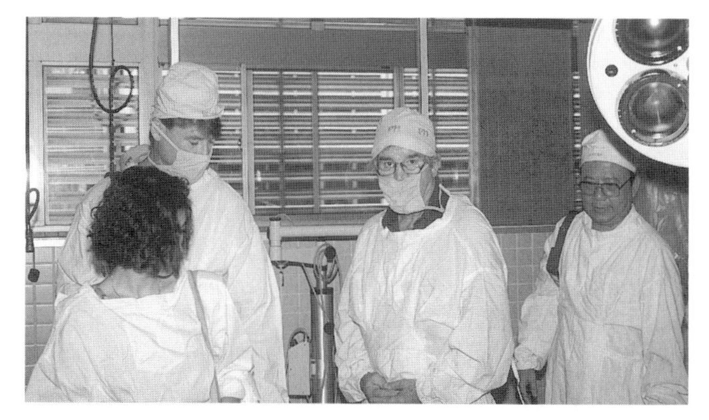

Top: Demonstrating cataract surgery, Hanoi. The interpreter, an ophthalmologist, is on my right. The banner reads *Long live the Communist Party of Vietnam*. *Above:* With Hollows Foundation director John Cooper and Vietnamese surgeons in the very busy National Institute of Ophthalmology, Hanoi. *Right:* With Professor Nhan, Vietnam's top eye man.

With General Giap in the State Guest House, Hanoi, Mrs Bruce Dover is the interpreter and my son Cam shares the General's chair. General Giap signed my copy of his book, *People's War, People's Army*.

The tieless Aussies. *From left:* Federal Treasurer John Dawkins, me, Peter Corris, Senator John Button and Ambassador Michael Potts at an Embassy 'do' in Vietnam.

The AIDS Conference. *From left:* Julian Gold, Dr John Kalder, Professor Ron Penny, me, Brian Howe, Dr Bruce Shepherd.

Dr Bruce Shepherd, one of the first people to write in support when I spoke at Alice Springs, and Brian Howe at the AIDS conference.

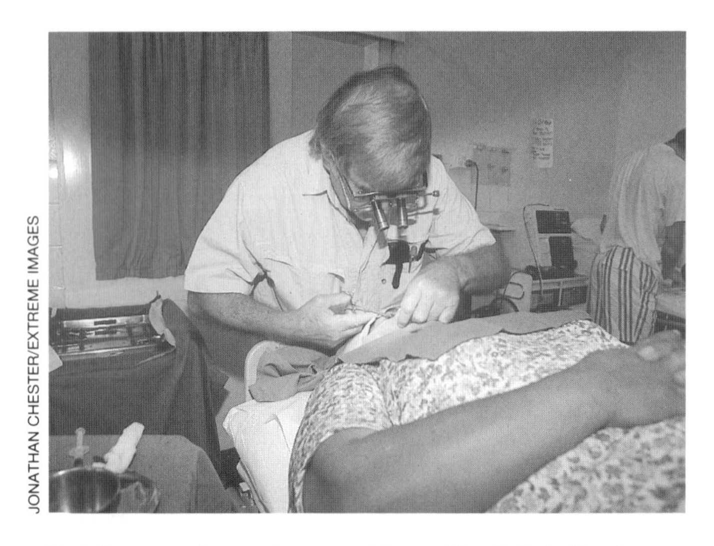

JONATHAN CHESTER/EXTREME IMAGES

Back home, and operating at my bi-monthly clinic in Bourke, NSW. Gabi and the kids came with me — as usual. Good country, great times.

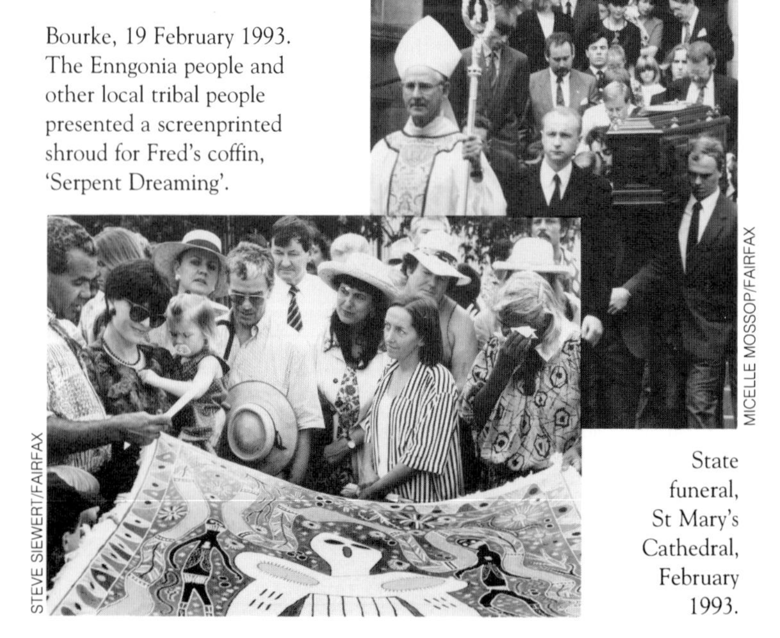

Bourke, 19 February 1993. The Enngonia people and other local tribal people presented a screenprinted shroud for Fred's coffin, 'Serpent Dreaming'.

STEVE SIEWERT/FAIRFAX

State funeral, St Mary's Cathedral, February 1993.

MICELLE MOSSOP/FAIRFAX

CHAPTER 14

The Trachoma Program 2

> The visually handicapped, that is, those who are pensionably blind or who have poor vision form a group who do not have good vision in either eye . . . Overall, 9 in every thousand non-Aborigines seen and 38 in every thousand Aborigines seen fell into this group.
>
> *National Trachoma and Eye Health Program*

There was nothing new about trachoma in the bush. Known as 'sandy blight' in the early days of European settlement, the disease affected whites and blacks alike until the early decades of this century. With the improvement in living conditions it began to disappear within the white population but, in the 1940s, Father Frank Flynn, who was an ophthalmologist based in the Alice Springs army hospital, found that around 90 per cent of the Aborigines of the Centre had some signs of the disease, with up to 7 per cent being blinded by it in one or both eyes. These findings were backed up by Professor Ida Mann's work in Western Australia in the 1950s. In some Aboriginal communities almost every individual exhibited trachoma signs; incidences of 60 per cent were not uncommon; in some places 70 per cent of children had follicular trachoma. She found that 3 per cent of Aborigines were blind in both eyes (with trachoma as a contributing cause) and about the same percentage were blind in one eye. The overall blindness rate for whites was 0.2 per cent.

Flynn and Mann were followed by other ophthalmologists

who attempted to combat the disease by treating school children, using mobile units to reach adults and pressing for educational programs and for microbiological research into the trachoma organism. Ida Mann, in particular, laid stress on the necessity of improving Aboriginal living conditions as a first requirement towards eliminating trachoma. Progress was slow though. Bad pun, but out of sight was out of mind, and it wasn't until the climate of opinion about Aborigines had changed in the 1970s, that it was possible for a program of the size and expense of the one we proposed to have a show of being accepted.

It was on a plane between Alice Springs and Darwin, travelling with Pip Ivil, that I drafted the five points that were later ratified by the College of Ophthalmologists. It's my belief that clarity and brevity are at the heart of the best poetry, the best writing generally. And there's nothing like a bit of pressure to bring these qualities out. And the pressure was on then. For one thing, we'd started to spend money but the overall aims and objectives of the project hadn't been spelled out. Secondly, we knew that the Northern Territory was going to be one of the biggest areas of operation and Pip Ivil made it clear to me that I had to have something in writing to convince Charles Gurd — the man in charge of the NT health department — to lend his support.

Pip said, 'He's not antipathetic. He thinks you're all right, Fred. He thinks you're a doer. But you have to have it down in a way that he can understand and get on the books.'

The result was the 'Aims of the National Trachoma and Eye Health Program':

1 The elimination of trachomatous blindness in Australia.

2 Presentation of the ocular health status of persons in rural Australia to interested agencies.

3 Provision of immediate eye care to persons in rural Australia.

In the light of the above and experience gained, that consideration be given to:

4 Establishment of ongoing eye care programs for rural Australia.

5 Training of medical, paramedical and interested lay persons in the skills necessary to provide eye care in rural Australia.

That carried the day with Charles Gurd and, for the most part, we got excellent co-operation in the Territory. The aims were moderate and diplomatic, as I saw them, and this reasonableness stood us in good stead in the long run, although we had problems with people who chose to put a different interpretation on what we were doing, particularly in Queensland.

Of equal importance to the official aims and policies of the program were what might be called its operational principles and style. In this regard, the most important thing was liaison with the Aboriginal communities. Ideally, a few weeks before a team reached an Aboriginal settlement, a black liaison officer had been in there first — explaining what the work was all about and getting the people organised and interested.

This massive operation was organised by Gordon Briscoe and worked brilliantly. The number of times it broke down could be numbered on the fingers of one hand which was extraordinary, given that over four hundred Aboriginal communities were visited. Trevor Buzzacott was the first liaison officer appointed and served the longest, working in South Australia, Western Australia, the Territory and Queensland. Other key men were Emmanuel Ebsworth, Greg Davis and Reg Murray in New South Wales; Mick Miller and Clarrie Grogan in north Queensland (at the suggestion of Charles Perkins); Michael Mace and Lindsay Black in southern and western Queensland; Lionel Turner and Don Ferguson around the Red Centre and Allan Mallard and Kevin Cox in the West. Dr David Moran, the program's epidemiologist, was involved in liaison as well as testing vision, report writing and so much else.

Trevor Buzzacott's final report gives some idea of the way the work was done:

> Each community the program visited had to be treated individually. Different groups spoke different languages; housing and lifestyle were frequently radically different; many communities were physically isolated from other centres. Within the communities, there would be different authority structures, and different input and control from outside agencies, including the Department of Aboriginal Affairs, other government departments, local non-Aboriginal resource personnel, and various religious institutions. All these factors had a strong bearing on how contact was made with each community. In some cases the hostility of some outside agencies meant that special efforts had to be made to reach the Aboriginal community itself.

On other occasions, the teams' movements were influenced by factors such as Aboriginal ceremonies, deaths within the community, link-ups with other surveys, and the movements of populations acording to a number of factors.

The rather bureaucratic language may mask the fact that liaison work was time-consuming, delicate and onerous. Looking back, it is almost impossible for me to contemplate what it would have been like to lead teams into communities that had not been visited by the liaison men. The problems we had, and there were plenty of them, would have been magnified into the realms of impossibility.

Some of the local liaison people were remarkable individuals who I consider it a privilege to have met. Such a one was

Poster announcing impending arrival of a Trachoma Program team.

Mrs Avey Curly of Meekatharra in Western Australia. She was sixty-one years of age and had given birth to eighteen children, thirteen of whom had survived. In the bad old days, when the police had routinely driven all blacks out of town at six o'clock, Mrs Curley, although a matronly lady at the time, had collected together a big group of Aborigines who passively, but resolutely, broke the curfew. She insisted on being gaoled with the others and this action did something to help change community attitudes. She was a leading figure in the Bundi Club, an Aboriginal progress group. I wonder how many other women in the country had a record to equal hers — bearing children from the age of fifteen until well into her forties, and tirelessly active on behalf, not only of her own large family, but the wider communuity.

Each team consisted of up to nine full-time staff: (1) a trachoma grader, usually an ophthalmologist, (2) a senior Aboriginal field officer, (3) an ophthalmologist, usually a volunteer spending several weeks on the road, (3) an orthoptist, (4) a trained nurse, (5) an optical dispenser, (5) a microbiologist, (6) a field secretary, (7) a mechanic and baggage handler. Often, the teams were smaller with staff members doubling up on some jobs. As a general rule, about half of the workers were Aborigines and in places where local people helped with clerical duties, liaison and interpreting, the proportion was higher.

Outback Australia had never seen anything like that degree of scientific and organisational expertise. It was tiring work and no two days were alike, but after a while we became super-professional. We could lob into a place, see the logical spot for the grader to work, the vision fields to be taken, the palavering to go on, and get right into it. The 'Vietnam tents' were terrific; we could throw them up in no time, link them if we needed to, provide treatment and sleeping areas. Each team was self-sufficient as to food and supplies and we tried not to interfere in the local economy — either by way of providing largesse or being a drain.

SURGERY CARD

1	2	3	4	5	6	7	8	9	10	11	12	13	14
1	4	4	3	7	0	6	2	6	1	2			

NAME [redacted]

ADDRESS THURSDAY ISLAND. HOSPITAL.

AGE 90 yrs SEX Male.

Surgical diagnosis: 1. (1) Senile cataract 2. 3. 4.

DATE 14.7.78

PLACE T.I. Hosp

SURGEON [redacted]

ASSISTANT [redacted]

ANAESTHETIST [redacted]

PREMED Attempted LA Droperidol / Fentanyl Converted to GA

TRACHOMA R. ☐ L. ☐

NON-TRACHOMA R. ☐ L. ☐

Description of procedures:
1. (L) I/C cataract X[illegible] (GA)
2. Corneal section
3. Sector iridectomy
4. [illegible]
5. [illegible] 8.0 BSS

NATIONAL TRACHOMA AND EYE HEALTH PROGRAM
OPHTHALMOLOGY ACTION CARD

1	2	3	4	5	6	7	8	9	10	11	12	13	14
1	5	2	5	1	0	4	0	1	1	5			

NAME:

ADDRESS Yandeyarra

AGE 57 SEX 1

DATES:		Examiner
1st Exam.	6/6/77	1
2nd Exam.		
3rd Exam.		

R1 X R2

Right 07 V/A 05 CPM

Left 07 V/A 05 CPM

SURGERY	X
GLASSES	
TREATMENT	
OTHER	
NO ACTION	

Remarks:
1st Exam: R+L Pterygia 3724 corneal [illegible] due to trichiasis

2nd Exam: Surgery: R+L trichiasis surg.

3rd Exam:

Action cards and surgery cards: part of the simple, effective paperwork the NTEHP used.

I have to admit there were exceptions, places where we had a definite social impact. I hope, a beneficial one. Some of the spots that I travelled to that carried some kind of missionary-inspired notice stipulating that alcohol was not to be consumed, became places at which to hold a party. We refused to collaborate with the repressive, moralistic regimes that operated in some districts. We didn't do anything outrageous. We celebrated life, and I make no apology for that.

That leads into another of our social attitudes. Some time before we got started, I discussed with an Aborigine named Yami Lester the attributes the blacks would look for in a community adviser — an educated Aborigine from the outside who could help a community get what it needed from the white authorities.

The first thing Yami said was, 'He should have a woman, his own woman. And children, to show he's fair dinkum about the woman.'

Yami's statement stuck with me and I thought it was important that, as much as possible, the male doctors and bacteriologists and others in the teams, should be accompanied by a woman. The last thing we wanted was to be seen as competitors for the Aboriginal women — that had been the prime cause of trouble between the blacks and whites in the early days. I asked Gabi O'Sullivan, the senior orthoptist at the hospital, if she would go on the road with me. It was a sort of contract — to commit ourselves to be monogamous for the duration of the work. It was important. On all sides, loyalty and support were going to be crucial to getting the job done, and I wanted to have them solidly grounded in my personal and professional life. Gabi, a beautiful young woman to whom I was strongly attracted, agreed and that was the tentative and provisional beginning of our relationship.

I discovered what an unusual person Gabi was early on, when I worked with her in a blacks' camp in the Territory. I was examining eyes and grading for trachoma; Gabi was taking visual fields and I can tell you which is the harder job

— hers. You have to deal with linguistic and cultural differentials and be patient and pleasant if you hope to achieve anything. Gabi must have examined two hundred people that day, and she was as soothing and agreeable to the two hundredth as she had been to the first. I noticed something else: Gabi's tone of voice, manner and body language didn't change, whether she was dealing with the station manager or the oldest, most withered Aborigine in the camp. That kind of innate goodness is rare. Gabi and I were married in 1980 and we now have five children — Cam, Emma, Anna-Louise and the twins Rosie and Ruth. I also have a fifteen-year-old son, Ben, from Tracy Ellison who I lived with for a time after the break with Mary.

There is a very good record of the trachoma work, on film and in print.[8] Shaun McIlwraith, the medical correspondent for the *Sydney Morning Herald* travelled with us at various times, and his reports and feature articles helped to advertise the program and build the widespread public support we enjoyed. An extract from one of Shaun's reports will serve to give an idea of what went on when we visited a settlement and some of the local factors we had to take into account:

> A dozen hollow-bellied dogs sprang from nervous repose beside the Aboriginal wiltjas, and ran barking in the dust of the three strange vehicles as they drove into Amata, a dot in the centre of a continent.
>
> The sun was still high over the broad, flat valley, yellow with dry grass and flanked by the yellow-brown hills of the Musgrave Range which rises abruptly from the valley floor.
>
> Land stretches for hundreds of miles in every direction. The Pitjantatjara people who live there must at one time have regarded the apparently boundless expanse as the entire world.

---

[8] Published as *The National Trachoma and Eye Health Program*, (Royal Australian College of Ophthalmologists), Sydney, 1980

From within the wiltjas a few Aborigines looked curiously after the small convoy. Their crude shelters, made from scraps of canvas, iron, wood and other odds and ends, are known in the east as humpies.

Professor Hollows, leader of the field team of the National Trachoma and Eye Health Program, was on the job as soon as the heavily-laden four-wheel-drive vehicles pulled up outside the aluminium visitors' huts.

Seeking out Amata's three white nursing sisters, he asked to be shown the small local hospital which they ran with the help of Aboriginal health workers. We walked there through thick, red-brown dust.

Clearly, there was enough room in the first of its two buildings for the team to carry out its task of examining the eyes of the 300 or so people settled in the area.

'But how will the people feel about it?' Hollows asked Sister Chris McCall in his gravelly voice. Hollows turned to Reg Murray, the Aborigine in charge of the team's transport. 'What do you think, Reg baby?'

'Better put up the tent,' Reg answered laconically.

Beside the hospital was a broken-down tin shed used for picture shows. They looked at that on the way out. The walls inside are lurid with paintings and scribble. Hollows studied the local graffiti with interest.

Gabrielle O'Sullivan who tests visual acuities for the team, thought it might distract the people from her eye charts. But having established there was no hex on the building, Hollows decided that was where the clinic should be. It was a non-threatening place, and Gabi could hang a sheet to hide the wall motifs.

In the event the concrete floor of the shed was so uninviting in the chill of the next morning that, by unanimous consent, the team transferred to the hospital. Tribal unease about death scenes did not prevent more than 200 people flocking to the clinic in the next two days.

I can't resist throwing in some more statistics. Working under optimum conditions, an experienced examiner could screen up to 500 children for trachoma signs in a single day. Each child was also tested for visual acuity and ear problems. Clinics which covered substantial numbers of older people were slower affairs because many of the people needed to be tested for spectacles and there were questions of surgery and other forms of treatment to be discussed. Overall, an average team would see more than 100 people per day and in places where they really got up speed, such as in parts of Queensland where eye health was good, the statistics are very impressive — two teams saw more than 20,000 people in 80 locations in a two-month period. All up, we visited 465 Aboriginal settlements, performed a thousand operations, treated 27,000 people for trachoma and delivered 10,000 pairs of individually prescribed spectacles.

But the statistics can't convey the real essence of the work. I wish I had kept a proper diary but the pressure of work made that impossible. But there are records. The head of each team wrote a brief report on every location visited. Some of these were bland and uninteresting, but some are the stuff of fiction. Looking over them, I see that a team consisting of Gabi, Allan Mallard, myself and others were caught in a cyclone near Yackabindie station in Western Australia and suddenly found that the road we were driving down had turned into a lake. At the clinic we held there we saw some Pintibi tribespeople who had only recently come in from the desert.

The disparity between places was very striking and served to confirm the overall findings of the survey: 'Aboriginal groups suffering from high prevalence of ... diseases are outside any effective Australian health system', and, 'Most of the problems of ill-health encountered were due to to poor standards of hygiene, crowded living, substandard housing, ignorance concerning health matters and alcohol abuse.'

In my report on Wiluna, Western Australia, I wrote:

> The Community Health Sister was on long leave and the Sister at the hospital was a locum who was leaving in a couple of days . . .
>
> The attendance at the clinic was not encouraging and it was decided to visit the 'reserve', about a mile out of town. This was done early in the morning as it was found that people became inebriated before noon. . .
>
> An intensive treatment of the entire population is indicated . . . The aboriginal population at Wiluna suffer serious deprivation of the basic requirements of shelter. The majority live in tents and humpies. There is no running water.

By contrast, in Croydon, Queensland:

> We saw 32 children in the school and another 20 or so people in the hall. Croydon is a very small town of about 150 people with a history of gold mining. It is rather like an eastern goldfields ghost town which has mysteriously acquired the benefits of a hotel, garage and several other amenities. I met the Matron of the hospital, Sr White, and we worked in the shire hall.
>
> The Aboriginal people of Croydon all live in new houses on stilts and seem to be very well integrated. Most of the children read and appear to be interested in their schoolwork. There is no trachoma among the children of Croydon.

CHAPTER 15

The Trachoma Program 3

'Until they share the same basic conditions of hygiene, sound diet, insect-proof houses, sanitation and clean water which whites take so much for granted, Aborigines in rural parts of the country will continued to be afflicted with avoidable diseases . . .'

Statement made at the time of the release of the NTEHP Report, Sydney Morning Herald *2 April 1980*

The trachoma program brought out the best and the worst in people — great events do that. We weren't saints and there were disagreements along the way. In every case though, they were resolved without damage to the work. Early on, for example, some of the workers felt that travelling time should be counted as work time. I was against that, knowing that the hours on the road were going to be long but would have to be discounted if we were going to cover the ground and stay within our budgets. In the end, situations developed like the one in Bourke. We'd come down there after a long stint in the Territory and Queensland, working without a break for six weeks. There was a bit of a celebration going on in Bourke — foot races and cycle events and plentiful piss-ups. I thought it'd be a good chance to have a few days off.

After the first half-day break Reg and Rose Murray, who had originally backed this 'travel is work' proposal but had since done tireless, first-class liaison stuff and a hundred other things, came to me and Reg said, 'Look, Fred, we've had a bit of time off and we're getting sick of sitting around. There's eight hundred people to see in Dubbo and we're not too sure about the liaison. Why don't Rose and I head off to Dubbo now and make sure everything's all right?'

It wasn't all self-sacrifice. One night, at Ernabella, at a mission in the Pitjantatjara country, we were invited to dinner. The woman who invited us — the wife of the mission accountant — was plump with very delicate hands and feet and precise, petite movements. Life has taught me not to refuse a dinner invitation from a plump woman, because it's odds on the food's going to be good. We'd been living out of cans and cooking over the fire, and when she said there'd be wine and a couple of courses, I was keen to go. We got dressed up, big change from the shorts and grotty shirts we spent most of the time in. I had a white suit and I put on a polo-neck and hung my George III shilling around my neck — those were the days when you wore things like that — and we went off to have a six-course dinner with wine on a beautiful, crisp evening in Central Australia. It was a great night.

I don't want to gloss over the difficulties. I wasn't popular with everybody all the time, I'm sure of that. For one thing, I insisted that a complete record of everything we'd done at a stop be typed up in triplicate — names and ages, who had trachoma, who needed glasses, who needed surgery, who had perforated ear drums and so on — and a copy left with the Aborigines along with an explanation. Those reports often contained comments on the state of hygiene, the delivery of medical services and so on. They were critical and evaluative and they pointed to action. The blackfellows were fed up with whites screaming into their camps, rousting out everyone to be examined and pissing off saying, 'Yeah, we'll let you know our results.'

I didn't want a bar of that. Often it was a hard grind for the secretary to type out the report on a machine clogged up with sand and with sweat running into her eyes. There were tears and protests. But I insisted on it and I think I was right.

All this makes it sound as if I had no doubts, fears or

hesitations and as if no mistakes were made. That's a false impression. I had plenty of misgivings and I'm sure we made mistakes. But I had great faith in the people I was working with and I was constantly seeing evidence that we were going about things the right way. The Aborigines, I believe, could see value for themselves in a visit from a team. They knew that they weren't just the objects of another scientific survey for the benefit of a few white sinecurists and careerists. Those with crook eyes didn't want them to get any worse and looked to us for help. And word spread. Aborigines at one place heard of improvements in health that had followed our visits to another and welcomed us.

The hands-on, grass roots problems were nothing compared with the villainy and betrayal that went on at higher levels. The trouble blew up in Queensland, as most Australian political difficulties did in those days. Our two senior liaison officers for north Queensland were Clarrie Grogan and Mick Miller, both members of the North Queensland Land Council. Charles Perkins had recommended them and Penny Cook, our field secretary, had worked for Jim Keefe who had been an ALP Senator for that region. She had the contacts and arranged for us to attend a meeting of the NQLC to see if it could help us with liaison — it had delegates from twenty-three communities.

So there was an ALP connection of a sort between us and Miller and Grogan, but that was as far as it went. Nevertheless, Grogan and Miller were seen as ALP activists and when Joh Bjelke-Petersen heard that they were moving around the black communities on behalf of a federal program he went spare. Politically, the area was a series of rotten boroughs which the National Party machine delivered to Joh. The Aborigines who were on the roll had their votes bought by pathetic hand-outs, and there was certainly no effort made to get more blacks on the roll. Clarrie and Mick may have been encouraging enrolment, I'm not sure, but Bjelke-Petersen was calling an election and he didn't want to take any chances.

Pressure was applied on me to sack Grogan and Miller. I got a message to that effect from Jim Fair, the national Secretary of the College of Ophthalmologists. I ignored it. Then, when we were working at Weipa, seeing hundreds of people every day, more messages started to come through. Eventually at Weipa airport, just as I was about to fly out to Thursday Island, I got a phone call from Jim Fair.

'Fred,' he said, 'you're going to have to sack Grogan and Miller.'

'Whose orders are those?' I said.

'I can't tell you.'

'When you send me a letter over someone's signature saying that I have to sack them and why, I'll consider it. Until then, they're working for me.'

Then I flew off to the Torres Strait. Organised by Dr Peter Holt of the Thursday Island hospital, the Torres Strait expedition was one of the most exciting and rewarding experiences in the whole program. Peter arranged for the transport — fixed-wing planes, helicopters, catamarans, outboards — and the facilities, and we saw almost everybody in the group. We ran into some heavy seas, landed in the mangroves at dead of night, were winched into the hold of ship along with all our gear — stirring stuff.

With only one more day's work to do in the islands I was standing on the jetty at Thursday Island when I saw the last person in the world I expected to see — a senior office-holder in the College (who had better remain nameless).

'Fred, I've come to take those two fellows out of the field.'

The humour of it struck me immediately. This person was diminutive in stature and he was obviously totally uncomfortable, inappropriately dressed, suffering in the heat.

I said, 'Oh yeah,' and I called Clarrie and Mick over. Clarrie Grogan had been the national light-heavyweight boxing champion. He had the reputation of having broken more police jaws than any other Aborigine in Australia and at that time he must've weighed seventeen stone. Mick Miller was a big, fit man who'd played rugby league for north Queensland. I told them that this was the bloke who was going to put them out of action. They were polite. Either one of them could've picked him up with one hand and tossed him off the pier.

He said, 'Fred, I think we're going to have to talk about this.'

'You talk about it,' I said, 'I've got work to do.' I went off to do a clinic at the high school. In the Torres Strait there was a lot of follicular trachoma among the teenagers but very little scarring in the adults. There were about four hundred of these kids, brought in from all the islands, and it was important to see them in order to understand the different courses the disease could take. I was working away and my supposed colleague came up and we struck a deal. I agreed to take Grogan and Miller out of the field for a couple of weeks (they needed a rest anyway) until the state election was over. In return I was assured that no more political pressure would be brought to bear. Seemed fair enough, and we shook on it as a gentleman's agreement.

But he ratted on me. Malcolm Fraser called a Federal election and the Queensland Nationals got very edgy about our presence in the north of the state, with or without Miller and Grogan. The College of Ophthalmologists was a very conservative body, responsive to that sort of pressure. A few weeks later I was in Brisbane with Charles Perkins addressing a meeting of the Federation for the Blind, the major organisation for blind people in Australia. Three members of the College were in the audience and they came up to me after the meeting with a formal document, signed by Dr Nameless, saying that, as of now, the trachoma program was not going to operate any further in Queensland.

I was speechless with anger. I went back to the hotel where

I was staying with Gabi and I was in very low spirits. Charles Perkins was there too and he said the only thing to do was get some publicity. He grabbed the phone in my room and rang the ABC saying that his name was Hollows and that he was running this program and political interference had stopped it. He raved on for a bit and hung up.

'What now?' I said.

'They're going to ring us back. D'you reckon I sounded like a professor, Fred?'

We got the answer to that a few minutes later when the ABC rang back to make sure it hadn't been a hoax call.

'You're not much of a fucking professor, Charlie,' I told him, 'but you've done the trick.' I confirmed what Charlie had said and the next thing I know I'm in a car heading for the ABC television studio. Paul Murphy interviewed me. I showed him the letter and told him about the trachoma program and rattled on in a fairly heated way. When we finished up, Paul Murphy thanked me and said, 'That'll be headline news tomorrow.'

I doubted it. I went back to the hotel, grumbled about the food Gabi had ordered and went to bed. At five o'clock in the bloody morning the press started hammering on the door and, sure enough, the story was in all the papers. The publicity got us some protection but a lot of damage was done. We were subjected to delays in places where nervous officials wanted to check with the higher-ups that it was OK to deal with us. I got sick of it and we diverted down into New South Wales for a while until the federal election was over and the heat died down. Ralph Hunt, the Federal Minister for Health, was very co-operative then and later. In the end, partly as a result of the publicity, we got a better coverage in Queensland than anywhere else, but we could have done without all the flak.

That was in 1977. The other major political hassle came four years later when the government in Canberra proposed to move most of the federal responsibilities for health back to the states. Included in that, of course, was the whole area of Aboriginal health and the on-going work of the trachoma program. It was very depressing. Such improvements in Aboriginal health care as there had been only came about because the federal government could claim a mandate in that area. Left to the states, nothing would have happened, and here we were, looking backwards.

Peter Baume was the Minister for Aboriginal Affairs at the time which made matters worse. He was a doctor, a gastroenterology specialist, and my contacts with him had been amiable and productive. I could not believe that he could be a party to this, but my eyes were opened when I attended a meeting at the Redfern Aboriginal Service at the invitation of Gary Foley and a few other Aborigines. I wasn't that keen to go because it was my view that the Aborigines were running their medical services and it was their business. This was a meeting between representatives of the services in New South Wales, South Australia and Victoria, and the Minister.

Foley said, 'We want you there so you can see how he treats us.'

I went to the meeting and sat there for two hours. Every time an Aborigine made a point, Peter Baume would stand up and contradict him or her, completely disregarding the facts and the circumstances. A woman from the Davenport Reserve stood up and told a story about their attempts to establish a medical service. They'd run it on a shoestring with a visiting doctor and the police had come and confiscated all their records and notes, kept them for three months and returned only photocopies, not the originals. Now I knew that Aborigines are very sensitive on those questions of privacy and confidentiality, as are doctors, so I thought, *Here's a chance for Peter to show sympathy with these people.*

He stood up and lectured them on the duties of the police.

I was incensed; here was a privileged, middle-class professional who had never had a copper's hand on him, telling black people about the police who had been their natural enemies for generations. Bruce McGuinness, an Aborigine, was in the chair and he asked me if I had anything to say. It was another of those occasions when I was almost incoherent with anger. I couldn't trust myself to speak — the result would have been too violent and obscene. I had some papers in my hand, notes I'd been taking. I walked up to the table where Baume was sitting and threw them down in front of him.

'I will never work with this man again,' I said, and I left the room.

There were some reporters outside. I was about to march past them when Foley came out and said, 'Talk to them, Fred.'

A woman approached me with a microphone and asked me for a comment.

I said, 'Peter Baume is a dissembler.'

I don't know how the word popped into my head but it did, a sheer fluke, a trick of consciousness, and it was exactly the right expression. A dissembler can never be trusted and has no honour. My father was staying with me at the time, and I could hardly wait to get home and sit out on the porch with someone I knew to be a decent human being. I've had no further dealings with Peter Baume.

The upshot was that Gordon Briscoe and I resigned from our posts as Assistant Director and Director of the trachoma program. The move was actually a culmination of a number of things — difficulties running the program in the face of political opposition in Western Australia, financial cutbacks and so on. The resignations were big news, coast to coast. I made statements like the one that appeared in the *Sydney Morning Herald* on 23 May 1981:

> We will no longer co-operate with a Government that is deliberately placing Aboriginal health at the feet of State

> Governments, the very people who nearly succeeded in the genocide of Aborigines . . .

Or:

> As a white doctor and a man with a conscience, I cannot understand how men in authority can stand by and watch the appalling state of Aboriginal health problems which would cause a huge outcry if they occurred in the white community.

You don't have to be Einstein to see who the target of that second commment was.

Malcolm Fraser let it be known that he'd like to see us. Briscoe came up from Canberra and we had a confab and nutted out seven points, to do with on-going health care, funding and so on, that we'd need reassurance on if we were to reconsider. We went over to Kirribilli House and had a meeting with Fraser. It took place in a big room with only Fraser, Briscoe and me, Peter Baume and Fraser's secretary present. Gordon and I told him where we stood, went through the points and he agreed with us all down the line.

Specifically, he agreed that the allottment of $50 million over the next ten years for 'environmental health' was bull-shit. The money was being used to build airstrips for mining companies, to seal roads, and the phrase meant nothing. We wanted that changed to 'Aboriginal Public Health'. Fraser agreed and told Baume he wanted these things done. Baume said nothing but, 'Yes, sir, no, sir.' Briscoe and I rescinded our resignations and the work went on.

The trachoma work had its moments of high comedy, like the time in the Queensland town of Capella. I hadn't been expecting to see that many people there but, as a result of all the publicity, the church hall was chock-a-block. It was a tiny little place and you had to wonder where they all came from, but there they were. And standing in the front of the queue was a woman holding a poodle. I approached her and the dog snapped at me.

'Professor Hollows,' she says, 'this dog has got cataracts and I want you to have a look at it.'

Speaking sternly, I said, 'Madam, I will examine your dog when I've finished seeing all these people, on the condition that you make sure it doesn't bite me.'

I worked all day and, sure enough, there she was at the end of the line with her dog. She'd tied a handkerchief around its snout. You had to give her credit for stubborness. So I took a look and I told her that she needed a vet and a very good one, because taking cataracts out of dogs' eyes is a tricky business, especially with poodles.

There were very important scientific gains made as well. Hugh Taylor did some important work in South Australia when he personally examined a hundred and sixty-seven of the relatives of a young Aboriginal boy who had presented to us with signs of Hurler's syndrome, an inherited metabolic misfunction that results in physical and mental disabilities. He was able to describe a form of the disorder never before found in humans. At Jiggalong mission on the edge of the western desert, Taylor tested a twenty-six-year-old Aboriginal woman who was found to have the sharpest human vision ever recorded. I encouraged Hugh to write an MD thesis on Aboriginal sight which was a fascinating topic raising some controversial issues. Hugh Taylor is now the most published ophthalmologist in Australia and holds a chair in Melbourne. The external examiner for his thesis was my old mentor, Archie Cochrane, who told me that Taylor's was the best MD thesis he had ever examined.

It is inescapable that superior Aboriginal vision indicates a level of racial supremacy. Aborigines exhibit short-sightedness only to the degree that they have non-Aboriginal ancestors. Their genes are better than ours — had to be to ensure group survival. And vision is, to a great degree, a matter of brain power. All things being equal, a person can read down an eye chart to about the same level with each eye, but can usually do better when both eyes are brought into play. This is called the binocular increment and it's a matter of brain function — the fusing of images and transmission of the data by the brain. Full-blood Aborigines exhibit a superior binocular increment, *ergo*, superior cerebration.

CHAPTER 16

High Profile and Friendship

My god, this is not the time to be accepting accolades for work in Aboriginal health.

Fred Hollows

Caroline Jones, the ABC radio presenter, asked me recently if there had been any moment in my life when I'd been brought up short, induced to take stock of what I was doing and consider my priorities. A scene popped into my head: I was hobbling around the streets of Chihuahua, in Mexico, in 1973. I'd torn a muscle in my leg. It was painful when I was sitting still or lying down, so I'd taken to hobbling around the streets, just to keep the muscle from stiffening up and getting sore. I don't know what it was — the slightly comic gait I had to adopt, the wholly exotic location in Mexico with all the remnants of Mayan civilisation in decay around me, or the occasional shafts of pain, but I had a sudden insight into the nature of things as far as Fred Hollows was concerned.

It was in the Plaza de Armas, at night. A sort of two-pronged enlightenment came to me: first, I suddenly realised or apprehended or appreciated, that it didn't matter if I published no more scientific papers in the journals that serviced the academic side of my specialisation. I'd made a respectable contribution to ophthalmology and there was no crying need to add to it. I felt I didn't need to feel threatened from that direction. Secondly, I perceived with great clarity that it was against my nature, and ultimately negative, for me to participate closely in academic and administrative politics. Put plainly, I decided not to attend meetings that I judged likely to be unproductive. I'm afraid that covered a great many of the deliberations of the Faculty of Medicine and its various committees.

The upshot of this was that I became notorious as a bad committee man, one apt to be absent or, at best, uninterested, when the rarified academic and administrative debates were going on. There were probably losses involved, opportunities missed, but I would contend that this decision freed me up to use my time more productively — to get involved in things that mattered and produced results! I have to admit that there was an element of self-indulgence in all this; from that time in 1973 on, it was very seldom anybody found Fred Hollows doing things he didn't want to do.

Since then I've done the work that I've wanted to do and the sorts of tasks that would make me feel good about doing them. I've tended not to do things simply because they might enhance my academic standing. I resolved not to go to meetings just so people would know who I am — which is a large part of what a lot of administrative meetings are all about. Associated with that, people say, 'But I wrote you a letter.' I have to tell them that I don't even *read* all my mail, let alone answer it. I believe that if someone really needs to get in touch, he or she will come and find me. I believe that this attitude has allowed me to be more useful. I know it has allowed me to get a lot more fun out of things.

It's ironical that, in the years after I put this policy into operation, I became a much more well-known figure than I had been before. I've never sought a high profile, except insofar as it has been of benefit to the work I've been doing. Notoriety is a curious thing; it appears to have a life of its own and to be self-sustaining. For example, some years after the first phase of the trachoma program had been implemented, I was offered an honorary (because I was still a New Zealand citizen then) Order of Australia, in recognition of the importance of that work. It so happened that I'd recently re-visited some of the settlements where Aboriginal health had been in a pitiable state. We'd identified these as communities requiring special effort and resources and put a lot of work into helping them establish their own medical services. I was distressed to find, on going back, that conditions were still very bad. Eye health had improved, but general health was still appalling. Statistics showed high prevalence rates of hepatitis B, syphillis, gonorrhoea and we observed tragic cases resulting from a poor social environment. From one small community, with fewer than five hundred people, there were twenty-nine children in the base hospital suffering brain damage as a result of petrol sniffing.

I was preparing a report on this for Clyde Holding, the Federal Minister for Aboriginal Affairs, and that document was lying on my desk side by side with a note from the Governor-General's secretary inviting me to front up to Government House and get this gong. This made me think: *My god, this is not the time to be accepting accolades for work in Aboriginal health.* I wrote to the secretary along these lines and the Governor-General, Sir Ninian Stephen, got in touch with the Health Minister and we got together and set up another program — which is still running — to work against communicable diseases among Aborigines. That program hadn't progressed beyond the planning stages when I was again asked to accept the award. I said, 'Setting up a committee hasn't changed the situation one bit.'

Word of that got around and I hope it helped the people in control to take more seriously the work we were trying to do. You can never be sure; the layers of cynicism over the imaginations and sensibilities of politicians and bureaucrats are very thick. It's only fair to say that this insensitivity didn't extend to the Governor-General. I later met him at a function to do with blindness, and he struck me as a very well-informed and sympathetic man.

An issue like Aboriginal health doesn't go away. Once I had become identified with it, and, somewhat inaccurately, tagged by journalists as 'Australia's leading expert' in the field, I was frequently asked to comment and became embroiled in controversy. Some of the things I had to say were very unpalatable to white society. In general, public health has improved through this century and it is one of the things that is always put up to people who lament the passing of the 'good old days'. No one regrets the absence of diphtheria, whooping cough and poliomyelitis. But for many black Australians the story is very different. I had a bit to say about this. A review of Aboriginal health showed that, whereas in 1890 life expectancy for white and Aboriginal males in New South Wales was about the same, by 1985 a big gap had opened up — the average life expectancy for a male Aborigine was only forty-eight or forty-nine years, about twenty years shorter than for whites. There were equivalent gaps between blacks and whites for females. Deaths from circulatory diseases in the twenty-five to forty-four years segment ran twenty times higher for blacks than whites. Statistics on lower infant mortality were being used to give an impression of improvement in Aboriginal health. The short life expectancy of *adults*, and the prevalence of infectious illness, gave the lie to that.

Also unpopular were some comments I made, about the time I refused the Order of Australia, on the role of women in preserving the Aboriginal race. Alcoholism was neutralising a great many Aboriginal men, but the women refused to stop bearing children. A great deal of pressure was put on them to do so. Mrs Avey Curly, the mother of thirteen, was a case in point. This capable and energetic woman had been offered every known birth control method and had resisted them all. It was a fact that a great many of the strong, confident black women I met all over Australia, who had made massive contributions to Aboriginal survival and dignity, had ten or more children. Uncomfortable stuff for modern-day birth-control pundits who, in my opinion, were unconscious racists.

But I came in for head-on criticism from blacks as well as whites, and was attacked on the flanks by anthropologists. At that time I also made known my views on the role of traditional Aboriginal culture. Addressing the national convention of the Royal Australian College of General Practitioners, I said:

> We await the movement within the Aboriginal organisation that is going to modify Aboriginal culture so that they can survive, so that they can avoid illness. Right now, Aboriginal culture does not enhance group survival.

My ideas on this very important question owe a lot to Gordon Briscoe, but I take full responsibility for them in the form that I have put them forward for public and professional debate. The basic proposition is that anthropologists have not usefully analysed traditional Aboriginal society. Rather, they have textualised and contextualised it.

The greatest danger lies in romanticising the Aboriginal past. Over the whole continent a system prevailed in which the labour of the women and children was disposed of by the old men to serve their interests. The men controlled the knowledge essential for group survival — knowledge of weather, water, animal and vegetable food resources, as well as the social mechanisms of ritual initiation, marriage and breeding rights. As I understand it, the Aboriginal 'skin system' is a means whereby through matrilineal links, groups are assured of access to land and its resources over a wide area. Marrying outside the group, according to rules administered by the male gerontocrats, extended the resource base. Thus the females, as well as providing the bulk of the day to day food, were an essential, but unenfranchised, feature of Aboriginal economics. This system was wrecked by the intrusion of white males. Suddenly, Aboriginal females had bargaining power and in some cases their white partners accorded them something very close to equal status.

The role models for most of the part-Aboriginal male descendants of these unions are their white grandfathers. Nor do the females seek to return to the traditional patterns. The only people who want to return to the pre-1788 structures are those who wish to reinstate the male gerontocrats, that is, the male gerontocrats themselves and some anthropologists. Traditionalism is much spoken about by many 'activists' and supporters of Aboriginal movements, but Aboriginal women, and where they can, children, especially teenagers, have strongly resisted such moves. The notion that the only 'real' Aborigines are full-bloods wearing ochre, beating clap sticks and sitting out in the red dirt and mulga, is a very negative one. From personal experience I can testify that Aboriginal communities that have been left or driven into these traditionalist cul-de-sacs are in very bad shape — almost every health indicator is bad in these communities.

I put these ideas forward at a scientific conference — and ended up by being a bit provocative. I said:

> Some of you may be of the Roman Catholic persuasion. The origins of Catholic Australia were in the most oppressed group of whites ever to exist on this continent, but today Catholics are represented at the highest levels of society in proportions unimaginable 200 years ago.
>
> It is my hope that such a group escalation can occur for Aboriginal Australia. It is our task to help get it started.

Of course, I *knew* a lot of the people in the audience were Catholics, and I derived some amusement from watching their reaction. Many politicians and anthropologists, it seems to me, deal in and accentuate the differences between people. I think it's more helpful, and it certainly behoves a doctor, to emphasise our common humanity — even if some people don't like to be reminded of their kinship with others.

In 1991, some years after delivering that address, I am still waiting for signs of this wholesale improvement in the lot of Australian Aborigines. I recently made a statement which was highlighted in the press, to the effect that Aborigines should be stockbrokers and be driving BMWs. Stockbrokers as well as stockmen. I still believe that.

Involvement in controversy is very distracting and time-consuming and there have been occasions when I should have spoken out for and against things and haven't, begrudging the time. The question of the effects on Aborigines of the British atomic tests of the 1950s in South Australia, however, wasn't one to duck. This surfaced in the early 1980s when stories began to circulate about the 'black mist' which the Yankunyatjara group claimed had enveloped certain people after a test in 1953. Among the effects blindness was mentioned and that inevitably brought me into the debate. I met a man named Yami Lester who was totally blind. He'd apparently been blinded by trachoma at a fairly young age, his corneas ulcerated and scarred.

That was unusual. In the whole scope of our work we saw very few young people actually blinded by trachoma. It is not the way the disease typically struck and progressed. In fact he'd undergone enucleation — that is, removal — of one eye: there's a different story attached to that. But, with reference to radiation, Yumi was a member of a community that had been exposed to a plume, or cloud, of radiation fall-out from one of the British tests. No doubt about that. The question was: did the exposure to radiation contribute to his blindness? It comes down to possibilities and probabilties. There's a formula: the likelihood of unusual things being unrelated is the product of their probabilities. Now here, we had a rare event — an Aboriginal kid blinded by trachoma and the same kid exposed, at a particularly vulnerable age in respect of his immuniological system, to radiation. How many such subjects were there? Babies and adults aplenty, scandalously. But how many young people, infected with trachoma, moving into the age zone when the immune system will contain or repel the disease, but not quite there? Very few. Of course, the authorities argued that the two things were unrelated. The South Australian authorities claimed that Yami Lester's blindness was caused by measles — but that was their explanation for almost all Aboriginal eye disease. They were the people who told me to expect a 1 per cent trachoma incidence among Aboriginal kids whereas I found 80 per cent.

Yami Lester worked as a stockman on properties south of Alice Springs through the 1960s. He had been at Wallatinna station, north of Emu Field at the time of the Totem One test there. On 15 October 1953 a ten kiloton device was detonated in a tower. Yami Lester testified that he had seen a cloud:

> It was coming from the south — black, like smoke. I was thinking that it might have been a dust storm, but it was quiet, just moving through the trees and above the trees. It was just rolling and moving quietly.[9]

This man had almost no vision in one eye but sufficient in the other to control a horse and follow stock. He was sent to Adelaide for examination when his vision drastically deteriorated, and the procedure that was followed — enucleation — was the most common form of eye surgery experienced by blacks in Australia at that time. This helps to explain some of the reluctance we experienced in the trachoma program among blacks who were advised to have surgery. Eye surgery for an Aborigine in the centre of Australia meant having your eye out. They feared the loss of their eyes! Yumi Lester

[9] See Robert Milliken, *No Conceivable Injury: the story of Britain and Australia's atomic cover-up*, Penguin, 1986.

contended that the eye he lost in Adelaide was his 'good' eye. However that might be, this drastic procedure, often without reference to ophthalmolgical opinion — an unthinkable medical situation as far as the white population was concerned — was still being routinely carried out in the mid-1970s. I and others made a strong protest against it, and the practice has been stopped.

The debate, and the legal proceedings which were begun on Yami's behalf, were inconclusive. But I listened to his story, heard the anecdotal evidence of the course of his eye disorders, and I have no reason to doubt that the formula holds. Were the two highly unusual events — early-age blindness through corneal damage and exposure to radiation — unrelated? I don't think so.

I wasn't only involved in life and death issues. Some things just plain get up your nose and I couldn't keep out of it when plans to demolish the Randwick Ritz theatre were announced. The theatre was coming up for auction along with two adjoining shops, and the agent emphasised the potential of the site and mentioned the possibility of opening a medical centre there. The matter had come up before and a Ms Diane McGee had bought the site precisely for the purpose of saving it from destruction. Business reversals and changes in the marketing of films had forced her, reluctantly, to sell. A 'Save the Ritz' committee was got up and I was happy to throw in my two cents' worth. Among other things, I said that 'Randwick has enough medical centres' and 'a suburb is not a suburb without a picture house'.

When I went to the pictures, I went to the Ritz. You could buy popcorn there and ice cream for the kids. Sit in beautiful plush seats and always be sure of a seat. It reminded me of the theatres I went to as a kid in New Zealand and I didn't want to see it ploughed under. That was a victory. The Ritz is still there. Gabi and I took our son Cam there to see *Silverado* — great picture, and the first movie he ever sat through from go to whoa.

My financial circumstances improved through the 1980s, from lamentable to adequate. 'Farnham House' provided the sort of living quarters I'd been hoping for, but it was only by a stroke of luck that I was able to keep the house. Some time after I'd taken possession I was out in the backblocks, working on the trachoma program. The team crossed from Queensland into north-western New South Wales — the strategic withdrawal at the time of the trouble with Joh Bjelke-Petersen and his crew — and we lobbed into a little place called Hebel. A real speck on the map, it consisted of a pub, a store where you bought petrol and supplies and one house. When we arrived in three heavily-laden vehicles we outnumbered the townsfolk.

We were heading for an Aboriginal settlement named Weilmoringle but nobody knew that we'd be passing through Hebel. We'd only decided on it a day or so before ourselves. It was a hot day and we went into the pub for a drink. The barman pulled me a beer and said, 'Are you Professor Hollows?'

I admitted it and he said there was a phone call for me.

I said, 'Where's the phone?'

He pointed through the window and I saw the phone box outside with the road sort of bending around it. I carried my beer out to the phone box. The receiver was off the hook so I picked it up.

'This is Fred Hollows. Who's that?'

It was my bank manager in Randwick. He told me that my finances were in a hopeless shambles — that I was overdrawn in several accounts and going down the gurgler.

I was astonished and all I could think to do was state some

facts. I said, 'Look, I'm out on the road running this program and I'm likely to be at it for a year or more. That's my job. Your bank holds my mortgage. Your job is to run the bank's finances. I'm doing my job, why don't you do yours?' And I hung up. I had a bit of protection because the chairman of that bank happened to be a patient of mine, so I knew they wouldn't just chop me off without thinking. Still, it was worrying. But within a month of that phone call the property boom hit Sydney and my equity in the house shot up so that the bank's mortgages were secured and it got off my back. But I never did find out how that bloke knew I was in Hebel.

The first person to share the Randwick house with Gabi and me was Michael Johnson, someone I met through a mutual friend. Like me, Michael enjoyed running in Centennial Park, and in our first conversation I suggested that the course he ran, around the lower part of the park, was a touch wimpish and that he should tackle a 10-kilometre route that included some hills. The first time we ran together I left him on the first hill and came in about five minutes ahead of him. The next time I didn't get away from him until we were close to the top of the first hill; he ran with me all the way the time after that and then he beat me by a couple of minutes. Subsequently he had to handicap himself a few minutes if we were going to finish together.

Michael became a very firm friend and he moved into the house along with his then girlfriend. He was an oil company executive, but devoted most of his energy and a lot of his time to outdoor pursuits like bushwalking, white-water rafting, rock climbing and so on. I called them all the 'butterfly people', meaning that they put more into their recreation than their work. They were mainly Brits, like Michael. Good party people and we got into some strange activities like Scottish country dancing for which we had the space at Randwick. We ran and cycled together and he came mountain-climbing in New Zealand with me a few times. He was somewhat eccentric as a mountaineer, often declining to make it to the absolute summit.

Michael hadn't enjoyed school and, from a few things he told me, I gathered schools hadn't enjoyed him, but he underwent a change of heart and enrolled as a mature-age student at the University of New South Wales. He was a phenomenon, doing a double honours degree in sociology and economics. One year he tackled eleven units and finished with eight high distinctions and three distinctions. There was nothing butterfly-like about the way he worked at his degree and he finished as the second highest mark-getter in the Arts faculty in the year he graduated. He became Farnham House's resident intellectual. He's now a much-published economist and head of the Department of Public Sector Economics in the University of New South Wales. His other distinguished appointment is as godfather to my son, Cam.

Max Williams became the resident poet at Farnham House. Max was a country boy, born in Guildford, New South Wales, who got into trouble early and spent twenty-eight years in the gaols of this state. Pat Fiske, a mutual friend, met Max at a poetry reading, saw him afterwards at a party and brought him along to a party at my place. Pat took the photograph of a row of back-lane brick shithouses in Newtown which appeared on the cover of one of Max's books of verse, *Poor Man's Bean*. We hit it off straightaway and I invited him to move in.

He said, 'I live with a woman and her child.'

'Doesn't matter,' I said. 'You can all move in.' That was my policy in those days and Max, apparently, was 'stunned'. He moved in and stayed for some years. Max was a great story teller and I was fascinated and enlightened by his stories about the criminal milieu — the corruption at all levels and the brutality of the prisons. He was in Grafton 'tracs' — the section for intractable prisoners — for many years, some of them in solitary confinement. By law, no prisoner was supposed to be placed in solitary confinement for more than six weeks at a stretch, but this regulation was flagrantly ignored at Grafton. The treatment was frankly sadistic and Max was savagely beaten on many occasions and carried some serious internal injuries as a result.

Darcy Dugan, long-term prisoner and escape artist, actually witnessed one of Max's beatings. In evidence given to the Nagle Royal Commission into New South Wales prisons, he said:

> I inadvertently entered what I thought was my cell but discovered it was that of Maxwell Williams. Williams was back up against the rear wall, he was covered with blood. His right eye was an open raw mark, the skin was flapping down, pouring blood. Three warders were attacking him, one in front and one on either side. Williams was trying unsuccessfully to protect himself.[10]

Once, when we were doing some carpentry in my workshop downstairs, I asked him how close he had come to being broken in spirit, because that was what the brutal treatment was designed to do. He said that they might have got him to knuckle under but for Kipling's poem 'If-':

> If you can keep your head when all about you
> Are losing theirs and blaming it on you,
> If you can trust yourself when all men doubt you,
> But make allowance for their doubting too;
> If you can wait and not be tired by waiting,
> Or being lied about, don't deal in lies,
> Or being hated, don't give way to hating,
> And yet don't look too good, nor talk too wise:

[10] Quoted in Jan Simmonds, *For Simmo*, (Cassell), Sydney, 1980.

It can sound corny until you think of it from the prisoner's point of view. Those words and ideas sustained him somehow and Max didn't become emotionally dependent on, addicted to, the criminal and gaol life, the way so many people do. He must always have had some objectivity about it because he explained to me that he had given up thieving (which he had gone in for on a rather grand scale), because it ultimately didn't pay:

'Fred, by the time you pay off the security men at the places you're going to rob, and the police and your solicitor and every other bugger's solicitor when things go wrong, it's hard to even make wages.'

There was more to it than that, of course. We see quite a few Long Bay prisoners at the Prince of Wales and I've asked some of the long-termers about Max. They all describe him as 'willing', meaning independent and never ready to play the informer. He led an escape from Goulburn goal once and it was that experience that enabled him to write the great lines:

> The hound bays from the depths of his ancestry
> Frightening those who expect to be hunted

I think the compression of information and emotion in that is terrific. Max is one of those people — there have been many of them down the ages — saved from wasting their lives by the magical power of language. Those were relatively enlightened times, once the excesses of Grafton and Goulburn had been exposed, and Max started to write in prison, attend writing and reading groups. When he got out there were literary friends to encourage him and various support mechanisms. He got several writing grants and was able to find a point and purpose to life, apart from avoiding or confronting people like a certain strongman who was out to get him.

The other factor, ironically, that helped with his 'rehabilitation' was the widespread use of drugs in prison. Apparently, that changed everything. Drugs governed who did what to whom and why, affected the politics of the prisons, and Max didn't want any part of it. Drugs obliterated the old political system in the prisons and made life much more dangerous. Max was smart enought to see that there was absolutely no future in that kind of life.

Max has published pretty widely and he is an adornment to any occasion. He's a man of parts — a woodworker, a musicologist, a chess player. Chess is another of my enthusiasms which has given me great enjoyment over the years and cemented friendships. I enjoy the cut and thrust of chess, although with friends like Gordon Briscoe, Max Williams, John Stonham and others I always play a gentleman's version, wherein you are allowed to take your hand off the pieces. I've played it in mountain huts and desert tents as well as at home and a good game of chess and a few glasses of decent whisky constitute real pleasure.

Max Williams is also a naturalist. We were walking through a dreary paddock once and he pointed out to me an ordinary-looking bird hopping along ahead of us which he said migrated from Siberia every year. I was sceptical, checked, and found out he was right. Added to that, he's got balls. When we used to rig up flying foxes on climbs and bushwalks, 15 metres above the rocks and water, Williams would volunteer to test it. It's a pleasure and a privilege to know him and I've tried to learn things from Max and others like him — mainly, how not to be afraid. I haven't always succeeded, but their example has certainly helped.

CHAPTER 17

Peaks and Poetry

Rangi, the Sky Father, had union with Pohato-te-po before being joined with Papa, the Earth Mother. Pohato-te-po's eldest, Aorangi, with his younger brothers, left Hawaiiki by canoe, angry at Rangi's second marriage. Near the South Island their canoe struck a reef. Aorangi and his brothers climbed to the high side of the wrecked canoe so as not to drown. But rescue was long in coming: they turned to stone and became the Southern Alps.

From the Maori account of the creation.
Aorangi, cloud-piercer, is Mount Cook.

For nearly twenty years after I took up the appointment in Sydney, I tried to spend part of the annual vacation in New Zealand. Apart from wanting to get out of Sydney, which is not usually a pleasant place in January, my objects were to see my family and to climb mountains. I made many climbs in those years, some of them unsuccessful, some routine and some quite creditable ascents of difficult peaks by unusual routes.

One of my frequent companions was Tom Barcham, an excellent mountaineer who kept journals of some of the climbs. A perusal of some of these reveals that Tom was generous in his assessment of my capabilities. I have never claimed to be a great mountaineer, but most people who have climbed with me would agree that at least when you climbed with Hollows you climbed rapidly.

I had a lot of adventures in the mountains and some close shaves. The most unpleasant experience came when I was at the Hermitage, a hotel which provided a base for excursions and climbs on Mount Cook. I joined a party trying to rescue two women who had been caught on the mountain in a weather change. The conditions were too bad for helicopters to be used and we went out to locate them and bring them back. We reached an icy ridge which had to be crossed and it was very ticklish work. There wasn't time for all the usual precautions and we had to cross the ridge individually, unroped. Meanwhile, there was a break in the weather and a helicopter came in and winched the two women to safety. Then, without so much as a by-your-leave, the chopper began rescuing us as well! I was chest-roped and hauled up into the helicopter, completely terrified.

I prefer to remember a climb which encapsulates a lot of the pleasures of climbing — the skill, the danger, the camaraderie. This was a grand traverse of Mount Cook done in 1971 with Pat Barcham, Tom's brother, and Kevin Rainsford and Paul Gaisely. The latter two, incidentally, were both killed mountaineering, Kevin in Patagonia and Paul on Mount Cook.

Mount Cook has two big quadrilateral faces, then a series of triangular faces coming off them. There are three peaks about a mile and a half apart and the summit is over 12,000 feet. The first person to make the climb described it as 'surely one of the greatest aerial highways in the world'. We left the last hut about midnight and began the climb in bright moonlight, traversing across the face of the mountain on thick, dry ice that you felt stuck to, like shit to a blanket. Very safe. We had a bit of trouble on parts of the way up because the two younger men, who were moving fast ahead of us, dislodged some rocks which came whistling down at us. Very unsafe — a decent-sized rock could brain you or knock you off the mountain.

It was partly a matter of technology. Pat and I had been brought up on sisal ropes which you did not trail in the ice and snow because they froze and went stiff. Kevin and Paul were using the new type of nylon rope that could drag on the surface without being damaged. Their rope dislodged the rocks and I had some very sharp words to say. A little later I attempted to soften the blow by taking a photograph of them working along a little arrete just as the sun came up. I've won a few prizes for mountain photographs, and this was one of my better efforts.

It was a beautiful day for a climb and the summit was a great place to be in the early morning. On the way down we stopped at a big rock face called the Jacob's Ladder and had a brew, using a litle portable primus. It was windless up there, you could easily light a pipe, and you could spit into the Tasman Sea on one side and see the Pacific Ocean on the other. I had a tremendous feeling of exhilaration and happiness.

The younger men, who were taller and stronger than Pat and I, went off ahead of us on the way down. We had the Linda Shelf to get over and the Linda Glacier to cross. In New Zealand terms it's the roof of the world up there — all the biggest peaks around you, Cook's 3764 metres, Tasman, Dampier. I was leading Pat down the glacier and I came to a deep blue crevasse. They're described as blue because of the colour of the air in them; this one was very blue, a 100-metre drop and no bottom in sight. It would have been about two metres across with the far side slightly higher than the near one — a very difficult jump. All signs were that Kevin and Paul had jumped it — roughed up snow, crampon marks, you could almost imagine the fingernail marks on the other side. I looked across and saw written in the snow by an ice axe the words JUMP FRED! They were getting back at me for rousting them about the dragging rope.

Pat and I knew we couldn't jump it but Pat spotted an ice fall way over to one side where the blocks were sort of teetering across the crevasse. We made our way there and got across on a long rope; it was still a very precarious manouevre. Pat, who was a rather strait-laced sort of chap, said that we shouldn't tell Kevin and Paul about how we'd crossed the crevasse. I agreed. We got to the hut, had a meal and I was washing the dishes when Kevin said, 'How did you and Pat get across that crevasse, Fred?'

'Which one d'you mean?'

'The big blue one.'

'How did you get over?'

'Well, Paul's six-foot-two, so he jumped across, just made it. Then I swung over on a rope.'

'Pat and me jumped it side by side, didn't we, Pat?'

My climbing days are over now, but on a recent trip to New Zealand I saw the peaks again, some of which I've climbed: Hooker, Brewster, Rolleston, Ward. Ward was massive and terrifying — a big, black, south-pointing face with a little runnel of snow going up the middle of it. The mountains of the world are places of awe and inspiration.

That's one sort of 'high' that's always been important to me — the physical kind, involving endurance, some nerve and paying off with a sense of something accomplished. There's also an aesthetic 'high' which is harder to describe and account for. I can get it from music, but mostly I get it from reading verse.

Shakespeare is important to me. A friend of mine named John Stonham has chunks of Shakespeare by heart and, after we've played a little chess and drunk a few whiskies, I have only to say to him, 'John, tennis balls,' and he's off.

What treasure, uncle?

Tennis balls, my liege.

We are glad the Dauphin is so pleasant with us;
His present and your pains we thank you for:
When we have match'd our rackets to these balls,
We will in France, by God's grace, play a set
Shall strike his father's crown into the hazard.
Tell him he hath made a match with such a wrangler
That all the courts of France will be disturb'd
With chases.

Henry V. I get a funny feeling at the back of my neck when I hear that, and when I saw Warren Mitchell, playing Lear, carrying Cordelia in his arms in the last scene, I'm afraid I blubbered uncontrollably.

I think verse is terribly important. It's to do with communication and the neopallium — that's the newest, in evolutionary terms, part of the cerebrum, the front and upper part of the brain, which is formed by the development of new pathways for sight and hearing. Our greater development in this area distinguishes us from the other animals. Verse lyricises human communication, or the kind of verse that I respond to does. I agree with those critics who say that verse works against the transitoriness of emotions and ideas and makes their expression universal and enduring.

For me, John Keats, at his best, epitomises lyricism in English. And lyricism contributes to that heightened form of consciousness which is what poetry is all about. It's to do with economy and rightness. The best lines of verse say things with the greatest possible concision and precision. Good surgery is the same.

O for a beaker full of the warm South,
  Full of the true, the blushful Hippocrene.
With beaded bubbles winking at the brim
  And purple-stained mouth;
That I might drink and leave the world unseen.
  And with thee fade away into the forest dim:

. . .

Forlorn! the very word is like a bell
  To toll me back from thee to my sole self!
Adieu! the fancy cannot cheat so well
  As she is famed to do, deceiving elf.
Adieu! adieu! thy plaintive anthem fades
  Past the near meadows, over the still streams,

Up the hillside; and now 'tis buried deep
In the next valley-glades
Was it a vision, or a waking dream?
Fled is that music — do I wake or sleep?

Great piquancy in the language and you could say that ending is very modern for a poem published in 1820, or timeless. I wouldn't be without 'Ode to a Nightingale' and images like

Through the sad heart of Ruth, when, sick for home,
She stood in tears amid the alien corn;

for anything.

CHAPTER 18

Looking further: Nepal

For all the World to See. Title of film on the life of Fred Hollows by Pat Fiske.

Although I continued to do work in Aboriginal health as I have indicated, events drew me into an involvement with eye health in developing countries — Mexico, Burma, Thailand, most significantly in Nepal and then Eritrea in the Horn of Africa.

I had met Dr Pararajah Seagram, a Sri Lankan and a great humanitarian, in London. In addition, he is an excellent eye surgeon and he and his wife, also an ophthalmologist, worked in the trachoma program for nine months. He came out because he wanted to see a project in operation that was actually doing things. He went on to run SEARO, the South East Asian Regional Organisation arm of the World Health Blindness Prevention Program. WHO provides some funds for blindness prevention work in Third World societies and they appoint short-term consultants to assess the worth of these projects. In 1985, Pararajah asked me if I'd do one of these stints for Nepal and Thailand, six weeks all up.

I declined immediately. I was sceptical about these flying

visits and rushed reports done on the basis of scanty knowledge, but eventually I agreed to go to Nepal for six weeks to look at things more thoroughly and to put in a token appearance in Thailand. I have to admit there was also an element of self-interest in this. I was fairly fit in those days and I thought I might get a chance to visit the Everest base camp and do a bit of trekking around, I wanted to see the south face of Annapurna and the Lohise face and so on.

My brief was to assess the Nepalese blindness prevention program, particularly the effectiveness of their ophthalmic assistants; to assess the extent of trachoma and evaluate treatment given; and any other matters relevant to blindness prevention in Nepal. Pretty wide terms and I worked very hard on both my visits trying to do the job properly. I examined thousands of people and demonstrated different operations to the Nepalese surgeons. The head of the show was Dr Ram Pohkrel. He was a fellow of the Royal College of Surgeons in ophthalmology, like myself, and he was the official ophthalmologist to the King and royal family of Nepal. The first time I met him was in a courtyard in which there were at least two thousand people waiting to be seen. He'd been working all day, seeing non-paying patients in a seemingly never-ending stream. I was impressed.

Our next meeting, after I'd been out in the field for a while, was in the same town but this time in a hall where an improvised operating theatre had been rigged up. He was doing cataract extractions — the old type of operation — taking only six minutes for each and doing them extraordinarily well.

He said, 'Professor Hollows you must help me. I want you to finish the surgery here this afternoon. I have done a hundred and forty today but the king has ordered me to be in Hatowda at seven o'clock tomorrow morning and I have 200 kilometres to travel tonight. So I must leave within the hour.'

And I thought, *Jesus, here's the top man and he's not sashaying around giving orders. He's in there, sleeves rolled up.*

So I got stuck in and did another twenty or thirty extractions. I found the assistants extremely good and the harder I worked them the better they performed. You had to be impressed by the way things were shaping up in Nepal. There was a team of very good young eye surgeons and they were making headway. A few years previously, fewer than one thousand cataract operations had ever been performed in Nepal and by the time I was there they were doing fifteen thousand a year.

Like many things, it was a matter of good organisation. The best blindness prevention survey ever carried out in a Third World country had been done in Nepal. The country had been divided up into grids, and, for certain things, they knew to a very accurate degree what needed to be done where and they had training programs on the go. All they needed was a little extra know-how, such as a good grading system for trachoma. I demonstrated that and the assistants picked it up as quick as a flash.

One of the men who'd worked on that survey was Sanduk Ruit, a Sherpa who had gone to an English school in Darjeeling. He'd shown such promise that, despite Sherpa being a relatively low caste, he'd been selected to go to India to study medicine. There were no medical schools in Nepal at that time. Ram Pohkrel had spoken highly of Ruit and that endorsement was borne out. We did a great deal of work together.

On one occasion we were working in a little hill village, close to Everest, and a dwarf came into the clinic. He had bilateral congenital cataracts, a divergent squint and he was blind. Removing congenital cataracts doesn't give as good a result as removing what's called senile cataracts, because the retinas in such people have never 'learned' to see. But it's worth doing because the person can see enough to get around. I said to Ruit that he should get this little fellow down to Khatmandu where I could demonstrate the use of a suction device I had to remove his congenital cataracts. We went on with the clinic and as we finished Ruit said to me, 'Fred,

I gave that chap 60 rupees and he's getting on the bus to Khatmandu tonight.'

'Good,' I said.

Ruit's smile was mischievous.

I can't tell you what he said. It would upset some important Nepalese and jeopardise his work. But he was on the right side.

I knew I'd found a soul-mate.

I did most of my work in the Terai, the plains of Nepal, where most of the population is now that they've got some control of malaria. The plains will yield two or three rice crops a year and people are moving down there because living in the mountains is rough. They are very tough, adaptable people. The villages can be beautiful with lovely courtyards, all constructed from local materials hauled on bullock wagons which are themselves impressive pieces of technology.

The strength of the Nepalese male and female is amazing. One day I examined the bundles of wood the women were carrying. These women wouldn't have topped five feet and they'd be lucky to weigh five stone; 150 cm and 32 kg. Using a headband they were carrying on their backs bundles of wood about a yard long and a couple of feet in diameter. In the middle of each bundle the woman would tuck her axe, quite a solid implement. The loads looked heavy but the women appeared to carry them easily. I asked the Nepalese doctor who was working with me what the bundles weighed and he said they were about a hundredweight. I couldn't believe that and I asked him to get one of the women to lower hers onto a bank, a place where she could conveniently take it up again, and to let me have a shot at carrying it. I put the headband on and took the weight and it was all I could do to stagger three or four paces before I had to lower it back down. The women had walked eight kilometres to where they had cut and split the wood and they had 20 kilometres to walk to the place where they were going to sell it. It's said that any Nepalese can carry his or her own weight and I'm inclined to believe it.

I didn't manage to do any trekking but when I was working in a hill station one day I was told that Kanchenjunga, the third highest mountain in the world at 8,603.4 metres, was visible from the next ridge. I'd read a good deal about this legendary mountain — about the German expedition in which every member of the party was killed and the ascent by Charles Evans in 1955 when they stopped a few metres short of the peak out of deference to the local peoples' veneration for the mountain. We knocked off for an hour and climbed the ridge. The mountain was covered by cloud but still an awesome sight. Later, I took a short plane ride that gave me a good sight of Everest. There was no lack of interesting experiences, from the sight of elephants making an airstrip to the matter of goat meat.

To make an airstrip in Nepal a number of elephants are brought in to simply walk up and down over the area for three months, pounding everything flat and stamping in their droppings.

I can never see a goat now without remembering arriving in a Nepalese village one day and being confronted by a man holding a goat by a string tied around its neck.

I was asked, 'Doctor, do you want goat meat for the midday meal?'

I didn't care one way or the other but I was pressed and eventually I said, 'Yeah, OK, we'll have goat for lunch.'

With that the villager pulled out a bloody great cleaver and cut the fucking goat's head off right in front of me. He chopped it up and charged me 35 rupees. There was nearly always a man with a goat whenever we entered a village and I could never look the goat in the eye after that. The meat was tough. You were eating it within an hour of the poor brute being killed. I didn't care for it much but the ophthalmic assistants were very keen on me giving the thumbs down — they didn't get to eat meat all that often.

There was a good deal of follicular trachoma in Nepal for much the same reasons as in Aboriginal Australia — poor living conditions, inadequate water for washing, overcrowding. We found a lot of quite young women with inturned upper eyelashes which is a scarring condition. Trachoma has reached a vision-threatening stage by then. Seven women to every man were in this condition because of poor hygiene in the creche. The women were spending a lot of time among pus and other secretions, passing the chylamidial infection around.

I insisted on visiting the blind schools in Nepal because that's where you can get a profile of the problem. A great proportion of the children in blind schools in Australia have other congenital abnormalities but that's not the case in Nepal. Here you had a great number of nimble-witted kids, good at Braille and with other skills, who could have been greatly helped by surgery. Those visits were both sad and encouraging.

In my report to WHO I stressed the need for better domiciliary hygiene, particularly the provision of water, the advisability of medication in the form of eye ointments and systemic drugs and vigorous provision of surgery. I was able to report favourably on the progress of the measures already adopted, particularly on the quality of the work of the ophthalmic assistants. I wrote:

> The vocational future of ophthalmic assistants must be assured. These men and women are eager to work, are well trained and are knowledgable. They are currently providing a large proportion of direct eye service in almost every eye institution and especially in the remote areas of Nepal. Without them the present impressive diagnostic and therapeutic anti-blindness work in Nepal would drastically fall off. It is also recommended that an adequately sponsored salary and promotional scale be established with appropriate university and public service certification put in place. It is recom-

> mended that training be continued so that there become available and be maintained about 200 ophthalmic assistants throughout Nepal.[11]

Although it sounds a little stilted in the bureaucratic language of such documents, I meant it when I wrote that I was impressed 'with the gentleness and sincerity' of the people I met and that 'all relationships were most cordial'.

Particularly cordial were my dealings with Ruit. He was a first-rate diagnostician, totally absorbed in the craft of ophthalmology. I said, in an off-hand sort of way that he should come to Australia to see how we did things here. He wrote to me indicating his eagerness and I was able to arrange it. For a good many years the money over a certain figure I earned in my private practice had gone into a fund controlled by the university. It had built up to a sizeable sum and I was able to tap this to get support for Ruit. He came out through Europe and America, stayed for a year and went back through Japan, so he got a world view of the technology.

Working in Sydney, Ruit did his first modern cataract operation with intra-ocular lens implant. He worked on Thursday Island and spent some time in Adelaide studying corneal banking, a procedure by which donor eyes are kept in a solution which contains antibiotics and other agents. In this way, the corneal tissue can be so preserved for five days.

When he went back to Nepal he started using and teaching the Prince of Wales hospital surgical techniques. On my second visit I found that he had refined and improved some of our methods so that at the Prince of Wales we now use what I call the Nepal technique.

Ruit and Gabi organised an Australian support group called the 'Nepal Eye Program-Australia', and Tim McCartney-Snape, the first Australian to climb Everest, became its

---

[11] WHO South-East Asia Region, 'Prevention of blindness in Nepal', Consultant's report, 15 July 1986

president. The idea is to support what the Nepalese themselves are doing, not go over there in a missionary spirit trying to tell them what to do. We have a permanent representative there, an Australian ambulance driver, who's in love with Nepal. We heard recently that the Australian ambassador has made a donation of $70,000 towards setting up a lens factory and he has supported the eye program out of discretionary funds in various ways. The Nepal Eye Program–Australia sponsors eye camps all over the country at which Ruit and the people we have trained perform their excellent surgery. Several hundred thousand dollars worth of equipment has been provided and, with Nepal, you can be sure that the gear gets to where it is supposed to go. Unfortunately, this is not the case in other parts of Asia, like Burma and Bangladesh, where graft and inefficiency can completely negate good support work.

There were some excellent health workers in Burma, but the economic, political and social structures seemed designed to frustrate any advances in medicine. For example, there was a very high rate of angle closure glaucoma — acute, blinding glaucoma. A much higher rate than in Australia. Everywhere I went the eye doctors would say, 'Oh, the people don't come in for treatment early enough. The people are stupid.'

I don't believe that people *en masse* are stupid, so I made some enquiries. I found that a person in central Burma, on average, was unable to get to an eye doctor in less than three days. So I asked what treatment was available in the villages for an attack of angle closure glaucoma. The answer was: pilocarpine drops. Now that treatment *may* relieve the pressure temporarily, but that's all.

'Have you ever cured an attack of angle closure glaucoma with pilocarpine drops alone?' I asked.

They admitted they hadn't. The nature of this type of glaucoma is that, if you can relieve the pressure, the eye will be all right until the next attack occurs. But if you don't, and the eye's been as hard as a marble for several days, that means the optic nerve will not get any blood and will decay. You may relieve the pressure later, but the optic nerve will not regenerate and its destruction means that the eye will never see.

'What do you do, here in the towns, when you encounter a patient suffering an attack of acute glaucoma?' was my next question. The answer was that they administered two Diamox tablets plus the pilocarpine which usually broke the attack and then they operated. It was obvious that what was needed in the villages was a sufficient supply of Diamox tablets to enable sufferers to take a course of these through the time it took them to get to an eye doctor. But the prevailing view was that the cause of the problem was the stupidity of the people.

What I saw there made me very angry. I saw people whose glaucoma was corrected through a simple operation, well carried out, but they remained blind due to cataract. No intra-ocular lenses were being implanted. Similarly with corneal grafts. There was a crying need for that form of treatment but there were no corneal banks, even though I was assured by paedatricians that healthy corneal tissue was available on account of the high infant mortality rate. There was a great deal of enucleation and nothing is better calculated to keep people away from eye clinics than wholesale eyeball removal, with the result that many people who could be helped do not get attention in time. Through no fault of theirs.

It seemed to me that the only thing that worked in Burma was Buddhism. The biggest lottery in the country was a crazy affair in which people bought tickets hoping to win the right to put gold leaf on the dome of a big pagoda in Rangoon. WHO had a fondness for Burma because there were no beggers on the streets. The place looked tidy by fastidious western standards. But that was because the only people *allowed* by law to beg are Buddhist monks and the impression of tidiness was misleading. As things turned out, my rejection of Burma as a model for the improvement of eye health in Asia was justified. The universities were shut down in 1988, the political parties were suppressed and I fear that the enlightened and forward-thinking health workers I met have either left or been shot.

Nepal, although an hereditary monarchy, was exhibiting signs of change at the time of my visits that have been to some extent fulfilled. The power of the King has been reduced, free elections have been held and parliamentary democracy is developing promisingly. It has a population of about 16 million people and, as a result of the excellent survey I've referred to, it can reliably be estimated that about thirty-two thousand people are blinded by cataract each year. Cataracts cause 96 per cent of the blindness there. That's a different situation to the Australian one where there is macular degeneration, glaucoma and diabetes at a much higher rate. The last time I looked at the figures, thirty thousand operations were being carried out per year, so they appear to be getting on top of the problem and that is encouraging.

CHAPTER 19

In the Horn of Africa

> With a flush of blood I remembered that the Ethiopians had promised to drive the Eritreans 'into the Red Sea'. 'Into the sands of the Sudan,' Mengistu had put it once. This grievous intention of the Dergue's had made the Eritreans into just warriors, a corps of the righteous. To feel an association with warriors was a new experience for me . . .
>
> *Thomas Keneally*, Towards Asmara

The Horn of Africa is one of the most interesting places on earth. Historically, it is close to the birthplace of civilisation in Mesopotamia, and it has been subject to influence from all the great cultural centres of the Old World — Arabia, Africa, Asia, Greece and Rome. The Europeans are real Johnnies-come-lately, compared to the Arabs and Indians. In political terms, the Horn's geography and history have meant that its people have been exposed to a vast range of diplomacies and intrigues in a variety of languages stretching back over centuries. They have acquired sophistication and wisdom.

These qualities have been dearly bought. The Amharic feudal rulers, based in Abyssinia, exerted influence from Egypt in the north down as far as Kenya. There are two important things to be understood about Amharic suzerainty over the Horn of Africa. First, it was always achieved and maintained because the people subject to it could not unite against it. Secondly, the Amharic rulers were always ready to call in outside forces to back them up. Those two factors have shaped the history of the area from the sixteenth century to the present. In the second half of the nineteenth century, Emperor Johannes of Tigray joined forces with the British to suppress the troublesome independence movement in the Sudan, where Britain had substantial interests. He did this to curry favour with the British and win their support for his annexation of Massawa and other parts of Eritrea that were then ruled by the Egyptians.

Menelik the Great, the so-called King of Kings, played off the rivals Britain, France and Italy to acquire massive quantities of arms. Some sources say that he got his hands on 7 million rifles and 44 million bullets — massive firepower in those days. He subdued the Oromos, the Somalies (of the Ogaden), the Sidama and other nationalities, incorporating them into modern-day Ethiopia. But, although he invaded and conquered territories more than twice the size of his original kingdom, Menelik was unable to realise the ultimate dream of Ethiopian expansionism — unhindered access to the Red Sea. The Italians were involved in the Eritrean area and thus the Eritreans managed to hold it. As Johannes failed there, so did Menelik.

It was not achieved until 1951. Haile Selassie, Emperor from 1930 to 1936 when Mussolini conquered Ethiopia, had returned from Britain after the Fascist defeat in 1941 and was reinstated by the allies. With the aid of the Americans, he was able to secure United Nations support for the federation of Eritrea with Ethiopia. Haile Selassie then demonstrated his fealty to the US by contributing money and men to the Korean War. Ten years after the federation was carried out, Haile Selassie forced the Eritrean Parliament to vote itself out of existence, and Eritrea fell under Ethiopian control. The Eritrean resistance began at that point. Addis Ababa and Washington signed a military agreement that stayed in force for twenty-five years. The US was provided with the Kagnew military communications base in Asmara, the capital of Eritrea, and naval facilities at the Eritrean port of Massawa.

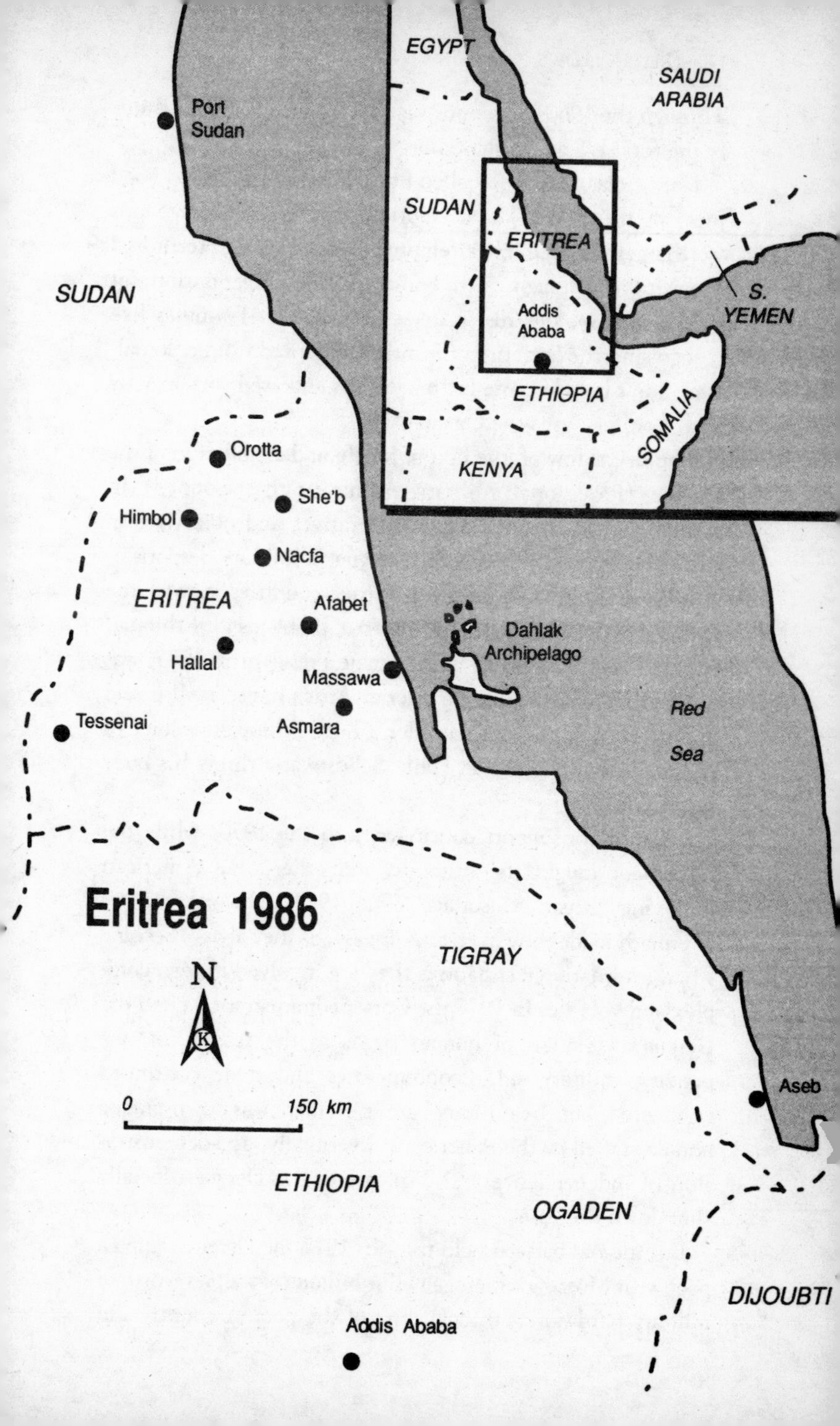
EGYPT
SAUDI ARABIA
Port Sudan
SUDAN
ERITREA
Addis Ababa
S. YEMEN
ETHIOPIA
SOMALIA
KENYA
SUDAN
Orotta
She'b
Himbol
Nacfa
ERITREA
Afabet
Dahlak Archipelago
Hallal
Massawa
Asmara
Tessenai
Red Sea
Eritrea 1986
TIGRAY
N
K
0
150 km
Aseb
ETHIOPIA
OGADEN
DIJOUBTI
Addis Ababa

Through the 1960s, Ethiopia was the beneficiary of two-thirds of the total US aid to sub-Saharan Africa.

Haile Selassie, the so-called Lion of Judah, enjoyed a good press in the West. His corruption, cruelty and repressions were largely ignored. He attempted to legitimate his territorial acquisitions through such bodies as the Organisation for African Unity, but his strategies went awry. Formulas like recognising the 'sanctity of frontiers inherited from colonialism' didn't help because Eritrea itself is endowed with exactly such frontiers, as is the Ogaden.

The overthrow of 'the lion of Judah' and installation of the Dergue (Provisional Military Administrative Council) in 1974 didn't change the basic imperatives and objectives of Ethiopian foreign policy. The Dergue, a military despotism, did all it could to ensure that other countries viewed the Eritrean and other dissent as 'internal' problems for Ethiopia. Mengistu Haile Mariam, who became President in 1977, was as repressive and arbitrary a ruler as Africa has seen. It is said one of his first acts was to order a huge Ethiopian soldier to strangle the octogenarian Haile Selassie and throw his body down a well.

US military support continued into the 1970s while the Ethiopians fought the Eritreans and others, but American misgivings began to surface. The 1974 upheaval and its aftermath made the Americans uneasy, as they always become when international situations they are involved in turn complex and volatile. In 1977 the Carter administration cited the Dergue's violation of human rights as the reason for suspending military aid. Economic ties and trade continued unaffected, but the military base in Asmara was down-graded and de-staffed by the Americans. Eventually, as a demonstration of independence and displeasure, the Dergue officially shut down the base.

But the old pattern held true. In 1977 the Dergue signed a pact with Moscow which gained it billions of roubles worth of military hardware. Ethiopia, one of the poorest countries in

Africa, became militarily the strongest. In the tradition of its predecessors, the Dergue called in the mercenaries. Over seventeen thousand Cuban soldiers were sent to the war in the Ogaden, ostensibly to ward off an invasion by the Somalis. The Junta's actions have made its lies transparent. For example, it claimed to have closed the Kagnew base to preserve its territorial integrity. How would it explain the Soviet naval base in the *Eritrean* Dahlak Archipelago which is off-limits ato Ethiopian personnel?

The war went on. Soviet and Cuban military support shrank. All indications pointed to the Eritreans and Somalies winning. Massawa fell under Eritrean control as the result of a brilliant land and sea raid. The Eritreans surrounded the Second Ethiopian army who are nearly starving. They could knock it out at any time. The Oromo are able to take all the airfields in Ethiopia, which will mean that the MiGs they've got left — the sixty to eighty or so — will be neutralised. Asmara, by the time Mengistu fled the country, could have been taken at any time over the preceding months.

The organisation that is poised to take control of liberated Eritrea is the EPLF, the Eritrean People's Liberation Front. This is a democratic, non-sectarian movement which embraces all of the nine ethnic groups in the country, the various religions and the multifarious shades of political opinion. It did not become the major force easily. In the early years of the struggle, a more traditionally oriented, elitist, narrowly Islamic body, the ELF, Eritrean Liberation Front, held sway. The ELF's position was that matters such as the emancipation of women, the abandonment of practices like infibulation and clitorectomy, the erasure of divisions and privileges based on ethnicity, could be left until the Ethiopians had been beaten. The EPLF insisted that the movement had to embrace and practise these freedoms from the outset. There was armed conflict. The EPLF prevailed, won popular support, and the ELF is now reduced to a sort of rump, operating only in the western flanks of Eritrea, near the Sudanese border.

But I knew nothing of any of this when I met my first Eritrean. Before that all I knew about the Horn of Africa could be summed up in two words — a song and a surgeon. The song was something I remembered from my childhood. It went, roughly:

There's a war in Abyssinia won't you come?
All you need is ammunition and a gun,
Mussolini will be there, shooting peanuts in the air,
There's a war in Abyssinia won't you come?

The surgeon was the celebrated Bietti, Professor of Ophthalmology in the University of Rome. He had described and given the name to climatic droplet keratopathy (popularly called Labrador keratopathy), as it occurred in Libya, Ethiopia and the Dahlak islands off the coast of Eritrea. I met Bietti in Rome in 1965, as I was on my way out to Australia. He was a brilliant, flamboyant surgeon and an Anglophile. He drove a Jaguar and had a huge office all done out in marble. I saw him perform some amazingly theatrical surgery, including the use of a cryo probe, a technique involving freezing, which was very new to me then.

So, I knew there had been a war in Ethiopia back when I was a kid and that there was another one going on now and that the Red Sea was a bad area for eye disease. That was the sum total of my knowledge in 1986 when I met Fessahaie Abraham, an Eritrean refugee who came to the Prince of Wales clinic with an eye problem. The complaint was relatively minor, but I did notice that he showed traces of Herbert's Pits, which is a condition associated with trachoma. We got into conversation and he told me that the Eritreans were winning the war and had recovered about three quarters of the country.

'The doctors must be busy,' I said.

'Yes, we have twenty-one doctors and they are very busy.'

That didn't sound like many doctors to me and I asked him how many eye doctors there were. He told me that there was one man in the country who did the eye surgery although he wasn't trained to do it. He just happened to have some skill at it. It sounded like a very serious situation to me — one untrained eye man in an area where there were likely to be a lot of eye problems, quite apart from the traumas of war. I suggested to Fessahaie that this Eritrean doctor should come to Australia to see how things are done here. He found that interesting and lent me some literature and a video which dealt with the EPLF and its role in the struggle.

There are hundreds of thousands of Eritreans scattered throughout the world — all over Africa and Asia, in Europe and America — and most of them are working like badgers for the cause. Fessahaie was studying chemical engineering and he had founded the Eritrean Relief Association in Sydney. We became friends and I got more and more interested in Eritrean affairs. I had a contact in ADAB (Australian Development Aid Abroad) and I knew they were interested in training people in the Third World. I wrote one letter and got allotted $20,000 to bring out the Eritrean eye man. It looked like plain sailing but in fact it took quite a while to organise, firstly because Eritreans can only get passports by buying them and there were some bureaucratic tangles over that, and, secondly, because the war had hotted up.

The man in question was Dr Desbele Ghebregioghis and he was not only doing eye work, but dealing with arms and legs and every other part of the carcass, as the Ethiopians threw everything the Russians had given them at the Eritreans. Eventually, Desbele was able to come. He's a small man, rather shy and modest. You wouldn't know he'd been at war for eleven years. He had been selected by the Ethiopian authorities to do medical training in Greece, at Salonica, where there is a very good medical school. He'd qualified, done one year as an intern and one day just didn't turn up for work. He had joined the EPLF.

As it happened, at almost the same time as Desbele arrived, I was invited to do another short-term consultancy, this time to help appraise the WHO World Blindness Program by attending a conference in Alexandria. I have a lot of criticisms of the bureaucratic structures in WHO and I doubted that going to a conference would do any good, but I was attracted by the idea of going to Egypt. I'd been interested in the excavations at Abu Simbel, where huge quantities of antiquities had been moved from areas that were going to be covered by the Aswan dam. I looked at the map and noted how close Abu Simbel was to the Sudan and then I thought, *I could nip down from there into Eritrea and get an idea of Desbele's working conditions*. I was going to be involved in his training and I reckoned that would be useful background knowledge. Fessahaie said it was difficult but feasible. If an Eritrean says something's feasible, you can pretty well bet it'll get done.

Trachoma was initially called in England 'Egyptian ophthalmia' because it was thought that it had been introduced into Britain by seamen returning from the Battle of the Nile. It was these cases that led to the establishment of the first eye hospital at Moorfields in London. Whether that account of the origin of the disease in England is true or not, it was certainly the case that trachoma was widespread among the poor in Egypt. We were taken on a tour of some villages about 30 kilometres from Alexandria by a professor of ophthalmology. I took my magnifiers and torch and I was shocked to see many five-year-old children with advanced conjunctival scarring. Many of them were certainly on the road to trachomatous blindness. The people were subsistence farmers living in the most appalling conditions — no clean running water to the houses and the water they washed in was downstream from where people and animals urinated and defecated.

On the bus during this tour we were treated to a lecture by a young assistant of one of the professors of medicine. He ran the line that the *fellahine's* diseases were their own fault, the result of superstition and ignorance. I was made very angry by this. We visited a hospital which boasted a hundred beds and modern facilities. An immaculately dressed woman told us that clinics were held at the hospital every morning. But the in-patients section was empty. We were told that they had had trouble getting a cook which made it impossible to house patients, but it was obvious that the hospital did almost no real work and was a showpiece, built by internationally donated funds. As we left the hospital a village kid walked along beside us and he was muttering away in Arabic. A Palestinian friend of mine translated. The kid was saying that this was a nonsense hospital. The doctors visited briefly in the afternoon and prescribed no drugs. He said that people like him went to the traditional doctors in the villages when they became ill.

We travelled back to Alexandria to a function held at the house of the professor. It was an elaborate Mediterranean villa with marble steps and a large marble bathroom. You could wash your hands, have a shower or a bath and clean towels were laid out. Then we went through the house to the back where there was a marquee and a lawn and tables laden with imported booze, cakes and other food. I was standing next to the professor of cardiac surgery and a pediatrician and other senior members of the medical faculty of the University of Alexandria were within earshot. I said, 'Isn't it great that this professor can show us the real problems of Egypt. We've just been to a village where most of the kids have trachoma and many of them are certain to be blinded by it. There's a total absence of even rudimentary hygiene facilities there, and now here we are in this beautiful place with its bathroom and all this clean food on the tables. It's good to see the real problems of Egypt so strikingly demonstrated.'

There was some tut-tutting and people turned their backs on me. It would have been easier to have just mingled and enjoyed the grog, but that was one occasion when I had to speak out and doing so has given me a memory to cherish. The political naivete of the Egyptian bourgeoisie is beyond belief and when the poor people, whose present condition is just about hopeless, rise up against them they won't have any understanding of what's happened.

I flew from Egypt to Khartoum and then down to Port Sudan. Representatives of the Eritrean Relief Association picked me up there and we began the journey into the field. The first stage is down the arid coast of the eastern Red Sea to the old Turkish slave port, Suakin. Chaos characterises the Sudan the way order characterises Eritrea, and the EPLF garage workshop and staging post at Suakin was order amid chaos. Very impressive. We then drove inland and south to Orotta. Tom Keneally has written a very good description of what travel is like in those parts in his novel, *Towards Asmara*:

> . . . the road was a scarcely perceived rumour. We followed river beds clogged with lumps of stone in which you could read, if you had some sort of divine sense, a history of Africa's uncertain rains. The insides of the truck hit us fierce blows on elbows and shoulders, the back of the head.

The drive took about fourteen hours, mostly at night because of the danger from the MiGs. At that time the EPLF had been driven back into the hilly country near the southern part of coastal Sudan, but they'd cut roads in the hills and were doing the most innovative things with captured Russian equipment — towing supplies across flash-flooded creeks and using derelict vehicles as foundations for ramps and causeways.

We got to Orotta at some time in the early hours and I got out of the Toyota, stiff as a board, black and blue from the jolts, and I seemed to be nowhere at all — just walking along yet another rocky creek bed. All of a sudden we came to some steps which led through a door to a big underground bunker.

There were a hell of a lot of people inside, black, white and brindle. It was the second meeting of the EPLF Congress and there were representatives there from Norway, Germany, Belgium, Britain and so on. It was a bit of a shock after that bone-jarring ride from Port Sudan, but what was even more surprising was that there was someone there I knew — an African named Voika Kunta who'd been a member of the Black Consciousness movement, the Steve Biko movement. He'd been in our house in Randwick and here he was again in a rock bunker in Eritrea. That was not the last of my surprises.

The most extraordinary thing was the attitude of the people, their dignity and poise. Although everybody was armed and the men, women and children had seen action, there was none of that swaggering bravado often associated with revolutionary movements. Quite the reverse. On one occasion, in Nacfa, I saw a small group of militia who were having a rest in the garden. The garden is an oasis of shade and peace after the heat and glare of the hills. The militiamen had their rifles with them, mostly Kalashnikovs which they customise — construct special slings and handgrips for, bind with tape and so on. Their guns reminded me of the .303 rifles which we used for deer shooting in New Zealand in the 1950s, ex-army weapons which were very cheap like the ammunition. We cut them down, modified the sights, put comfortable shoulder straps on them and so on. This group was arranged around the well and I thought the scene would make a terrific photograph. *Peace amid strife*, that sort of thing. They were willing and I got out the camera. When I lined the shot up I noticed that they had pushed their weapons out of sight. They wanted to be photographed as ordinary human beings, without bravado and props. I thought that showed an extraordinary development of consciousness.

This dignity and maturity is expressed in a hundred ways. The Eritreans don't wear badges of rank. Authority is demonstrated, not advertised. It appears to me that they are not addicted to war and its trappings, although they've been fighting for a much longer time than World Wars 1 and 2 put together. They haven't lost sight of normalcy. Amna Nur Hussein, a remarkable woman who'd seen a lot of action and always went about armed with a pistol and grenades, once asked me to photograph her with a friend. The friend was another handsome young woman, similarly armed. They removed all the hardware and posed under a tree, adopting 'feminine' poses. I find this encouraging.

I was there to investigate medical matters and I did. Orotta was the EPLF hospital base and medical administrative area. There are several dendritic, that is, branched, valleys, previously unoccupied, all surrounded by steep rocky hills. On the sides of the valley floors there are trees, mostly thorny acacias, and under these trees and partly dug into the hills are the different parts of the hospital. Each institution, such as the operating theatres, maxillo facial unit, orthopaedic ward, paediatric ward and so on, is placed separately to reduce vulnerability to air attack.

I met Alemo, who was doing eye work during Desbele's absence, and he explained that the work of the department was done at night, because of the MiGs. At six pm we started work in the eye clinic. A group of patients had gathered under the acacia trees and the staff had recorded their details and done some preliminary vision testing. The patients were a very mixed bag — young fighters with their weapons tucked away as I have described, children with their parents, old nomads. They reflected the immense diversity of races, religions, languages and customs that is Eritrea and all were treated with the same courtesy and care.

One family who brought in an old woman with a severe eye problem told me that they had travelled 1,000 kilometres to seek treatment from the EPLF facility. Given the difficulties of travel, you could not get a better vote of confidence than that. The clinic proceeded with quiet efficiency, nobody pulling rank, patients being treated well, explanations being given. The team of us worked on through the night until the last patient had been seen. The diagnostic equipment was rudimentary but functional. Most of it had been donated by European agencies. The saddest cases were those of the young people blinded by bomb, mine and rocket fragments. Modern microscopic eye surgery could have helped some of them. Much of the surgery that was being carried out was inexpert.

I was shown through the whole complex by Dr Nerayo, who had trained in London and the US as well as in some of the best hospitals in the Middle East. He'd given up a prestigious job in Asmara to join the EPLF and you could tell that the patients and staff saw him as a friend and fellow fighter, not just as a medical superintendent. He spoke good English and was able to point out things to me that I might have missed. For example, he showed me that the medical staff were helping in the construction of a new building, real hard masonry work, because they felt that their medical jobs were soft, compared to the things the fighters had to do.

I was particularly struck by the sophistication of the chemical and pharmaceutical manufacturing. In a semi-underground, camouflaged building, they were turning out up to fifty thousand tablets an hour — anti-malarial, anti-tuberculosis drugs as well as vitamins. I also saw the day's yield of intravenous fluid — more than a thousand half-litre packs of fluid — what's called five-stage pyrogen-free pH exact. This is life-saving stuff in this area where wounds and fevers increase the chances of death from dehydration of people who can't take anything by mouth. I couldn't help thinking back to a discussion we'd had at the conference in Alexandria. We'd spent half a morning on a great advance that had come from some mission workers in Tanzania or Kenya who'd perfected a way of using phials that had contained penicillin as containers for eye drops.

We ooh'ed and ah'ed about that. It looked impressive. Once the penicillin has been extracted from it the container is sterile and, with the addition of a little plastic device, you could convert it into a sterile eye-dropper. Or close to sterile;

with an eye-dropper, a little non-sterile matter shouldn't be a problem. Very useful for everyone except people who might happen to have a reaction to penicillin. Very bad news for them. But here I was, four or five days later, seeing a process that was producing utterly sterile intravenous fluid in a cave! I was impressed.

I also visited the Nacfa front because I wanted to see the conditions under which the fighters were working. I didn't want to just drift in, do my thing in the hospital and wander off. At that time, I had no idea that my involvement with the Eritreans would become as intense as it has. It was one of those long, bruising night drives that ended about three am A woman named Chuchu was my minder and she showed me into the basement of what had once been a house. The town of Nacfa has been levelled from the air, but the Eritreans have re-created it, as it were, underground. I was shown a cement floor and given a blanket. I thought, *Shit, no chance of a sleep here*. I was so tired I was asleep within minutes.

Chuchu woke me up just before dawn and we drove up a valley and reached an underground bunker where a lot of fighters were sitting around. We got into a trench-line and followed it up a ridge. I noticed that, at some points, the trench appeared to cut through solid granite. I wondered about that. The Eritreans are slim and I was rather overweight so I had difficulty getting through at various points, but we worked our way up. Every so often there was a sentinel point, occupied by two Eritreans, sometimes two men, sometimes two women or one of each. Invariably, they were helpful and pleasant to this puffing gent. Eventually we got to a point where we could wriggle up through a hole to a dugout and look through an agricultural pipe down the ridge.

Chuchu said, 'Fred, look through this pipe and you'll see the Ethiopians. But don't let your head completely cover the opening, or they might see the shadow from below.'

I was very nervous, not only worried about being shot at, but at the thought that I could get stuck in the hole on the way down. I took a quick, sideways sort of look. I could see the soldiers moving around, about a hundred metres away. That was enough for me.

We went back to the dugouts and Chuchu told me that the troops who weren't up in the trenches were 'at their lessons'. That was a new one on me and I asked her what she meant. She took me down to a big dugout, not more than a hundred metres from the actual front, and I found thirty or forty people all having an animated discussion in Tigrinian. I asked her what they were talking about.

'Hygiene,' she said.

CHAPTER 20

The Amazing Eritreans

Spill your sweat to save your blood.

Eritrean saying

That first visit to Eritrea gave me a lot to think about. It seemed to me that here was a bunch of people actually getting on top of some of the worst health problems in the Third World and equipped to do even better than that.

Take the matter of malaria. Through the 1960s it was thought that WHO and other agencies were getting on top of malaria and that it could be eradicated from the planet, like smallpox. But that hasn't happened: malaria is on the increase. About 5 million children in the Third World get malaria each year and it is still killing people. It's treatable if you can identify it. The Eritreans are producing the drugs *and* they have developed a little plastic microscope which just consists of two lenses and a hinged barrel. With the sun for illumination you can put a slide with a blood sample in and make a diagnosis of malaria. Cheap, simple effective technology.

On the question of hygiene they are remarkable. You don't see any food scraps, paper, plastic wrapping or anything like that lying around an Eritrean camp. Partly this is for security reasons, to cut down on the risk of the site being seen from the air. But it's more than that. It is a recognition of the relationship between dirt and disease.

I was doing a ward round one afternoon and I kept hearing explosions — *boom*, *crump*, *boom*. I asked what it was and they told me not to worry about it. I insisted and the only answer I got was that it was Tuesday afternoon. After some more questioning, I discovered that the noises were bottles and aerosols exploding in the rubbish pits. On Tuesday afternoons all the rubbish is cleared up, burned and buried. Why Tuesday? Because it's a day that won't offend the sensibilities of either Muslims or Christians. They have created a sort of brief weekend comprising of Tuesday afternooon and Wednesday. Very pragmatic, the Eritreans.

I couldn't help thinking of the strides we could make in Aboriginal health if we could collect the young people together and get them to engage in a serious discussion about hygiene. The effects of this attitude can be readily seen in the eyes. Among the first batch of patients I saw were two young men, one eighteen the other twenty-seven years of age, who had trachoma so advanced that it required eyelid surgery to save their sight. Obviously, they had grown up in a home environment where rudimentary hygiene was not possible. I was alarmed and examined all twenty-six children in the hospital valley. Only two of them had signs of trachoma and the cases were very mild, not requiring treatment. I inferred that, in spite of the remoteness of the area, the scarcity of water and the problems caused by the war, the EPLF organisation has achieved good home hygiene. This was not the case everywhere. In one refugee camp the incidence of follicular trachoma among the children was 35 per cent, but the difference between Eritreans and others is that when a problem is pointed out to them they are not happy until they find the means of solving it.

The Eritreans' capacity for work amazed me. I still don't know how they managed to dig through the granite to construct their trenches. Some of the wells appeared to have been dug through solid rock, too. One of them told me that they have a saying: 'Spill your sweat to save your blood'. I suppose that explains it. The day after I had done my first stint of night-time surgery, which I found pretty exhausting, I went for a walk past the operating rooms. There, drying in the sun, were the operating gowns and drapes. I realised that the staff hadn't knocked off with us surgeons, but had done the theatre laundry before going to bed.

I came back all fired up and got stuck into helping to arrange support for the Eritreans. I joined the committee of the Eritrean Relief Association. The Australia-Eritrea Health Link and the Eritrean Blindness Prevention Program, partly under the auspices of Austcare, are the organisational arms of that support. Desbele completed his training and did a lot of good work on Thursday Island with Dr Gary Brian, a senior lecturer in the University of New South Wales medical school and an excellent teacher of surgery. He wanted to go to Eritrea, the way a lot of people do who hear about the remarkable things going on out there. We raised $15,000 to buy a teaching operating microscope which is a big piece of equipment, weighing about half a ton. Desbele, Gary and the microscope went off but the Sudanese wouldn't let the equipment through customs. Gary arrived in Eritrea with a supply of intra-ocular lenses and other things that he couldn't use for want of a microscope. That was very disappointing.

I made my second trip to Eritrea in January of 1990. I had a lot of equipment with me and my intention was to do some intra-ocular lens implants and other operations, assess what Desbele needed and so on.

I got to Orotta and Desbele wasn't there. I was absolutely furious, after all the effort we'd put in to train this surgeon and he wasn't on the job. I had a suspicion that he was away fighting and that made me even madder. I went around saying that any ratbag can take up a gun and shoot people. I'm afraid I was rather rude about it. The Eritreans were polite but refused to tell me where Desbele was. I was interviewed by a woman from the EPLF radio, which is broadcast in all the hill camps and is a most important form of communication, and I spoke my mind. I said that Desbele had only taken one set of instruments for cataract operations with him and that I suspected he was doing front line surgery instead of setting up the blindness prevention program. As far as I know, my remarks weren't edited.

Nothing for it but to get to work. On my first visit I'd shown Alemo and another doctor how to do a ketesey, which is an eyelid operation to relieve the effects of trachoma. Done properly, it's a very good operation and I was delighted to find that they had done a lot of them and done them excellently. They were very good eyelid surgeons but weak in intra-ocular work because they lacked proper magnification and illumination. But the good work I saw helped to mollify me somewhat.

In fact, I had gone in pretty ignorant on that second visit and, apart from doing a lot of surgery, I also learned a great deal more about the Eritreans' struggle. In the first place, I learned that Desbele had not just gone off to fight in some skirmish but had been present at the capture of Massawa, one of the greatest tactical victories of the twentieth century. Attacking from the sea, the Eritreans sank sixteen of the twenty-three ships in the Ethiopian navy and subdued the naval base. The EPLF land forces got the Ethiopians in a cross fire and caused nine thousand casualties. Eritrean casualties were light. It was all due to meticulous planning executed with the tightest security, so I could understand why, in the days preceding the battle, the Eritreans didn't tell me where Desbele was or what he was doing.

Likewise in my dealings with Amna Nur Hussein. I'd become uneasy about her going around, well behind the lines, with a big Soviet or Chinese pistol strapped to her belt, along with a couple of grenades. I asked her why she was so heavily armed.

'That's to protect you, Fred.'

I'm a bit funny about firearms, I suppose. I've had a lot to do with them but I don't like them. I reckon they should be kept somewhere and only brought out for use, not toted about. I thought the pistol-wearing might be some kind of officer mystique, the sort of thing I'm very impatient with. Amna Nur Hussein is a great woman, much admired and respected and, like Ascarlu, another woman I worked with, a member of the EPLF Central Committee which is an important office. But, for all that, I thought she could take a little ribbing. I sang the song that goes:

> Drinkin' beer in a cabaret and dancin' with a blonde,
> Till one night she shot out the light and bang that
> blonde was gone.
> Lay your pistol down, babe, lay that pistol down,
> Pistol packin' mama, lay that pistol down.

That caught on with the Eritreans and they all started to sing it to Amna. But I was wrong. I didn't understand the situation until a good deal later. At that time, in the area we were in, the ELF was still operating and it was not unknown for them to ambush a small, vulnerable truck convoy or take pot-shots at people. So Amna *was* armed for my protection.

I'd taken photographs around the town of Nacfa on my first visit, including one of a valley with a lot of prickly pear. The landscape reminded me of parts of South Australia. Back in Sydney an Eritrean told me that I'd actually taken a picture of the nerve centre of the Nacfa front — the place from which the defeat of the biggest army in Africa had been masterminded. By the time of my second visit the Nacfa front had moved 200 kilometres to the south, reflecting the Eritreans' success. The battle of Afabet had been fought and won. There were thirty thousand Ethiopian casualties and the Eritreans captured scores of Russian tanks and vast quantities of military equipment. I saw hillsides where battles had been fought and the bones of the dead were poking out through the rocks and grass, bleached by the sun.

War is a dreadful and inhumane business by definition, but, as far as I could tell, the Etritreans did all they could to mitigate its horrors. They certainly didn't use their own keen, young fighters as shock troops the way the Iranians, or the British generals in World War 1 had. And their treatment of prisoners was humane. I was frequently asked to examine and treat Ethiopian prisoners and the people conducting them to the clinics treated them with compassion. I saw several POW camps in which the treatment of the prisoners was good, in complete contrast to the brutality the Ethiopians inflicted on EPLF prisoners.

But now I was really seeing the trauma cases and they presented me with a dilemma. In particular, I met two young fighters who had been blinded by the foreign bodies blasted into their eyes. They were Ahmed Umer who was twenty-six, and Teklu Tesfamichael who was only twenty-one. I thought that modern surgery might possibly restore some vision to them. In both cases the right eyes were incurably damaged, but each could distinguish between light and dark with the left eye.

What was required, firstly, was a special kind of x-ray to determine the nature and location of the foreign bodies. Then I could do a vitrectomy, that is, operate on the vitreous humour, the jelly-like substance that fills the back of the eye. Retinal detachments would probably be necessary and possibly corneal surgery. Expensive equipment and prolonged and difficult surgery. It would cost, say twelve thousand dollars to bring them to Australia and who was to say that would be money well spent? There were so many medical problems and competing claims on the resources. Twelve grand buys an awful lot of antibiotics. I put it to Narayo and his opinion was that nothing was too good for those young fellows. I knew of a good hospital and top surgeon in Saudi Arabia and I thought I could arrange to have the work done there and payment made from my private practice fund in Sydney. But the Saudis never responded to requests for visas and other documentation and in the end we, that is the Eritrean Relief Association, had to bring them to Australia.

That was a sad business. Each of them had more than twenty foreign bodies in their eyes and I had thought that some of this might be ferrous, magnetic material. As a result of the industrial revolution a whole set of skills had been evolved for removing ferrous foreign bodies from eyes very dextrously. When I was trained this was one of the basic areas. The story is that foreign bodies cause fibroblastic activity, the growth of fibrous tissue. This doesn't happen much in older people but in the young there can be vigorous fibroblastic activity and it can cause great damage in the retina. The effect is like crinkling the film in a camera, destroying the image-preserving capability.

The stuff in these men's eyes was mostly rock fragments and bits of cordite and nitrates and nothing could be done for them. Their arrival generated some publicity which was helpful, but I was greatly distressed by my inability to help them. That's the hardest thing in eye work, to have someone go blind or be unable to restore sight. There are lots of jokes about doctors burying their mistakes, but there is no such relief in ophthalmology. Every blind patient is a reproach and a cause of anguish.

CHAPTER 21

Beyond Asmara

Liberation, a human phenomenon, cannot be achieved by semi-humans.

Paulo Freire, Pedagogy of the Oppressed

It would be nice to be able to say that the idea of establishing an intra-ocular lens factory in Eritrea came to me when I woke up in a bed which had been occupied by an Ethiopian general who had been personally executed, with a bullet in the back of the neck, by Mengistu. I did indeed sleep in such a bed, but the idea had no such dramatic genesis.

The Eritreans' manufacturing and adapting skills made a deep impression on me. I could never forget the first time I saw the 'garage' at Himbol — it consisted of several kilometres of creek bed lit by neon lights strung along in the acacia trees. The mechanics were taking out differentials and gear boxs and replacing axles in trucks and jeeps and earth-moving equipment. It was the most basic, and most efficient, 'workshop' I had ever seen.

The underground plastics factory, where hundreds of items were stamped out per hour, and the pharmeceutical manufacturing plant, never suffered a power failure or a significant mechanical breakdown. In a way, this expertise was not surprising. The people from the Horn of Africa began to take an interest in European industrialisation as soon as it got underway. I've read a report on a group of 'Abyssinians' visting the Lancashire cotton mills towards the end of the eighteenth century and exhibiting a keen interest in steam-driven cotton cloth manufacture. The Arabs had introduced weaving and metal-working and, after the Italian occupation in the 1930s, the Eritreans were throughly industrialised.

The Eritreans manufactured intravenous fluids which we used with great success in eye operations. The eye has to be kept spherical by the administration of a fluid during a lens implantation procedure and I have found the Eritrean-manufactured fluids to be excellent. If the fluid is the slightest bit too alkaline or is pyrogenic or too concentrated, the cornea can be damaged. I have not had one case of 'hazy cornea' as a result of imperfect fluid. Given this, I could see no reason why they couldn't manufacture intra-ocular lenses in Eritrea. These are the most expensive little bits of plastic in existence. In Australia each lens costs $140, which is a prohibitive price for Africans. In Eritrea they could make them for a tenth of that price, or less. This would be of enormous benefit to the Eritreans themselves, but they could also export them to the rest of the Third World at an affordable price. I became very excited by this idea of Eritrea becoming a model of the way a Third World country could break the cycle of First World exploitation and privilege, and further its own economic development in the process.

I sold this idea to some of the EPLF leaders like Assaias Afawerkie, who is the general secretary and commander in chief. It has his total support. I don't pretend that it is an idea that arose among the Eritreans themselves, although I do believe that they would have come to it. When they reached the point of having ten surgeons implanting lenses and making inroads on the blindness problem, they would have seen the benefit. But I've tried to push it ahead a bit and it has become the centrepiece of my efforts in Eritrea. I say 'centre-piece' because the lens factory will be only part of a whole process, some of which is going on now. On my third trip to Eritrea I mainly concentrated on the training of 'barefoot doctors' — men and women with good hands who are capable of performing cataract extractions and implanting lenses. On the fourth visit the team took back about $200,000 worth of equipment — five operating microscopes, five sets of instruments, two thousand intraocular lenses and other things to push this process along.

Eye surgery, unlike other operations, can be performed without having a large sterile field. It can be done on a table in an ordinary room and even, as in Eritrea, in bunkers and dugouts, because you're not up to your elbows in offal. In eye surgery no part of an instrument that is touched by hand touches the eye tissue. And the instruments are easily sterilised either by heating, which can be done in a small hot-air oven or even an ordinary pressure cooker, or by wiping them with alcohol. Ruit has done thousands of operations in Nepal in schools and halls. You just set up your operating microscope and do it, wiping your hands and the instruments with surgical spirit between cases. I mentioned before that Ram Pohkrel had done one hundred and forty cataract extractions in one day — they were all done with the same set of tools.

The point is that the technology is appropriate to the circumstances and the effect is dramatic. In Eritrea I saw Desbele operate on a patient, a forty-year-old farmer from Danakil, said to be the hottest place on earth. This man, in his prime, was led into the clinic, totally blind. Within a very few days he had some vision and was walking around unaided. This is a common occurrence in Australia, but not in Africa.

In Australia, cataract extraction is the next most common operation to abortion, and no-one is blinded by cataract alone. We have 400 eye surgeons in this country; the whole of Africa has slightly fewer but its population is 500 million against our 17 million. In Africa about 3½ million people per year go blind for want of eye surgery. Africa cannot wait the twelve or so years it takes to train an eye surgeon in the developed world. Looking ahead, to a period after the war, I can envisage a Horn of Africa microscopic surgery workshop. A hands-on affair that could draw people from East Africa, Ethiopia, the Sudan, the Yemen, Somalia, Djibouti. It's a kind of dream — to think of this clinic being held in Asmara and the eye doctors being shown over the lens factory.

But the idea is entirely practical and there are precedents. A group of Eritreans, who had lived in the United States for a time, went back home with machinery and materials to establish a dry-cell battery factory. The plant was worth more than US$1 million and it's been a winner. The efforts of myself and many others to raise A$1 million to finance the lens factory appear to have been successful, and on my proposed visit in 1991 we were to select a site in Asmara.

I have been unashamed in my efforts to advertise and promote the Australia-Eritrea Health link, to the extent of stunts like the construction in the Hyde Park barracks in Sydney of a mock-up clinic, a thatched tent something like the sort of rural health facilities you get in Eritrea. We had some Eritreans acting as patients and the actor Jack Thompson, in his role as a goodwill ambassador for the UN High Commissioner for refugees, came along to give it a bit more clout.

If it helps real, living people then I am not going to worry about professional decorum, good taste or anything else. Suggestions that the work is somehow tainted by the adoption of modern marketing methods, or accusations of staging political stunts, don't cut any ice with me. These things are inevitably political, and I made no bones about how I felt about Australia supporting an oil-rich emirate in the Persian gulf when there were crying medical needs at home and abroad.

The publicity has been beneficial and, in fact, the idea is undergoing a kind of expansion. Plans are afoot for lens factories in Nepal and India and there are funds available from various sources. If we're talking about three factories we can

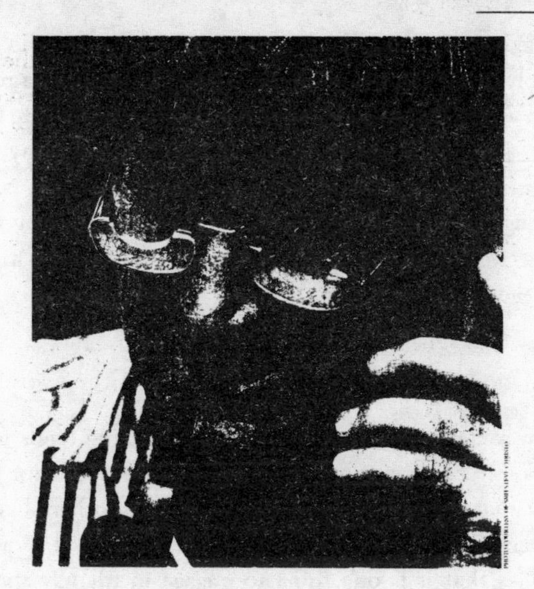

You don't need to be a surgeon to restore someone's sight.

It's a simple operation.

Professor Fred Hollows, eye surgeon and 1990's Australian of the Year, initiated the AUSTCARE-Eritrea Blindness Prevention Programme.

By using a simple artificial lens, sight can be restored to around 30,000 Eritreans blinded by cataracts each year.

However, the cost of these lenses is extraordinarily high.

Fred Hollows' bold plan is to build an Intra Ocular Lens Factory on Eritrean soil.

The cost of the lenses would then drop from around $150 each to less than $2 each for the Eritreans.

Give now to the Austcare-Eritrea Blindness Prevention Programme.
Ask at your nearest OPSM or call Austcare - 008 021 103.

PROUDLY SPONSORED BY

OPSM and Austcare helped with a fund-raising exercise for the lens factory, using this poster.

do a better deal with the American engineers who are to supply the necessary equipment. Dr John Cooper, a medical man with an exceptional business brain, is going along to help with some of the managerial arrangements. In my wilder moments I can imagine a whole network of lens factories throughout what is sometimes called 'the developing world'. That would help to make the word 'developing' a reality instead of a euphemism.

I am sometimes asked, as I go about seeking funds for this work, why I am so optimistic about the prospects for Eritrea now that the war is over. Why do I, and others like Tom Keneally, have such faith in the Eritreans? The question implies that it is one thing to engage in friendly shoulder-bumping, to appear to love and respect your leaders and to be tolerant towards all shades of opinion under the pressure of war, and quite another to maintain these virtues under conditions of peace. It has to be admitted that the peace offers new challenges to the Horn Of Africa's people.

I am optimistic because I believe the Eritrean intelligentsia has thoroughly analysed the situation and been able to communicate the results of the analysis to the population at large. I have seen an infibulated woman as I was in the process of removing some skin from her leg for a graft. Like clitorectomy, infibulation — the partial sewing-up of the vagina to prevent intercourse — is an horrific practice which was deeply rooted in the traditions of Eritrea. But it is completely rejected by the EPLF on the grounds that the emancipation of women is a cornerstone of their revolution.

In Eritrea it is almost exasperating to find out how thoroughly ideas from outside have been discussed and digested. English has been spoken in the Sudan and Kenya for a long time and is widely understood; the Ethiopians sent their intellectuals to the Soviet Union and the People's Republic of

China and they know the difference between the two forms of socialism. To their great discredit, the Ethiopians brought in East Germans to advise about security arrangements, so something is known of East German Communism. They learned about Cuba when the Cuban mercenaries came in, and people return from all over the world — America, Australia, southern Europe, northern Europe, Scandinavia. The place is a sponge for ideas and influences. People from all over the world are attracted to what they hear about Eritrea. Something of this comes through in Tom Keneally's novel and I've seen it myself. You stop somewhere, generally early in the morning before sunup, to gas up or change vehicles, and you're likely to be thrown in with all sorts — people making a film for American television, or aid workers from Germany or a geological survey mob — and ideas get floated. About AIDS, or the ozone layer, or any bloody thing, and there'll be some Eritrean there who's heard about it, read about it and has something useful to say. You can be sitting in a camp, hot and dirty after a day's travelling, and hear Eritreans discussing Japanese audio-visual technology or Swedish movies.

This sophistication augurs well, I think, but it's not going to be a bed of roses, even assuming that foreign powers, which so far have done nothing but harm in the Horn, stay out. Over the decades the Eritreans have absorbed and developed an extraordinary amount of idealism. For example, when Desbele was out here, he won $12 in a darts game. He was very reluctant to take his winnings.

'You are trying to make a capitalist of me,' he said. This over a prize of $12!

They are going to have to overcome some of those scruples to adopt an effective mixed economy which is what they'll need to get their country out of the Third World slough. When you think about it, First World countries experience earthquakes and droughts and floods but the citizenry, as a whole, doesn't succumb to starvation and disease. Why not? Because they have industrialised economies and can *buy* the means of survival and *finance* the rehabilitation of devastated areas. Even improve them. That's what the Third World countries are going to have to do. At present, subsistence agriculturalists in dependent, unindustrialised economies are helpless in the face of natural disasters.

I believe that the Eritreans are equal to this task and I want to help them. They are certainly ready to help themselves. I can recall being in an Eritrean Relief Association guesthouse in She'b, knackered after a night's travel, and hearing a group of Eritrean lawyers, just back from the US, discussing an Eritrean constitution. They were talking about Roman and Greek law and the constitutions of the western democracies and Islamic law and the whole gamut of relevant historical experience. Whatever happens in Eritrea now that the war is over will be hotly debated and the debate will be very informed. The people have fought so hard for so long that I very much doubt that the opportunists and self-seekers will get a look-in.

It has been a very long time since that meeting with Garfield Todd in Palmerston North, when I naively asked about the possibilities of cooperating with the ANC and had Todd walk out on us. I've learned a few lessons since then. Chief among them is to avoid the bureaucrats and deal directly with the people involved if at all possible. This approach has not always made me popular — within the university I know that my reluctance to fill in leave forms has caused some consternation — but I think it bore fruit in the trachoma program and it suits the situation in Eritrea where the separation of functions between bureaucrats and doers is close to non-existent. There is something immensely refreshing, even inspiring, in Eritrean social and political habits. To help restore sight in their people and possibly contribute to the creation of, in Tom Keneally's phrase, 'the first democratic republic in Africa' is to go some way towards thanking the Eritreans for reinforcing a Kiwi-turned-Australian eye-doctor's belief in our common humanity and the essential goodness of human beings.

CHAPTER 22

Cataract Triangle — Eritrea, Nepal and Vietnam

> 'Unity, the great unity, for victory, the great victory'; this slogan launched by President Ho Chi Minh became a reality, a great reality during the long and hard resistance.
>
> *Vo Nguyen Giap*, People's War, People's Army

Two republics and one kingdom, each subjected to intense colonisation in the past, each fighting its way towards a vision of the future. The choice of Eritrea and Nepal as areas in which to work was, as I have explained, partly accidental and personal. The same was true of Vietnam. As a young medical student in Dunedin, I recall attending a party in May 1954 at the home of Bill Glass, a well-heeled fellow student. He startled everybody present by proposing a toast: 'To General Vo Nguyen Giap and the forces of the Viet-Minh who have this day defeated the French at Dien Bien Phu.' I had followed the forty year struggle of the Vietnamese people with interest and admiration and, when it seemed likely that the idea of the transportable lens factory would benefit from an economy of scale, Vietnam was an obvious choice as a possible third location.

I made my first trip to liberated Eritrea in August 1991 along with Drs John Cooper, Mark Gillies and Gary Brian. We were accompanied by several journalists and my friend the documentary film-maker, Pat Fiske. We transited smoothly through Khartoum airport, normally an unthinkable thing to do on account of the rife corruption and inefficiency, but things appeared to be changing fast in this part of Africa. We caught a Fokker 50 charter flight to Asmara — a bumpy ride and landing which brought us in at 1 a.m. to a tremendously warm welcome. All 56 pieces of equipment we had shipped arrived undamaged, a remarkable feat due to Gillies' application.

The beautiful Italianate city of Asmara, so emotionally described to me by Eritreans over the years, lived up to their glowing portraits. I was astonished at the lack of tension in a city so recently liberated after such a long and bloody struggle. The military presence was muted; the citizenry appeared busy and cheerful and everything I saw confirmed my hope that the Eritrean People's Liberation Front means to put its egalitarian, democratic and civilising principles firmly into practice.

I met with Assaias Afawerkie and the heads of the foreign affairs and security departments as well as many senior administrators and was impressed by their confidence and dedication. As an example of the spirit prevailing, the EPLF has determined that its members will continue to work without payment for a further two years, receiving only food, shelter and clothing when what they have wears out. In practical terms this means that Desbele, now working in a large hospital, will have an Ethiopian colleague who owns an Alfa Romeo motor car. Desbele is unconcerned.

We took $140,000 dollars worth of equipment, some of it paid for by the Australian government, some by money raised from other Australian sources, to Eritrea. It all functioned perfectly. The video attached to the teaching microscope had great clarity and will be of enormous value in the instruction process. Our team set about training and honing the skills of eight Eritrean surgeons with good results. A great deal of modern cataract surgery was performed, incorporating the implantation of intra-ocular lenses (IOLs) with outstanding success.

The drought eased in the Horn of Africa in 1991 and this, plus the end of war, has meant that the herders returned to their former occupations. In Eritrea many of the goat-herders are children. Tragically, they are being blown up by mines of Russian, American and Israeli manufacture left behind by the Dergue forces. I was introduced to this disaster by Michael Ghebrehiwot, a front-line surgeon who said to me, 'Fred, what are we going to do about the mines? In the past week I've amputated limbs from five children.' No location maps of these deadly mines exist and, as many of them are plastic, they cannot be found by metal detectors. The mines will remain active for at least ten years and will cause untold casualties unless Eritrea receives some outside help. It seems to me that if a hereditary plutocracy like that in Kuwait can rid itself of mines the people of Eritrea should be helped by western military expertise to do the same. There are large debts to be paid in the Horn of Africa.

Among the equipment we took was a B-scanner, an ultrasound device that enables the condition of opaque eyes to be investigated. A B-scanner can determine whether or not the retina is still in place in a damaged eye and indicate patients suitable for surgery. I had thought this would be employed in cases of Eritrean fighters blinded by bombs and grenades. So it proved, but the B-scanner will help assess the damage in the children injured in mine explosions — a useful tool until the scourge of the mines is removed.

In medical matters, as in all areas of administration, some problems are already surfacing. Which area of medical work should have priority? There are various levels of medical experience and skill — the 'barefoot doctors', the nurses, the 'war doctors' (non degree-holding front-line surgeons who have dealt with the most grievous injuries) and medical officers. The question as to how these splendid human resources are best deployed is something I have been asked to advise upon.

A suitable site was found in Asmara for the lens factory and word had spread rapidly about this piece of practical and developmental aid being supported by Australia. I made several radio broadcasts and was presented with an award of honorary citizenship of free Eritrea — the first foreigner to be so honoured. Eritreans place a great value on the family and are intrigued by the case of a considerably mature person like myself having such young offspring. I was told that my children have thousands of cousins in Eritrea.

Perhaps the most exhilarating experience was to move around the country during the day without fear of attack by MIGs. To see a hospital working smoothly and efficiently with a reliable power source and dedicated staff is an inspiring sight anywhere in the Third World; to see it in Eritrea, where until recently a medical centre was as fit a target as a tank, was like a miracle.

I had some health problems, most annoyingly a shortness of breath. Asmara is over 2000 metres above sea level and the air was too thin for my damaged lungs. Stair-climbing was a misery. As a result, to my regret, I had to pass up the opportunity to visit Addis Ababa, which is somewhat higher. I would have liked to have seen the ancient centre of civilisation from which so much has flowed — for good and evil — to shape history in the Horn of Africa.

In December 1991 I made my fifth visit to Nepal to help with the training of eye surgeons, discuss the establishment of a lens factory and renew the links formed by the Nepal Eye Program-Australia. A television team from the Nine Network accompanied us to film the proceedings and they got dramatic footage of the work being done in the eye camps.

Dr Sanduk Ruit has now carried out more than 5000 cataract extractions with the implantation of IOLs under what might be called 'field' conditions — in village huts, meeting houses, schools and the like. No one surgeon in the world has performed at this level and Ruit's rate of success is extremely high. No-one else does the operation quite like Ruit for speed, dexterity and precision and fortunate indeed is the Nepalese patient who comes under his care.

In the 1990s, in every developed country in the world when the crystallised, opaque material known as a cataract is removed from the front of the eye it is replaced through extra-capsular surgery with an intra-ocular lens. Typically, the recipient of this piece of plastic can see well enough to cross busy streets, play golf, drive a motor car or operate machinery. Not so in the Third World. There, following old-style intra-capsular surgery, the patient is usually given a cumbersome pair of thick spectacles. Sight is restored in the treated eye but not field of vision nor peripheral vision. The experience has been described as 'like imagining the first third of your footstep falling through space'.[1]

Because people know about this far from satisfactory result, there was never been a strong demand for cataract surgery in the developing world. People have preferred to work with their failing, but familiar, vision to the point of blindness, rather than cope with the spectacles and imperfect sight which is the best that intra-capsular surgery has been able to offer. Nowhere was this more true than in Nepal, where flat ground is the exception. The ability to travel over uneven surfaces is almost the first requirement of survival and the Nepalese whose sight has been restored by *modern* surgery has been given a new lease of life, quite literally.

The television crew filmed the story of a woman from a

---

[1] The terminology, which relates to the details of the surgery, is confusing. For ease of understanding, intra-capsular equals old surgery equals thick glasses; extra-capsular equals modern surgery with lens implant.

high mountain village who was blinded by cataract in her forties, a comparatively early age. Cataract for the most part is a condition associated with age but it can be accelerated by exposure to excessive amounts of ultra-violet light, a hazard not uncommon in snowfall areas. This woman was assisted down to the eye hosptial, quite blind. She was operated upon by Ruit with all his customary skill and was able, very soon afterwards, to take the track back to her village, carrying a bundle, to spin and weave — an independent operator once again.

The film captured other, sadder histories, such as the case of the small boy blinded by keratomalacia. This is a progressive disease in which the cornea is softened and may become perforated. It has a single and easily correctable cause — Vitamin A deficiency. There is not only an urgent need for appropriate Vitamin A capsules in the developing countries, but also for a better understanding of how people in these societies live. I recall getting into an argument with a researcher who had made a considerable reputation by showing the dramatic improvement in general health experienced by African children who were fed green, leafy vegetables. I was prompted to ask him why the mothers hadn't fed their children in this way and he replied that they were too ignorant to do so. This made me angry. People are never, in my belief, too ignorant to guarantee their own survival. On a little reflection better answers to the question emerge, for example that green, leafy vegetables may well have provoked diarrhoea and digestive disorders *more threatening* than the vitamin deficiency. When respect for the dignity of human beings is omitted from medical assessment, medicine ceases to become a science and is in danger of becoming a set of formulas, as arid and unhelpful as spells, curses and other hocus-pocus.

In April 1992, I travelled to Vietnam accompanied by Mike Lynskey and Dr John Cooper, fellow directors of the Fred Hollows Foundation, an organisation we set up to raise funds for the work in developing countries. We went to Vietnam to investigate the feasibility of establishing an intra-ocular lens factory in that country, along the lines of those underway for Eritrea and Nepal.

The need is great. Every year, approximately 150,000 people go blind from cataract in Vietnam and fewer than 15,000 cataracts are taken out. That is a telling statistic of under-privilege in itself — in Australia cataract removal is available to all. But the full reality is worse. Only the very wealthy get intra-ocular lenses in Vietnam. The rest must cope with the baffling, immobilising results of the old style of cataract surgery.

The struggle of the Vietnamese against the Japanese, French and Americans was protracted, like the Eritrean opposition to Ethiopia, and had the same result — the victory of nationalist democracy over colonialism and imperialism. For me, as a resister of bureaucrats, believer in democracy and worker for human rights, the Vietnamese victory was an inspiration. But the American trade and aid boycott still continues and the country is in economic difficulties. It seemed to me only natural that those of us who had supported the Vietnamese in their military struggle who were in a position to help them in their economic contest should do so.

I am, I suppose, a theoretical Marxist who recognises the productive capacity of capitalism. The collapse of communism, lamentable in some ways, drives the point home. Indications were that Vietnam, never run on doctrinaire Marxist lines, would be disposed to manufacture the sight-restoring intra-ocular lenses at a fraction of the present cost (about $US150), use them to combat cataract blindness at home and export them at a profit to the rest of Asia and beyond. The profit, which I would prefer to call a 'surplus', should be reinvested — more manufacturing plants, more lenses, fewer blind people, reduced dependence on interest-hungry First-World capital.

So the visit to Vietnam was a feeler. I wondered whether we would see signs of the Eritrean nobility of spirit, the masterly surgical skills of Ruit in Nepal, or the corruption and conservatism that had turned me off in Burma and Bangladesh.

From the first, the signs were positive. The Director of the National Institute of Ophthalmology, Professor Nguyen Trong Nhan, Russian-trained, quadri-lingual, friendly and forceful, had fought as an artillery-man against the French. His two brothers were killed in the conflict. During the American war he had operated in Hanoi in bomb shelters, a stressful experience familiar to me from Eritrea. Professor Nhan is a man you can work with.

Most of my time in the first phase of the visit, in the north, was spent talking to the eye surgeons in Hanoi and inspecting operating conditions and techniques in the provincial hospitals and commune health centres, pushing the view that intra-ocular lenses could and should be made in Vietnam. The visit had been well publicised and attendance at the lectures was strong. There were press conferences in which Vietnamese politeness was scrupulously observed before the tough questions were asked: 'Why has it taken you so long to get here?' and 'Vietnam is a poor country and we have been told we cannot afford these lenses. Why are you saying something different?'

Vietnam is well supplied with eye doctors, about 600 trained to varying degrees. They are paid approximately $US10 per month and work long hours. Private practice is permitted, but time and appropriate premises are a problem. Wives work; government employees are enjoined to have a maximum of two children. The doctors yearn to improve their own material circumstances and the quality of the services they can provide. At one lecture I asked a batch of them: 'Do you want to implant intra-ocular lenses?' Hands shot up from the normally reticent and undemonstrative audience.

The country appears to be developing fast. In the cities and towns the air is thick with building dust. Some of the activity may be repair or replacement of war-damaged structures, but the people are disinclined to talk about the war and it is hard to tell. Trucks, most of them very old, carry huge loads of sand, timber and reinforcing rods. In the temperate north and tropical south, men and women sweat — excavating, laying bricks, mixing cement. In the hotel bars and embassy function rooms the talk is of deals, joint ventures, aid packages and investment . . .

I was encouraged by our reception and we got quickly down to the nuts and bolts of modern eye surgery — the necessity for operating microscopes, stable high-quality fluids and instruments.

Early on in the piece, I put an urgent, non-professional question to Professor Nhan: 'When can I meet General Giap?'

From what I saw in the commune health centres, I concluded that the Vietnamese surgeons were deft and confident, although the equipment and techniques were sadly outmoded. Cataracts were being extracted by the old Chinese method, in which a heated silicone ball is used to remove the capsule and crystallised lens. This is not done through innate conservatism, but because the surgeons do not have modern instruments. 'If you're good,' I said in one lecture, 'the surgery can be done with a razor chip (which is what I saw in use several times), 'but a 64 Beaver blade is better.' Heads nodded affirmatively. Vietnam can make the instruments, given the transfer of capital and skills.

The team travelled to the port city of Haiphong to see eye-doctoring in the surrounding provinces and to be received by a group from the People's Committee of this region which suffered severely from bomb damage in the war. The Vietnamese are not puritanical, and at a lively lunch I attempted to tell an improper joke. 'In France a French letter is called an

English cap,' I began. 'Why?' asked the interpreter. That got a much bigger laugh than my joke.

We went to Halong Bay up near the border with China, and took a boat trip to the Thousand Islands, remarkable upthrusts of rock thinly covered with vegetation that run for many miles up the coast. The people who fish in these waters live a very traditional life aboard their boats which were fragile-looking but well maintained and clean. The children, I was encouraged to see, looked healthy. With one of the Hanoi doctors acting as interpreter, we learned from a fisherman that his family had followed the occupation for 'many generations' and that the only major disturbance in their lives had been the American war. They had to run for the cover of the islands when the B52s filled the sky.

After the inspections and lectures and working meals and before the departure for the south there was one more appointment to keep — the hoped-for meeting with General Giap. On the first day in Hanoi we made the obligatory visit to Ho Chi Minh's mausoleum, an intensely ugly building. More interesting than the waxy, embalmed remains was the house Ho had occupied in a garden setting nearby. After the defeat of the French he had rejected a rococo French building in favour of a simple timber structure with an austere bedroom and study above and a plain meeting room below.

General Giap's style was the same as that of his former comrade. The meeting was held in a large, tastefully decorated room in a stylish but functional wing of the government guest house. A pair of young women served refreshments, but otherwise the General had no attendants. A small, dignified figure in a plain grey uniform, he appeared to be well-briefed and to have a clear understanding of why these somewhat scruffy looking foreigners were in his country.

General Giap is a legendary figure in Vietnam. A former Professor of history, he has entered the history books himself. No modern account of Vietnam omits to mention his military and political achievements. Now 82, he still holds a ministerial position in the government of the republic. Books were signed and exchanged. The general was no shirker of the truth. Through an interpreter he said: 'Australian soldiers fought against the Vietnamese people. But that is in the past and many things have changed . . .' He seemed to be particularly taken by my son, Cam, and had him sit next to him. He said he would remember the visit and hoped for a strengthening of ties between Australia and Vietnam. Lynskey, Cooper and I responded and photographs were taken.

I have met 'great' men before and said my piece, but something about General Giap humbled me. I'm told I was uncharacteristically quiet as I led the party out, holding my dog-eared, yellowed paperback copy of Giap's famous essay *People's War, People's Army*, containing a salutation in English and the general's elegant, almost ideographic signature.

A part of the strategy for the visit was not to appear as a well-funded, highly bureaucratised aid-team promising the world. When we arrived in the tropical heat of Ho Chi Minh City the point was amply made by the open-neck shirts and shorts favoured by the some of the members and the complete absence of ties and jackets. I had not packed a tie. Happily, the Vietnamese doctors did not seem to attach great importance to sumptuary rules. Tie-wearing among them noticeably dropped off as we spent more time together. More importantly, elitism was not apparent. As we boarded a river ferry, a man struggled to balance an enormous load of fibro roofing sheets on the handlebars of his bicycle. Two of the doctors jumped forward to lend a hand.

Dr Hoang Thi Luy, director of the Ophthalmology centre in Ho Chi Minh city, was an impressive woman who had several female lieutenants. Ophthalmology in the south appeared to be dominated by women, and several of the female surgeons in the eye departments of the southern hospitals asked me the most searching questions I had so far encountered. Like their counterparts in the north, they were anxious to do modern eye surgery. Several had trained in the US and were familiar with the procedures.

There is a long way to go before a Vietnam intra-ocular lens factory is a reality. At present, transportable lens factories are being built at Fairy Meadow, near Wollongong. A South African engineer named Steve Miller happened to be watching Clive Robertson's *The World Tonight* TV show when I appeared talking about the need for lenses in the developing world. Steve had been working as a production manager within the structure of the American-Australian joint venture enterprise which had built an IOL factory in Artarmon, Sydney. In fact it was Steve who got the factory up and running by modifying and adapting the existing imported equipment.

Then working at the University of Wollongong, but anxious to exercise his talents in a humanitarian direction, Steve got in touch and offered to build us a transportable lens factory. In effect, faced with the problems of devising gear which would function reliably in the Third World, he had to re-invent the wheel — do his own drawings and plans, build the plant up from scratch. He has been sensationally successful, producing a lathe for cutting the basic material of the lenses, a perspex-like substance known as PMA. The lathe is arguably the finest piece of machinery of its kind in the world. Two eminent engineers, one from the University of New South Wales and one from the CSIRO, have declared it worthy of whatever prizes may be offered for tool-making design. Andre Mescal, an Eritrean tool-maker and Siraj, a Nepalese, are working with Steve in the construction and testing of the equipment.

At the Vietnamese end a location and a support administration will have to be decided upon and a tool-maker found who could join with Steve, Andre and Siraj. There is no reason why a third factory cannot be 'piggy-backed' onto those already underway. In Australia, Vietnamese surgeons will have to be trained, funds will have to be raised by the Hollows Foundation and a scheme devised to transfer the whole operation by stages into Vietnamese hands. I am optimistic that these things can be done. The Eritrean IOL factory will be running within a month or so of the publication of this edition of this book.

CHAPTER 23

The Scourge of AIDS

> Acquired Immune Deficiency Syndrome (AIDS) has captured the public attention in a remarkably short period of time.
>
> *Brian F. and Lawrence McNamee*, AIDS: the nation's first politically protected disease

I was pleased to see that my successor as Australian of the Year, Archbishop Hollingworth of Brisbane, was a man who had taken on the former Prime Minister in a debate about social welfare and made a compassionate statement about Cambodian refugees soon after his installation. If the Australian of the Year, with the automatic claim on a certain amount of media attention, can be relied on to be a bit of a stirrer rather than a yes-man (or woman) for the establishment, things might look up.

Some people were surprised to find me still alive by January 1992 and some were discomfited, particularly when I entered into the debate over Australia's policies and attitudes towards the AIDS epidemic.

My contribution to the AIDS debate has aroused controversy and confusion. I am no stranger to controversy, but confusion is not helpful to rational, scientific discussion. Since my address to the first National Aboriginal HIV/AIDS Conference in Alice Springs in March 1992, I have received a large amount of mail endorsing what I said. In face-to-face contact, however, two questions have been consistently put to me. First, to state it colloquially, where am I coming from? Second, what risk does AIDS pose to the heterosexual population?

My specialisation is ophthalmology; my expertise is in treating large numbers of people; my interest is in the disequity between the 'haves' and the 'have-nots'. This, in part, is where I am 'coming from' — a background in the treatment of major public health problems. But what credentials do I have to talk about AIDS? Over the past 11 years I have studied the available medical literature on the subject. Initially, before the HIV virus was isolated, it was thought that the damage to the immune system was caused by an overwhelming disease load swamping its resources.

Back then, the syndrome was called Gay Related Immune Deficiency (GRID) and appeared to be affecting people with a prolonged and repeated history of sexually transmitted diseases such as syphilis and gonorrhoea. It is an unhappy fact that in metropolitan Australia at that time, syphilis was almost exclusively a disease of male homosexuals.

My initial interest was scientific. When the 'disease load' theory was current, I wondered if the immune systems of rural Aborigines, living in unhygienic conditions and subject to high levels of sexually transmitted and other infectious diseases such as scabies, impetigo and trachoma, were under attack. I was not to know then that AIDS and Aborigines would become more closely associated in my work. In a paper I wrote in 1986 on the subject of dealing with introduced diseases among Aborigines, I discussed AIDS — evidence that my concern went well back beyond the Alice Springs meeting.

An Aboriginal friend who had AIDS had developed one of the disease's most distressing infections — a blinding condition called cytomegalovirus retinitis — approached me for help. The drug he was being treated with was destroying his precious white cells. I had read in the American literature that injecting the drug into the eye arrested the condition and did not destroy the white cells.

My Aboriginal friend and patient volunteered for this treatment and received repeated injections. He died, but he was sighted, able to read and move about until the end. My colleagues and I have used this method on more people afflicted with this sight-destroying AIDS infection than any other medical unit in Australia.

No-one can yet claim success in AIDS treatment and no-one who has witnessed the suffering of the victims and their gallant friends, could fail to be deeply moved. It is some small comfort, however, that our treatment saves sight and requires relatively short visits to the clinic, so the patients can use what time they have left more profitably than hanging around in hospitals.

As knowledge of AIDS increased it became clear that it presented different characteristics in the First and Third Worlds. In developed countries AIDS is a disease that males give to males and rarely to females, or a disease that is spread amongst intravenous drug users of both sexes. An attack rate of about 1 person per thousand and with 95 per cent of the cases male is the typical profile in what is called 'the Type I Pattern'.

In parts of Africa and Asia up to 40 per cent of the population can be affected and women can make up 50 per cent or more of those infected. This is called 'the Type II Pattern'.

To Australia's shame, many Aborigines live in Third-World conditions inside our ring of affluence. It was obvious to me and others that, if the HIV infection spread to rural Aboriginal communities, those populations would be decimated. They have sexually transmitted disease rates, states of hygiene and general infections similar to those in Type II Pattern countries where the AIDS attack rate is more than 300 times greater than in urban First-World communities.

Following an approach by the Federal Minister for Aboriginal Affairs, I agreed to chair an Advisory Panel on Communicable diseases affecting Aborigines. Stanley Nangala, a gifted Aboriginal administrator with whom I have worked in the past, succeeded me as chairman of this panel. It was at his insistence that I eventually agreed to discuss AIDS as a single issue. The outcome was the now notorious Alice Springs address.

Before making clear what I said at that time, I would like to revert to the second of the questions most often put to me as a doctor. At fund raising meetings, book signings and other events anxious people question me about AIDS. In my opinion AIDS is at epidemic levels amongst male homosexuals. This is because, next to blood, semen appears to be the best host body fluid for the HIV virus, and the act of anal receptive sex is the most effective means of spreading the infection. The predominance of male homosexuals among HIV and AIDS sufferers has remained constant since the mid-1980s. Many homosexuals have recognised this danger and now desist from anal sex. For monogamous heterosexual people the danger of HIV infection is slight.

The Alice Springs meeting was an emotional occasion. I had lost a relative and several friends to AIDS. Moreover, I was disappointed by the reluctance of some of my medical colleagues, some of them homosexual, to state plainly the facts on AIDS. Plain statement is what I attempted in making the following points (I have stuck fairly closely to the text of the talk, omitting only matters covered earlier in this chapter):

> AIDS is a fatal virus infection which in Australia first appeared in Sydney in male homosexuals. Presumably it was brought in from the United States. Sydney remains the major source of AIDS in Australia.
>
> AIDS is caught by receiving infected white cells (T4 lymphocytes), which are mostly in semen, blood and vaginal secretions. The virus is called the Human Immunodeficient Virus

or HIV, infection from which may not be noticed for many years. Eventually, all HIV+ people develop infections that don't occur in other people. Infection follows infection until death.

Treatment now available can keep AIDS sufferers alive longer than before but all die of the disease. The sufferers become wasted and it is a very unpleasant way to die.

Women with the HIV virus who become pregnant have between one in two and a one in five chance of giving birth to a HIV+ baby. Most such babies will die.

Humans become infected because they do certain things, not because of spirits or bodily defects.

In Type II countries AIDS is, first, a disease of those who have many different sexual partners such as prostitutes and men who use prostitutes. Anal sex is a less important factor in these countries.

In Australia now, a man will get AIDS if:

1 He has anal receptive sex without condoms with an HIV+ male

2 He has had an infected injection into a vein or ulcer

3 He has repeated vaginal sex without condoms with an infected woman.

In Australia now for a woman to get AIDS she will have:

1 Had vaginal sex without condoms with an infected male

2 Had anal sex without condoms with an infected male

3 Received the virus from HIV+ blood in a vein or ulcer.

For an infected male to give the HIV virus to others he will have:

1 Had non-condom anal sex with a man or woman

2 Had non-condom vaginal sex with a woman

3 Transferred his blood or semen into a vein or sore of a man or woman.

For an HIV-infected female to infect others she must have:

1 Had repeated sex without condoms with a male
2 Had anal sex without condoms with a male
3 Transferred her blood into a vein or sore of another person
4 Given birth to a child when infected.

In Type II countries because many more women are infected, many more babies are born with AIDS.

Having many different sexual partners and having sexually transmitted diseases such as gonorrhoea, syphilis, Donovanosis and Herpes Simplex seem to be associated with AIDS.

So far in Australia AIDS is the Type I pattern. This includes AIDS in Aborigines. So far it seems that Aborigines are the same as other Australians as to whether they get or do not get AIDS, but if Aborigines are more likely to:

1 Become male prostitutes
2 Be intravenous drug users or blood-spreaders
3 Be promiscuous with non-condom-users then there is cause for alarm.

Some experts in the field think that all Type I countries will become Type II countries. Experts I have spoken to think that a Type II pattern of AIDS could quite quickly become established in parts of Aboriginal Australia.

If this happens it would be disastrous for Aboriginal Australia and may lead to selective depopulation along the lines of the smallpox epidemics of 1789 and 1829 which eliminated certain tribes.

How can Aboriginal Australia protect itself from this introduced disease? By behaving in a way that makes the catching of AIDS impossible.

So far rural Aboriginal Australia is relatively free of AIDS. In my opinion the following measures should be considered:

1 Direct intervention to prevent young boys becoming male prostitutes. The work of Medicine Sans Frontieres in Bangkok to extract children from prostitution provides a model.

2 Direct intervention to prevent intravenous drug use among males and females

3 Direct intervention to prevent young girls becoming prostitutes

4 Action to reduce promiscuity, especially drunken sexual activity

5 Action to ensure that all at-risk sex occurs with condoms

6 Action to stop all procedures where blood, semen or vaginal discharges are spread from person to person

7 Non-HIV infected people to avoid sex with the infected

8 The movement of people between the city and country to be watched and controlled. Some rural groups may wish to monitor the movement of HIV-infected people

9 The indication of Aboriginality and non-Aboriginality on HIV test forms with anonymity being preserved.

It has been said that AIDS is an individual infection with some public health implications. In my opinion AIDS is a public health issue with some personal implications. We will all die — some of us quite soon. Those who have AIDS must be asked the hard question: who might you have infected? Some prominent white Australians have died and others will die of AIDS. They have had and will get the best possible nursing and treatment in their final days. I suspect that the average Aboriginal AIDS death occurs in much less comfortable conditions.

This plague must not be allowed to contaminate Aboriginal Australia. The HIV virus has not yet penetrated remote Aboriginal communities and the development of a Type II pattern in Australia is still preventable.

The storm that broke over my head after this address was not caused by the talk itself — discussion of Aboriginal issues seldom wildly excites the media — but by comments I made afterwards. In response to questions from reporters, I remarked that the gay lobby had 'hi-jacked' the AIDS debate and I mentioned the late Stuart Challender as one prominent Australian who, given the opportunity of a national TV program, had not made clear what his sexual practices had been after he had discovered he was HIV+.

A paper and broadcasting war broke out that lasted until the end of March when I announced that I would make no further statements on the AIDS issue before a conference organised by the Australian Doctors' Fund (an alternative organisation, embracing doctors with widely divergent political positions, to the AMA) to be held in Sydney in May 1992. I had been castigated for attacking a dead man who could not defend himself, and branded a homophobe and publicity-crazed 'poofter-basher'. I was involved in an intemperate exchange of derogatory personal remarks with Brian Howe, the Federal Minister for Health. I also received strong support from some columnists, editorialists and letter-to-the-editor writers. What I was trying to do was focus attention on the way in which a dangerous epidemic was being handled. Badly, complacently, self-interestedly, 'softly' in my view, with potentially disastrous consequences for very vulnerable black Australians.

A gay man communicated with me from Melbourne. He was in great distress as a result of watching repeated acts of unprotected sex in a bath house. He urged me to continue questioning the assumptions, statistics, treatments and politics underlying the AIDS debate and I was willing to do so, although I was advised that adverse reaction would threaten the fund-raising power of the Hollows Foundation. This argument, and my awareness that participation in the AIDS debate was sapping my energy and deflecting me from work in the clinic and the Third World projects, made it necessary for me to stop talking about AIDS for a time. The Vietnam visit and a brief trip to the UK to attend a family wedding took me out of the firing line for a few weeks. The Doctors' Fund conference in May attracted headlines but not hysteria.

I did not, I believe, back away from the essential difficulty associated with discussion of a sexually transmitted disease epidemic. In an article published in the *Sydney Morning Herald* on the eve of the conference I wrote:

> May I recommend to all parents and to all who have influence with the young that they urge their children and charges to avoid anal intercourse. It is especially important that all boys be so advised because this practice is the forcing house of the disease.

My involvement in this debate has disrupted my life considerably and hampered my work as an eye doctor when there is so much to be done. However, I do not regret my participation. We must rid our community of AIDS by whatever means possible. Although I hope daily for a 'breakthrough' in the research, it seems unlikely that there will soon be a vaccine or an effective treatment for this deadly retroviral disease. I trust that, when the smoke clears, the suggestions I have made will have revitalised the AIDS debate in this country and properly focussed it.

CHAPTER 24

To have Succeeded

> If you can meet with Triumph and Disaster
> And treat those two imposters just the same . . .
>
> *Rudyard Kipling, 'If-'*

One of my great pleasures was to go for a bike ride on Sunday mornings. I'd ride my custom-built Tollis ten-speed down to Centennial Park, meet up with some friends, and we'd cycle 36 kilometres around the hills of the Eastern Suburbs. One morning, late in January 1989, I wasn't up to the ride. I had pains in my chest and difficulty in breathing. Gabi called Dr Paul Torzillo, who is a specialist in respiratory disorders and an old friend. Paul took me off to the Prince Alfred Hospital for a series of tests. I could tell he was worried about my condition. So was I.

I was in bed, reading, the following afternoon, feeling rather better, when Paul called with the results of the tests. The CAT-scan (a close-focus computerised x-ray which records soft and hard tissue) showed a large tumour on the left kidney and on part of the diaphragm and secondary tumours in the lungs. Very bad news. This kind of cancer is known as Grawitz tumour or hypernephroma. It is a malignant tumour of the kidney cells which spreads via the bloodstream.

We broke the news to Gabi when she got home that night

and it was a very sad time for us. But we also made certain resolutions, principally that we weren't going to pussy-foot around pretending things weren't as they are. If you do that, you have deception and concealment and cowardice to worry about as well as the facts. So we told the children who were old enough to understand as well as my friends and colleagues and attempted to get on with things.

I was particularly saddened by the thought that my youngest daughter, Anna-Louise, who was only a year old when the cancer was diagnosed, wouldn't remember me. That fear is past but, in one of those strange twists of fate that have characterised my life (I am thinking of taking the job in the Porirua mental hospital and turning up at the Frank Hardy meeting), Gabi and I are now the parents of twin girls who were conceived, we calculate, on Anzac Day, 1990. Ruth and Rosa may not remember me, but, then again, they just might. Gabi has a theory that I am stubborn enough to stick around long enough to make sure they do, and she might be right. Meantime, my policy has been to continue on with as many of my professional and personal activities as possible. To my regret, mountain-climbing and bike-riding are out but I enjoy a swim and an occasional round of golf. The big goals, the establishment of lens factories in Eritrea, Nepal and Vietnam, keep me going. The treatment for the cancer is by surgery and radiation, both of which I have had. The affected kidney has been removed, and I have undergone a form of radiation treatment known as Brachy therapy, in which radioactive iridium rods are inserted into the lungs to halt secondaries there. This involves sitting still for many hours. These treatments, carried out in Brisbane where the facilities for them are excellent, had very positive effects. They have bought me time.

A secondary cancer which developed in my brain was successfully treated and I appear to have entered a period of remission. I am acutely aware, however, that the next CAT-scan or the next unusual pain could herald dire news. But to tell the truth, this threat, distressing though it is, adds piquancy and value to every day. Each day of survival is a small victory and I am resolved not to waste the winnings.

In recent years I've gathered a few honours — Companion of the Order of Australia, the 1990 Australian Human Rights medal, the 1991 Humanist of the Year award, several honorary degrees and the Australian of the Year award for 1990. I've been surprised by the amount of personal gratification these gongs have given me. No-one is without vanity. But accepting them has also given me a platform from which to speak out about the things that most concern me — Aboriginal health and the social and political position of Aborigines, and the responsibility we, as privileged citizens of First-World countries, bear to the people of the Third World.

To my mind, having a care and concern for others is the highest of the human qualities. It distinguishes us from the other animals and deserves to be paid more attention and to be more exercised. Some of the things I've done have been designed to kick-start an awareness of what privileged people we Australians are.

Taking up a question from a non-medical friend, Mike Lynskey, a stalwart publicist and worker for the cause, was a good example. He asked, 'How do you make someone feel like a cataract victim?' This led to the cataract simulator. After a bit of trialing, Mike, and Peter and Sue Wilkinson, came up with a proto-type and got the world's only cataract simulator mass-produced. It is a cardboard and plastic mask which gives the wearer a very good idea of what cataract blindness feels like from the inside. I've given fund-raising speeches to a variety of professionals, from advertising executives to veterinary surgeons, accompanied by distribution of these masks designed to drive the point home: cataract blindness is severe, traumatic and yet curable! I usually begin these addresses, after the pin-striped gentlemen have donned their masks, with a line like this, 'You thought you knew what bad habit caused blindness, didn't you?' It always gets a laugh.

The effect of putting on the mask is no laughing matter. You are plunged into the world of the blind, where only light and dark and vague forms are discernible — no distinct shapes or features. In an ordinarily lit room you can grope-touch your way around familiar things, but that's all. As one ad-man put it: 'You can find your cock to pee, but aiming it at the toilet bowl would be an impossibility.' The response from these professional groups has invariably been extremely generous.

Against that, the Australian government is not doing enough. As a percentage of gross national product, overseas aid has shrunk from 0.5 in the first Hawke Labor government's budget of 1983 to 0.35 in 1991. This is ignominious. Being Australian of the Year gave me the opportunity to make this point over and over again, on radio and television and to groups like the National Press Club and powerful individuals like the former Prime Minister. Of course I recognise that there can be degrees of tokenism in this. When I met Mr Hawke, as part of the 'tour of honour' the Australian of the Year makes, I saw it as an opportunity to raise the issue of youth unemployment with him. He said something like, 'Fred, why don't you stick to being an eye doctor?'

In a way, that was fair enough. I'd already got a commitment of government support for the Eritrean lens factory from him. But I thought, *Hollows, this is no time to wimp out*, so I said, 'Look, I'm Australian of the Year for now, and this is probably the only chance I'll get to talk to you about this. You and I come from the same sort of background, and we both know that a political party that doesn't make work for young people a top priority should look to itself.' Mr Hawke heard me out and said he agreed with me.

Obviously, I don't believe that charity — defined by the

Macquarie Dictionary as 'the private or public relief of needy or unfortunate persons' — begins at home, but God knows there is a need for that spirit in Australia. The Aborigines continue to be needy and unfortunate. The problem now is not that there is widespread hostility towards them, but that the efforts to improve their condition are misdirected.

Nothing demonstrates this better than the Royal Commission into Aboriginal deaths in custody. Depressed Aboriginal living conditions resulting in poor health, inadequate education, low self-esteem and drunkenness, combined with unimaginative and unsympathetic police action to make these individual tragedies inevitable. But the Royal Commission was an expensive circus, a bonanza for lawyers, a soapbox for ranters, and a fountain of platitudes which did no good at all. The money wasted on it could have been more usefully spent on Aboriginal housing, health services and training.

When the media want a comment on Aboriginal affairs they are likely to contact Charles Perkins who has made great contributions since the 1960s. But where are the Aboriginal lawyers, writers and teachers of the 1990s? Why are they not speaking out or why are they not being heard? In a recent address at Macquarie University, I said that 'the most stupid thing' Aborigines had done was to allow themselves to become de-politicised. The use of the word 'stupid' caused some uneasy stirring among the audience as it was intended to. I was referring to the present situation where Aboriginal affairs are handled in an allegedly 'bi-partisan' non-party manner in Canberra where the buzz-word is 'reconciliation'. That smacks to me of bullshit. Politics is about the relationships between groups and it provides mechanisms for the out-groups to force their way in. This is what the Aborigines can and must do.

Although I have been a reader and book-buyer all my life, I knew nothing about the publishing business, so everything about the production, launching and reception of the first edition of this autobiography astonished me. I had expected a certain short-lived ghoulish interest of the 'Australian of the Year about to shuffle off' kind, but not the sustained and genuine interest and support the book seemed to provoke. From the time of its launching by Mrs Hazel Hawke, on a sparkling spring day in the grounds of the Prince of Wales hospital, to the production of large-print edition early in 1992, the sales remained buoyant and I would have no idea of the number of copies I've signed in Sydney, Newcastle, Wollongong and other centres in other states. Signed copies are certainly not a rarity.

From the start the autobiography had an inside track. Few autobiographers would be privileged to appear on Andrew Ollie's top-rating ABC radio show, have their book launched by the wife of the Prime Minister and do half a dozen television interviews all on the one day. With the publicity brilliantly orchestrated by Mike Lynskey, and the help of favourable reviews, the book sat near on the top of the best-seller lists for many weeks. I have been known, in rare acerbic moments, to refer to the television receiver as the 'cretiniser', and indeed I do have doubts about the capacity of the two-dimensional coloured image, accompanied by the usually over-simplified and facile texts, to stimulate the imagination. It was very encouraging, therefore, to have first-hand evidence of the power of the written word to communicate with ordinary people.

The many appearances I made in connection with the book boosted my confidence and performance as a public speaker. It is always gratifying to please an audience, but as I have increasingly become a fund-raiser for the eye-health projects I am involved in, my better presentation became a useful asset. One of the more memorable occasions was the fully-subscribed ABC literary lunch held in the Hilton Hotel in Sydney on 25 September 1991.

I had no idea of how to adopt the guise of literary figure until I took a phone call from Frank Hardy the night before the event. It is ironic that I, who have never, in the truest sense of the word, written a book should be advised on this occasion by Hardy. Frank, who has lived for decades by his pen and is the author of several fine books, has never been honoured by the 'chattering classes' with a literary lunch. 'Talk about what you've read and how it affected you,' Frank said. That sound advice led me to take books down from my shelves at Farnham House, do some thinking and make some notes.

When the guests were seated and the glassware and cutlery were gently tinkling, I realised that I was sitting next to fellow ex-seminarians Tom Keneally and Terry Lane. That gave me my opening gambit and I found the words to express the joy reading had given me and the ways in which it had shaped my consciousness as a human being. Friends who were present have told me, with surprised looks on their faces, that I was eloquent. I certainly enjoyed myself and the novelty of talking about the power of ideas and feelings expressed in words — something outside my area of professional expertise but about which I felt strongly.

I told the guests about reading Frank Hardy's *Power Without Glory* as a young medical student and the reason I read it: 'Because it was banned, and I reckoned that if the bastards who were running this society had declared a book illegal then I was going to read it.' That was pretty much the theme — the right of the individual to think and behave independently, and many of the books that stick in my mind, like Tom Keneally's *Schindler's Ark* and the works of people like Ivan Illich and Bruno Bettelheim, drive that point home. I also talked about the influence Gordon Briscoe's analysis of Aboriginal-European relations had on me and touched on other writers like Eric Rolls, Max Williams and the great historian, E P Thompson. After the lunch Peter Corris and I signed hundreds of copies of the book — each sale significantly supporting the sight-preserving work in Eritrea.

One thing led to another. In my talk I mentioned Bob Gould, the one-time left-wing activist and more lately prosperous Sydney bookseller. In the 1970s, Bob had insisted that I read the Brazilian Christian Marxist Paulo Freire's *Pedagogy of the Oppressed* to provide an ideological context for my work in black Australia. I resisted as a freethinker who thought the Freire enterprise had a theological, categorising smell to it. I also found the title of the book appalling, but I was captivated by the accuracy and elegance of Freire's analysis of the mistakes middle-class intellectuals make when they attempt to help the under-privileged. I'm sure I made some of the same mistakes, but perhaps fewer than if I had not read the book. Bob Gould heard the broadcast of the address, got in touch with Corris and myself, and the result was three highly successful book signings in his two Sydney shops. More opportunities to remind fortunate Australians of the work in Africa and Nepal, more dollars into the fund and, incidentally, more faces swimming up from the past — former students, colleagues and patients lined up with the book in their hands and good wishes in their hearts. The ABC successfully marketed a cassette of the literary lunch.[1] Then, in March 1992 BMG Records released a CD and cassette[2] of my readings from the works of selected Australian poets. The proceeds were to be directed to the Nepal Eye Program-Australia. I spent about six hours in the recording studio; state-of-the-art technology erased my pipe-smoker's wheez-

---

[1] *Terry Lane talks with Fred Hollows*, ABC Spoken Word Cassette, ISBN 0-642-129 39-8

---

[2] *The Man from Snowy River and More Poems, Yarns and Ballads*, BMG, Cat. No. VPCD 0850 (CD) and VPK 10850 (cassette)

ings, and I hope I did justice to the talents of poets like Paterson, Lawson, C J Dennis, Bob Brissenden, Les Murray, Geoffrey Lehmann, Nigel Roberts, Judith Wright and my old mate, Max Williams.

Some years ago a friend sent me a card with a snatch of verse attributed to the American poet and essayist, Ralph Waldo Emerson, on it. I put it on my office wall. It goes:

> To laugh often and much,
> To win the respect of intelligent people
> And the affection of children,
> To earn the appreciation of honest critics
> And to endure the betrayal of false friends,
> To appreciate beauty,
> To find the best in others,
> To leave the world a bit better,
> Whether by a healthy child, a garden patch
> Or a redeemed social condition,
> To know even one life has breathed easier
> Because you lived,
> This is to have succeeded.

I regard that as a pretty good summary of what life is all about. I am a humanist. I don't believe in any higher power than the best expressions of the human spirit, and those are to be found in personal and social relationships. Evaluating my own life in those terms, I've had some mixed results. I've hurt some people and disappointed others but I hope that, on balance, I've given more than I've taken. I believe that my view of what a 'redeemed social condition' is has been consistent — equity between people — and I've tried always to work to that end.

I call myself an eye doctor, but, casting around for another word to describe my life's work, I am reminded of that teacher's question put so long ago: 'Well, Hollows, what sort of an engineer do you want to be?' The *Macquarie Dictionary* lists seven meanings for the word *engineer*. The sixth is one of particular interest to me — 'US an engine-driver', my father's honourable calling; but I am also attracted to the seventh meaning: 'to arrange, manage or carry through by skilful or artful contrivance'.

Farewell

Fred Hollows died at Farnham House, Randwick, his home for almost twenty years, at 8.15 am on 10 February 1993. I saw him three days earlier on a weekend when, a press report claimed, he had had more than forty visitors. I doubt that there have ever been fewer than ten people under the roof of that house since Fred and Gabi moved in, and there were plenty around at the time of my visit. Max Williams, poet and Fred's mate, Fr Frank Brennan, family members. Writers Tom Keneally and Frank Hardy had been by earlier.

Until that last visit I hadn't really believed that Fred would die in the near future. He had spoken of some peculiar medical balance associated with his cancer that meant that the longer he survived the greater were his chances of further survival, of outlasting the cancer, as it were. I clung to that hope. But at Farnham House that weekend it was clear that his physical strength was exhausted. Not his mental strength. He corrected someone who mispronounced a name and pulled someone else up on a matter of chronology.

Two weeks before I had seen him in hospital when he was stronger and told him that I was to interview Paul Keating the next day. 'What should I ask him, Fred?' I said.

We were drinking Black Douglas whisky and Fred put his glass on the hospital tray and sucked in a painful breath. 'I'll tell you what to *tell* him! Tell him not to take Australian manufacturing industry into oblivion the way he did that fuckin' rock band.'

I did as instructed. The prime minister smiled and didn't rise to the bait. I related this to Fred and he smiled himself and nodded, which was all his remaining strength permitted him to do. In the hospital he had boasted of once finishing a marathon. 'What was your time?' I asked.

'Bugger you, Corris. I'm a three-hour man. Three hours and fifty-eight minutes, if you've gotta know.'

That's the Fred I choose to remember—rebellious, yet enjoying his prestige (there was no other patient drinking whisky in the hospital, I'll guarantee); tuned-in to contemporary political and economic issues with his own idiosyncratic slant on them; modest about his professional accomplishments and proud of his physical and social achievements.

When I was helping Fred with his autobiography, I tested the marketing waters by asking taxi drivers if they'd heard of him. Almost to a man and a woman they had. A state funeral was an appropriate send-off for Fred, not for the pomp, but to give all those ordinary people who responded to his tieless, vernacular-speaking, pipe-smoking image a chance to farewell him. Behind the image was a dogged worker against what he called 'disequity'. The Eritrean lens factory, much referred to in his book, will soon become a reality and the Fred Hollows Foundation will bring similar facilities to Nepal and Vietnam, reducing 'disequity' by a measurable amount.

In my lifetime I don't expect to meet a bigger man than Fred Hollows.

Peter Corris
Sydney
February 1993

Index

ACKNOWLEDGMENTS

For help in the preparation of this book thanks to Gabi Hollows, Tracey Boughton, Pat Fiske, Jean Bedford, Mike Lynskey, Dr Paul Beaumont, Dr John Elder, Dr Paul Torzillo, Dr Jean Edwards, Lynn Prylinski and the Royal Australian College of Ophthalmologists for the right to use photographs from *The National Trachoma and Eye Health Program Report* 1980.

For help in raising funds for the Eritrea Blindness Prevention Programme, the following organisations and people have contributed generously of their time, energy and money: Austcare; OPSM; Celebrity Speakers; Australia Day Council; Mr Ray Martin; National Nine Network; Designs for Vision; National Mutual; an anonymous donor from north Queensland; an anonymous donor from Edgecliff; Gulf Air; Rotary Clubs of Australia; Lions Clubs of Australia; Apex Clubs of Australia; Graham Ross; Douglass Laboratories; the *Australian* newspaper; Pymble Ladies College Mothers' Club; the Coast Golf and Recreation Club Limited; Hamilton Island Enterprises; Sutherland Trade Union Club Limited; Dr Garry Brian; Dr Mark Gillies; Dr John Cooper; Mr Mike Lynskey; Miss Tracy Boughton; Miss Christine May; Miss Mora Main; and Miss Pat Fiske.

[illegible]

[illegible]

[illegible]